Rethinking Learner Support in Distance Education

Distance learning is becoming an increasingly popular way of studying, and most universities now provide courses using these methods. Today's students, though, are demanding high quality, consumer-focused and flexible courses and learning resources, and active learner support. This means that providers of distance education need to reconsider key issues about their learner support systems, to ensure that this is delivered appropriately and effectively.

This book considers the changing needs and demands of distance education students. It draws together contributions from the UK, USA, Hong Kong, Australia, Japan, South Africa and Botswana, to offer an international perspective on:

- The challenges and and oppportunities of Informational and Communciation Technologies (ICT)
- Quality assurance, commercialisation and the learner as consumer
- The impact of cultural differences on internationalised curricula
- The implications for learner support of a wider range of learners.

This book should be read by all those involved in developing and delivering distance education courses.

Alan Tait is a Senior Lecturer and Sub Dean in the faculty of Education and Language Studies at the Open University, UK. **Roger Mills** is the Regional Director of the Open University in the East of England.

RoutledgeFalmer Studies in Distance Education
Series Editors: Desmond Keegan and Alan Tait

Rethinking Learner Support in Distance Education

Change and continuity in an international context

Edited by Alan Tait and Roger Mills

RoutledgeFalmer
Taylor & Francis Group

LONDON AND NEW YORK

First published 2003
by RoutledgeFalmer
2 Park Square, Milton Park, Abingdon, Oxon, OX14 4RN

Simultaneously published in the USA and Canada
by RoutledgeFalmer
270 Madison Ave, New York NY 10016

RoutledgeFalmer is an imprint of the Taylor & Francis Group

Transferred to Digital Printing 2006

Typeset in Times by
HWA Text and Data Management Ltd, Tunbridge Wells

British Library Cataloguing in Publication Data
A catalogue record for this book is available from the British Library

Library of Congress Cataloging in Publication Data
Re-thinking learner support in distance education : change and continuity
in an international context / edited by Alan Tait and Roger Mills.
        p. cm.
    Includes bibliographical references and index.
    1. Distance education–Cross-cultural studies–Congresses. 2. Education–
Effect of technological innovations on–Cross-cultural studies–Congresses.
3. Educational technology–Cross-cultural studies–Congresses. I. Tait, Alan.
II. Mills, Roger, 1941– III. Cambridge International Conference on Open
and Distance Learning (2001)

LC5800 .R48 2003
371.3′5–dc21

                                                        2002027522

ISBN 0–415–30143–2 (hbk)
ISBN 0–415–30144–0 (pbk)

For John Davison

Contents

List of figures and tables

Figures

Tables

List of contributors

Louise Aylward has been an instructional designer at the Open University of Hong Kong (OUHK) for eight years, and during that time has worked on a range of courses in a variety of disciplines. She is a member of the working group on course development procedures, reviewing and revising the current procedures to accommodate the incorporation of new technologies. Prior to joining the OUHK she was an editor working mainly on academic and educational books. She holds an MA in Open and Distance Learning.

Clive Barrett has worked for the UK Open University since 1989 first as an Associate Lecturer and more recently as a Project Officer co-ordinating the development of learning support materials for students and tutors.

Carol Bertram is currently the academic co-ordinator of the BEd Honours programme at the School of Education, Training and Development at the University of Natal. Before working at the University, she worked with a non-governmental organisation in teacher development and did freelance materials development. She has developed a number of open learning materials in teacher education. Her research interest in open learning is how students interact with materials, and the role of the tutorial group in learning. More generally she is interested in issues around educational change, and teacher and curriculum development. She holds an MEd from the University of Natal.

Norma Corry has worked extensively in the field of education. Since 1994 she has been involved with teacher education at the University of the Witwatersrand, Johannesburg, South Africa, initially with pre-service teachers and more recently also with in-service teachers in the BEd (Honours) programme. She runs the programme and tutors in a module dealing with issues in school curricula. Her research interests include curriculum innovation, mentoring and learning, and the Graeco-Roman world of the first century CE.

Lee Herman is Mentor/Co-ordinator at the Auburn, New York location of the State University of New York/Empire State College, and co-founder of the ESC Mentoring Institute. He has worked with adult students for the past twenty years. For many years he has collaborated with Alan Mandell on understanding, practising and writing about mentoring.

Margaret Johnson has worked within student services in the Open University in London, UK for nineteen years. First, as a tutor, then as a Senior Counsellor and presently as an Assistant Director. She has devised schemes and produced university-wide materials on a variety of aspects of student support, most notably in the area of academic English language development. She is holder of a National Institute of Learning and Teaching Fellowship in recognition of her work in this field.

Brian Kenworthy is a Senior Lecturer and Coordinator, International Projects in the Flexible Learning Centre at the University of South Australia. As well as working in the fields of educational technology and distance education for many years, he has carried out numerous distance education consultancies for UNESCO, AusAID and the Asian Development Bank in Asia and Africa. He also worked as a consultant to the Commonwealth of Learning in Vancouver in the early years of its development.

Tony Lelliott is Deputy Dean of the Faculty of Humanities at the University of the Witwatersrand, Johannesburg. From 1995 to 2000 he was the Director of the Further Diploma in Education at the university, a professional development programme for teachers. He currently teaches on undergraduate programmes in the School of Education in the areas of computer literacy and curriculum. His research interests are in the areas of the public understanding of science, scientific literacy, ICT in education and open learning.

Helen Lentell. Before joining COL Helen was Head of Higher Education and Professional Studies at the National Extension College in the UK where she developed a number of innovatory distance education work-based learning programmes – including The FrontLine degree for Coca Cola Enterprises, a postgraduate course for Cadbury Ltd, and an acclaimed programme of study for small and medium-sized enterprises. Prior to this she worked at the UK Open University in a number of roles, including Staff Tutor in the Social Science Faculty – where she was responsible for delivering social science courses in the East Midlands region and for authoring a number of social science units. She was also Assistant Director Regional Academic Services with a responsibility for staff development and training for the Open University's part-time tutoring staff and the staff in the regional centres. She has also been a visiting scholar at Deakin University.

Alan Mandell is Director of the Mentoring Institute of the State University of New York/Empire State College, and Professor at ESC in New York City. He has been a mentor and administrator for more than twenty-five years, and has regularly published on adult learning, including the newly revised *Portfolio Development and Adult Learning* (forthcoming, 2002) with Elana Michelson. Ongoing collaboration with Lee Herman includes, 'On Access: towards opening the lifeworld within adult higher education systems,' a chapter in Roger Mills and Alan Tait's *The Convergence of Distance and Conventional Education: Patterns of Flexibility for the Individual Learner* (1999).

Robin Mason is Professor of Educational Technology at the Open University, where she has worked with on-line courses as course designer, on-line tutor, evaluator and researcher. In partnership with Cambridge University, she is currently developing a new Masters Level on-line course called Learning in the Connected Economy. This course is one of three to launch the UK government virtual university initiative, eUniversities Worldwide.

Roger Mills is Regional Director of the Open University in the East of England and has worked for the OU UK since its inception. Through work in a range of different institutions and countries he has developed an interest in different approaches to learner support and is particularly involved in management and staff development. He has been joint organiser of the Cambridge International Conference on Student Support in Open and Distance Education since 1983.

Chieko Mizoue is a professor of the Research Center for Lifelong Learning, University of Library and Information Science in Japan. After working for Ministry of Education, Japan, and national educational institutions, she studied at Graduate School of Education, Harvard University, USA. Her research concerns adult learning in post-secondary education in Japan and North America. As a member, she has worked for some research projects on education at UNESCO and the National Institution for Academic Degrees in Japan.

Evelyn Pulane Nonyongo is employed by the University of South Africa (UNISA) as the Head of the Institute for Continuing Education. Her interest and experience in open and distance learning are in the areas of learner support, staff development and programme evaluation. Her work at UNISA and some of her publications cover these three areas of interest. Before joining UNISA, she worked for a number of years in a non-governmental organisation, the South African Committee for Higher Education (SACHED), which provided support services for students studying with UNISA. She is also an active member of South African and SADC Region professional associations in open and distance learning and serves in various committees of these bodies.

Jennifer O'Rourke has been engaged in open and distance learning in many roles: course developer, administrator, writer, tutor and researcher. As a consultant, her work includes teaching, programme planning, evaluation, research and organisational development for universities and colleges, non-government organisations and ministries of education in Canada, the Caribbean, Africa and Southeast Asia. She is based in British Columbia, Canada, and as the result of curiosity about her surroundings, is the co-author of *Namely Vancouver: A Hidden History of Vancouver Place Names* (2001).

Jason Pennells' main specialisms are teacher training and nomadic/pastoralist education. He tutors on the University of London MA in Distance Education and MA in Education and International Development (Distance Education), and co-ordinates and teaches short courses in the UK and overseas. He has expertise in student support, writing and editing of distance education materials,

materials development and production, evaluation, planning, institutional administration and reporting.

Marion Phillips is Assistant Director of Student Services at the UK Open University (OU) and Head of the 'New Technology for Supporting Students' (NTSS) Unit. Marion set up the NTSS initiative in 1999 to develop a Learner Support Service on the World Wide Web (www.open.ac.uk/learners-guide/) for Open University students and prospective students. In this role Marion combines her two main educational interests, namely the development of students as autonomous, independent learners and the use of new technology to provide on-line guidance and learning support.

Alan Tait is Sub Dean in the Faculty of Education and Language Studies at the Open University UK. He is a member of the Centre for Educational Policy and Management (CEPAM), and has written for courses in the lifelong learning and educational guidance fields. He has spent his career in the OU UK, in a range of posts for the most part concerned with learner support in the East of England; was Editor of the journal *Open Learning* from 1989–98; and is Co-Director of the Cambridge International Conference on Open and Distance Learning. He has worked as a consultant in a range of countries, both indus-trialised and developing.

Mary Thorpe is Director of the Institute of Educational Technology at the Open University. Since joining the University in 1975, she has evaluated course materials, tuition and learner support systems, and authored course materials in Third World Studies, Adult Learning, Open and Distance Learning and evaluation. She has published widely in these fields. As Director of the Institute, she leads a centre of international excellence for the teaching, research, evaluation and development of educational technology in the service of student learning.

Introduction

It is a real pleasure and a privilege – far more than these hackneyed words might suggest – to contribute the Introduction to this book. The book addresses a theme of core importance to open and distance learning at the present time, namely that of change for learner support services. The range of challenges identified by the authors in this volume makes it clear that such an examination is both necessary and urgent.

The book derives from the 2001 Cambridge International Conference on Open and Distance Learning. This was the ninth in the series, and the great majority of chapters here were contributed in earlier versions as papers. The Conference has provided a focus for professional development in ODL, and in particular for learner support, over nearly twenty years. There have been few more sustainedly fruitful and enjoyable experiences in our professional lives than building up the network of colleagues and friends from all around the world through our role as Directors of these conferences. The Conferences have contributed enormously to our own capacity to reflect on ODL, and to escape the parochialism which can derive from never lifting one's head outside one's own institution (for details of the 2003 meeting of the Cambridge Conference see www2.open.ac.uk/r06/conference/conference.htm).

The theme of this volume is the examination of change in the conceptualisation, management and delivery of learner support services. The challenges to learner support in ODL stem at present from a number of sources. These include:

1   The impact of ICT on what is wanted by learners today, what can be provided by institutions, and what restructuring of organisations has to follow;
2   The impact of the change of status from student to that of customer and consumer, which necessitates a change from 'obedient child' to 'adult and equal', and the attitudinal changes necessary on the part of the institution;
3   The policy drivers in a number of countries to include a wider range of learners as well as a larger number, and the tensions between the drive to use new media for learning and the issues of access and Widening Participation;
4   The challenge to the well-established institutions in their capacity to change quickly or be outpaced by younger institutions with less history (particularly acute for the second generation distance teaching universities around the world, now seen in some instances as conservative);

5   The pressures on costs which drive fee levels and pricing in the increasingly competitive environments that many governments insist on for education;
6   The need to attempt more complex activities through ODL methods, including work-based education and training, with the workplace as a site of learning;
7   The organisational politics with both internal and external dimensions that have to be managed in this challenging change process;
8   The increasing recognition of the centrality of student support in distance education and its role in retention and income generation.

It can be seen that these challenges do not drive conveniently towards obvious policy and organisational solutions, but indeed work in tension with each other. This is borne out where for example many learners are ahead of their institutions in demanding ICT supported services, while in other cases institutions are having to maintain multi-channel systems of communication with all the concomitant costs, because some cohorts of students cannot keep up with the hardware demands and line charges. There is also the tension between 'building the business' in obvious and relatively easy areas, and maintaining the institutional mission which for significant elements within ODL has been about inclusivity.

It can also be seen that the range of issues that currently arise have much in common around the world, and this volume draws on African, Antipodean, Asian, European and North American perspectives. In all these parts of the world the same issues face managers and practitioners as they attempt to engage with change, improve quality, contain or diminish costs, and make progress in a tough and competitive environment. The evidence in these chapters points to the even greater importance of learner support, at the same time as insisting that change has to be addressed and delivered. Discriminating within the broad dimensions of change and continuity represents the core contemporary managerial task.

All the evidence from government as well as international organisations such as UNESCO and the Commonwealth of Learning points to the fact that it has never been more important to expand opportunity, at the same time as ensuring that students are successful in engaging with a personally worthwhile educational experience. We hope that this volume will inform practice, and contribute to change in policy and the delivery of improved service for the millions of distance learners around the world.

Alan Tait
Roger Mills

May 2002, Cambridge, UK

1   Constructivism or Confucianism?

We have the technology, now what shall we do with it?

Louise Aylward

Introduction

This chapter examines some of the issues that arise when a university with a strong 'second generation' Open and Distance Education culture, operating in a society that is technologically advanced yet still heavily influenced by its Confucian tradition, adopts, within a relatively short time, new communication technologies in course delivery. It looks at the likely impact of these technologies on tutor support and considers some of the institutional decisions that will have to be made if the new technology is to be integrated successfully.

Setting the scene

The OUHK

The Open University of Hong Kong (OUHK) started out as the Open Learning Institute (OLI), which was established by government ordinance in 1989. Its goal was (and is) to provide high quality and flexible further education opportunities for adults, primarily through distance learning. The Institute was granted self-accrediting status in 1996, and became the OUHK in May 1997. That first October 1989 semester, 4,237 students enrolled on the first eight courses; today the OUHK has more than 26,000 students and 16,000 graduates, and offers more than 100 postgraduate, degree, associate degree and sub-degree programmes. It is a self-financing, non-profit-making organisation.

The OLI took as its model the UK Open University, and the first courses it delivered used minimally adapted OU UK course materials. The medium of instruction was English and a typical course materials package consisted of printed study units, a textbook, possibly an audio or video cassette, and in some cases, TV programmes broadcast on Sunday mornings. On registering for a course, each student was allocated a tutor to support his or her learning; tutor groups contained up to thirty students. A flexible credit system was adopted – students earned credits for each course and accumulated credits towards a degree (a Bachelor's degree requires 120 credits; a bachelor's degree with honours, 160). Courses were run by course co-ordinators (CCs), academics who had dual responsibility for academic content and course administration. Hong Kong being much smaller in area than the UK, one of the ways the OUHK differed from its UK counterpart was in its decision not to provide summer residential schools. It was felt that those students who wanted to mix with their peers would easily be able to travel to tutorials or day schools, so this was the system adopted. Also, because the majority of people in Hong Kong have somewhat compact living accommodation, it could not be assumed that students had the space to study at home, so from the beginning, study centres were provided, and science students, rather than being given home test kits, did their practical work in the OUHK laboratories.

This is how the situation was in the early days, but in fact, there has not been a great deal of change. The facilities have improved and been extended with the establishment of the OUHK's campus, and a Learning Centre on Hong Kong Island. Perhaps the major area of change is course development; the OUHK now develops the majority of its courses itself, and offers programmes in Chinese language and English (students have to opt for one medium of instruction). Courses are developed by course teams comprising a developer (internal or external), academic co-ordinator and member(s) (OUHK faculty), an OUHK course designer and an external course assessor. The range of media used to present courses has extended to CD-ROMS and, of course, the Internet. However, the model remains funda-mentally the same, and indisputably 'second generation' (Nipper, 1989), and the institutional discourse continues to be heavily influenced by the ODE literature of the late 1980s and early 1990s; for example Holmberg (1989) defined the 'guided didactic conversation' – in OUHK manuals and documents, course materials are often defined as a 'simulated conversation' or a 'tutorial in print'. The concept of the autonomous learner (Peters, 1993) working through prepared course materials with the support of a tutor has become engrained in the OUHK culture. Perhaps it was enforced so strongly because there was a need to create a culture quickly; the OUHK was expected to become self-financing within a few years; it had to be up and running fast. And while its founding faculty all had experience of distance learning, the academics who became the backbone team of course co-ordinators generally did not; many had worked at local 'traditional' tertiary institutions and had to speedily assimilate the new teaching mode.

Hong Kong learners and OUHK courses

As the OUHK has an open access policy, its students have reached all levels of education: some may have left secondary school after finishing Form 3; others may have university degrees. The majority, however, are likely to have gone through the Hong Kong education system, which, it is generally acknowledged, is still influenced by the philosophy of Confucius. The Confucian tradition is teacher-centred, with a focus on the transmission of content (Robinson, 1999). In Hong Kong, Confucian values are blamed for the perceived tendency of Hong Kong learners to rely on memorising, rote-learning, surface learning, transmission modes of teaching and so on. These accusations are not entirely fair to Confucius, whose importance to education in Chinese culture derives from his conviction that everyone is educable (Lee, 1996); and Biggs (1996) suggests that some of the learner characteristics identified as part of the Confucian tradition are oversimplified and misunderstood. However, when I arrived at the OLI in 1991, the theory of the passive, rote-learning, teacher-dependent Hong Kong learner certainly held sway. The autonomous learner model that I have described, with its emphasis on independence and self-direction was consciously presented as a counterpoint to some of the problematic aspects of 'Confucian' education. Students were told that, while at school they may have been used to being directed by teachers, now they were responsible for their own learning. They were encouraged to engage actively with the self-instructional course materials, which had been specially designed to promote such interaction, with objectives, activities, intext questions, activity feedback and so on.

The teams producing these materials, until very recently, worked to a more or less standard format with course templates dictating the shape of the materials. Time constraints meant that it was not always possible to produce mixed media, so courses predominantly took the physical form of printed study units. Time constraints also meant it was easier to produce the tried and tested format (behaviourist objectives, clear introductions and summaries, topics interspersed with activities and self-tests with feedback at the end of each unit) than to develop something new.

Within these parameters, course teams made great efforts to produce materials that presented multiple perspectives and engaged students in active learning through the familiar devices, conversational style etc. However, it is in practice quite hard to write a text that does not present as authoritative. Indeed, it could be argued that the fact it is a printed text *makes* it authoritative; certainly students from a Confucian background would be inclined to take it as so. Marton *et al.* (1996), while challenging the rote-learning stereotype, maintain that memorisation (rather than rote-learning) is one of the methods that Chinese students use to move towards understanding. It is easy to see how this learning technique transfers well to the processing of printed ODE course materials, however many interactive devices they contain. Of course it is possible to develop different, more flexible models, but innovation takes time, and also tends to meet with resistance from those who have a set view of what an 'OUHK course' should look like. So, in the end, the model that was perceived as a counter-attack on the passive learning of Confucian culture, turned out to fit in with it quite well, as students accepted the authority of the text.

If the teaching is in the text, then what is the role of the tutor?

OUHK tutors

Despite the emphasis on the course materials as the primary source of learning, the OUHK has always acknowledged the importance of tutor support in the learning process. In the 'pre-new technologies' tutor training manual, tutors were told that they would be expected to provide this support in three ways:

1   Marking and commenting on their students' assignments.

2   Providing telephone support.
3   Running face-to-face sessions for their students.

The current tutor manual has been updated to include the use of technology (I shall come back to that later) but there is no real difference between the role of the tutor as it was perceived in the early 1990s, and the role of the tutor today. As an open learning institution the OUHK must provide flexibility and choice, so it is made clear that while learners are encouraged to make use of their tutor's support, they are not obliged to do so. Student must be free to choose to study a course and achieve a pass in assessment without ever consulting their tutor. In some cases, therefore, the learner–tutor relationship exists solely in the dialogue in which the student submits an assignment, and the tutor comments on it. Nevertheless, much effort is put into persuading students and training tutors to make face-to-face tutorial sessions worthwhile learning experiences. Fung and Carr (1999) note:

> As in many other distance education institutions, the OUHK advocates that tutorials should be participatory events, not straight lectures, and the message is strongly reinforced in the staff development sessions/materials for tutors.

In other words, the tutorials are intended to continue the 'active learning' approach adopted in the course materials. Students are expected to interact at face-to-face tutorials, not only with their tutor but also with each other. The students, however, are not always enthusiastic about this approach. The same study indicated that 'straight lecture' was what a lot of them prefer. They want their tutors to interpret the course materials, select the key points, tell them what to learn. Furthermore, there is evidence that many tutors feel obliged to respond to these demands, particularly in the foundation level courses. As an academic who came out from the UK in the early days of the OLI to conduct training sessions remarked to me: 'I expended a lot of effort in Hong Kong trying to get tutors to give what I regarded as student-centred sessions, and failed basically because neither tutors nor students believed in my value system for tutorial contact.'

Such a split between what is supposed to be happening and what actually does happen is by no means confined to the OUHK, as Fung and Carr are at pains to point out, but it does reinforce the view that OUHK learners, if not rote-learners, then at least prefer a transmission learning model. It is not that OUHK students do not value the support of their tutors; in many of the student profiles in University documents and the web site, while families tend to be the first to be credited with support, tutors often come a close second. However, they are valued for the individual feedback they give over the telephone or assignments, as well as for the knowledge they transmit in face-to-face tutorials, rather than for the facilitation of student-centred tutorials, which some students, it has to be admitted, consider a waste of their time.

To summarise then, the OUHK has, since its inception, subscribed to a western model of distance learning that in theory runs counter to the Confucian educational background of its students, but in practice has married with it quite well. The concept of the autonomous learner is embedded in the OUHK culture but the emphasis is perhaps more on self-direction of study path rather than the development of independent thinking. The main teaching, until very recently, was delivered through printed and a/v course materials (and still is in the majority of cases). Tutor support is considered central to the success of the learning process, but the only interaction students are *required* to have with tutors is the submission of assignments for marking and feedback. Tutors are trained to facilitate interactive tutorials, but, due to student preference, often end up transmitting information instead. What changes in this model might the introduction of new technologies effect?

On-line learning at the OUHK

The decision to introduce new technologies into course delivery at the OUHK was taken in 1998 and after that, things moved fairly quickly.

In 1999 the OUHK adopted Web CT as its on-line learning platform (in the OUHK it is referred to as the On-line Learning Environment – OLE). (In fact, Web CT does not support Chinese, so the Chinese OLE uses Lotus Notes; but as the two OLEs look identical in structure apart from the language I shall confine my discussion to Web CT.) A number of courses were selected in each school for the pilot presentations in 2000 and 2001. With the exception of one or two courses (at the technological end of the spectrum), the Web CT platform was added on to existing courses, as an additional means of student support.

Web CT enables the delivery of on-line course materials (including text, graphics, audio or video), the electronic submission of assignments, and the provision of updates and news. It also has a number of 'interactive tools' – email, discussion board, chat and whiteboard – which students can use to communicate with their tutor and each other. It is the communication tools that have dominated the discourse of many ODE commentators, who see the potential of computer mediated communication (CMC) to build a collaborative and constructivist learning environment. For example, Jonassen (1998) (cited by Murphy, 1999) writes:

> Contemporary conceptions of technology-supported learning environments assume the use of a variety of computer-mediated communications to support collaboration among communities of learners … Learning most naturally occurs not in isolation but by teams of people working together to solve problems. CLEs should provide access to shared information and shared knowledge-building tools to help learners to collaboratively construct social shared knowledge.

And Harasim (2001) values CMC because it enables students 'to construct knowledge as it is constructed in the knowledge communities they hope to join upon graduation'.

However, although today at the OUHK we have around 200 'on-line courses' the communication tools are not very much used on most of them. System administrators report low traffic, and course co-ordinators bear this out, saying that use of discussion boards is limited. Instead, the focus continues to be on delivery of course content, often by the provision of an on-line version of the printed text. In several of the Chinese medium courses, on-line interactive exercises and quizzes have replaced the activities in the printed version, but this 'interactivity' is between individual and course materials, so is pedagogically no different from its print counterpart.

This somewhat disappointing take-up of CMC cannot be attributed to difficulty in accessing the Internet. Hong Kong is a technologically oriented place with free local phone calls. Access to the Internet is very common and a survey of OUHK students in March 2001 indicated that 97 per cent of respondents had access to computers, 94 per cent had Internet access, 50 per cent had 56K modems and 35 per cent had broadband. Nevertheless, it has to be admitted that so far the CMC tools remain underused on most courses (with one or two honourable exceptions). Why?

As one of my colleagues memorably put it, 'we have new technology but the same old system'. Although the OUHK is keen to be at the technological cutting edge, its culture has not changed, nor has its model of what a distance learning course looks like (this is true at all levels of the University). Hence, the new technology is being used to deliver the course materials; but the change of mindset that would be required to shift the fulcrum of learning so that content delivery is at least potentially balanced by on-line interaction has not happened. This has made it very difficult for course designers to persuade course co-ordinators (and indeed Deans of Schools) to make access to the Internet mandatory on any of their courses. (The main reason they cite for this refusal is concern about excluding some students, but as we have seen, access is not really the problem.) Even if they are prepared to make access to the Internet mandatory (so that, for example, they can include links to external websites in their course), many course co-ordinators are reluctant to integrate on-line discussion or collaborative activities into the course. This goes back to the idea of the autonomous learner as one who works through course materials *alone*. Constructivist collaborative learning seems in opposition to their internalised model of a distance education course. This is a problem at institutional level too. For example, it would require the permission of the Senate and the OUHK Council to change the University regulations to allow collaborative assignments.

If the technology is not integrated with the course, it becomes an optional extra, which means that most students will not use it because their time is at a premium. In the 2001 survey of OUHK students two of the reasons given for *not* contributing to the discussion boards were that participation was not compulsory and it does not count towards assessment.

Tutors and the OLE

Much of the literature on on-line learning stresses the transformation of the teacher from instructor to facilitator (see Collis, 1996; Rowntree, 1999). As we have seen, in theory OUHK tutors have always been encouraged to see themselves as facilitators, though in practice, have often found themselves in the role of instructor. Tutor training has not changed much either since the introduction of the new technologies. Tutors are encouraged to use the tools in the on-line delivery system: discussion boards, newsgroups, email and chat. They are told that their duties as a tutor supporting an on-line course may include the following:

- Leading discussions and answering questions on the discussion board
- Organising on-line tutorials
- Handling tutor-marked assignments on-line
- Answering emails

However, although they receive some technical training on the use of the OLE, they get a simple checklist of guidelines for e-moderating. Skilled e-moderating is crucial to successful on-line learning (Salmon, 2000) and tutors need more than a set of guidelines, they need a training course, preferably one that gives them experience of teaching and learning on-line (Rowntree, 1999). Once again, the retention of the second generation model, even though third generation technology is now available, is the source of the problem. It is not surprising that CMC is under-used when those responsible for facilitating it are under-prepared for this role.

The way forward

Clearly, if on-line learning, and CMC in particular, is to develop further at the OUHK, a number of changes will have to be made. But should we be taking this path? In these days of the student as consumer (Tait, 2002), should we even try to change the product when the indications are that our customers might well prefer the old model but delivered via new technology? If they want a transmission model, should we just give it to them?

Aside from questions of whether satisfying customers' needs means what they think they need or what faculty think they need, it seems clear that the new technologies inevitably bring change in their wake – in modes of delivery for example. But if the underlying pedagogical model is not at least reviewed, that technology may not be used effectively. For example, one of my colleagues on the Chinese course design team voiced reservations about whether the benefits students received from doing multimedia activities in on-line courses made the considerable amount of work it took to design and implement them worthwhile.

It is also worth pointing out that although, as a whole, the introduction of CMC into courses has had only a modest effect, in the few cases where it is integrated properly into the course design, the results have been much more encouraging. While some learners choose ODE specifically because they want to work alone, it seems likely that feelings of isolation are at least one of the reasons for the high dropout rate that is seen as a major drawback of traditional distance learning programmes (Bernard *et al.*, 2000). Hong Kong students certainly value connection with their fellows (in a focus group discussion in March 2001, several noted that they actively sought such connection and found it beneficial). They are also highly likely to have the necessary technical skills, as use of email and the Internet is so widespread in Hong Kong.

However, as we have seen, CMC cannot just be an 'add-on'. What is the most effective way of using CMC for OUHK learners? Not, I think (despite the title of this chapter) a full blown constructivist model. A constructivist/collaborative approach would probably not appeal to learners who retain their Confucian respect for the teacher or authoritative text. Bernard *et al.*'s interesting distinction between collaborative and collective learning seems relevant.

> In cooperative learning, the result may simply add to a collection or incorporation of each individual's work into the final product. However final products based on collaborative should represent a synthesis of the whole.

Bernard dismisses cooperative learning; but given what we know about Hong Kong learners, perhaps it should be revisited? It is worth exploring the use of CMC, and if it is to be effective, it must be integrated into courses. But care must be taken to avoid overloading students; if new technology is added, something else has to go (see Tait, 2002). Insufficient time is one potential danger area, but so is loss of flexibility (one of the other claimed virtues of distance education). Having studied in an on-line programme myself, I can confirm that once there is a requirement to participate in on-line collaborative activities, distance education becomes far less flexible. This has implications for OUHK course teams, particularly course designers. In our current 'industrial' model, we work on the course package but have little to do with it once it is produced. But now, as Thorpe (2001) suggests, the advent of CMC in ODE has blurred the boundaries: 'Where for instance does one locate on-line interaction – within course design or learner support?' On smaller population courses, it may well be that the academics running the courses also become the tutors. But it is hard to see how that could happen with larger courses. In their case, course designers will have to move from designing fixed content (delivered by whatever media) to designing the environment in which interactive learning can take place. So, as the boundary between design and support blurs, the gap between course designer and tutor will have to be reduced.

Implications for tutor support

If the boundaries blur and some of the teaching shifts from the course materials to the on-line moderated discussion, the role of the tutor will change and the University will have to provide appropriate support for this process. A number of issues need to be addressed, including training.

Tutors will need a whole set of skills. The course design team, recognising from their own experience that one of the best ways of learning about e-moderating is to participate in an on-line course, is planning a course on e-moderating, initially to be taken by course co-ordinators. Salmon's (2000) five-step model may prove a suitable starting point for such a course:

1   Access and motivation: setting up system and accessing
2   On-line socialisation: sending and receiving messages
3   Information exchange: searching, personalising software
4   Knowledge construction: conferencing
5   Development: providing links outside closed conferences.

Lentell (2001) has queried whether this model would always transfer to other contexts, and Cox *et al.* (2000) found that on a large-scale computer course, participants rarely progressed beyond Stage 3. I think that Stages 3 and 4 represent a spectrum of interactivity which could probably be subdivided in different ways. This is very much a business model, each step building on the next. I suspect, however, that if Stages 1 and 2 are successful, knowledge construction on an individual but cooperative basis could occur at Stage 3. Notwithstanding these qualifications, it is coherent and convincing; and certainly the first two stages are essential if on-line learning is to take place on any level at all. It therefore will provide a useful *basis* for training tutors. The first cohort could then possibly become tutors in future presentations of the e-moderating programme.

There is a range of further issues to consider.

- *Balance of face-to-face and on-line tutoring*
  To avoid overload of both tutors and students, if on-line tutoring (whether asynchronous or synchronous) is added to a course, it makes sense to reduce the number of face-to-face tutorials. This suggestion currently tends to meet with opposition at various levels, from senior management to students. Furthermore, Vermeer (1999) has shown that Hong Kong learners are less inclined to engage in on-line communication if they have not met their fellow learners at least once face-to-face. It seems that, for some time to come, it will be necessary to start off with face-to-face tutorials if on-line communi-cation is to succeed at all, but equally, it will be necessary to persuade all players (including senior management) that some tutorials can usefully be replaced by on-line interaction.
- *Tutor:student ratio*
  This will have to be reviewed. At present, tutor groups have thirty to forty students, depending on the level of the course. If e-moderating is to be taken seriously, tutor group numbers will have to be reduced.
- *Assessment*
  Because assessment is so important, the OUHK (like other distance learning institutions) has fixed assessment procedures and processes. Tutor-marked assignments are central to the system. They were designed to fit the second generation model, and impose constraints on attempts to break away from it. However, if CMC is to be genuinely integrated into OUHK courses, assessment will have to be reassessed at an institutional level, and tutors, who may end up taking more responsibility for assessment, will need to be prepared (it is harder to give explicit marking guidelines for on-line or even group assessment activities).

- *Time and remuneration*
  In implementing the OLE, the OUHK did not substantially rethink the role of tutors. Meaningful on-line interaction will not happen without skilled e-moderation, and that takes much more time. At present, tutors are paid an 'honorarium' for adding e-moderating to their other duties. This is inadequate, and can only be a temporary solution.

Conclusion

The OUHK adopted second generation ODE theories as its pedagogical basis when it opened in 1989, and they have become part of its official culture, although it is clear that students and tutors find ways of subverting this culture to suit their own learning attitudes and needs. Perhaps because the second generation culture was established so successfully, when new and emerging technologies became available, debate about their use was slow to develop. Now, though, as it becomes evident that these technologies cannot just be 'added on', there is ongoing discussion about their implementation. It is by no means clear that the OUHK should simply strive to become a 'third generation' ODE university, taking on board current pedagogical theories, without additional enquiry. If simply imposed on our context (and come to that on any other Asian, or non-Western context) without examination, there is a good chance that they will be subverted to suit local needs. It may be better then, to focus on the strengths of CMC as they are likely to be experienced by Hong Kong (or other non-Western) learners, and build on those strengths and traditions, with a view to adapting current theory and available technology to provide appropriate, learner-centred courses. What is certain is that if effective on-line learning is to take place, OUHK tutors will play a crucial part in it, and the University therefore needs to review their role.

References

Bernard, R. M., de Robulcava, B. R. and St-Pierre, D. (2000) Collaborative on-line distance learning: issues for future practice and research, *Distance Learning*, 21 (2), pp. 260–75.

Biggs, J. (1996) Western misperceptions of the Confucian-heritage learning culture, in Watkins, D. A. and Biggs, J. R. (eds), *The Chinese Learner: Cultural, Psychological and Contextual Influences* (Hong Kong: CERC and ACER), p. 53.

Collis, B. (1996) *Telelearning in a Digital World* (London: International Thomson Computer Press).

Cox, E. S., Clark, W., Heath, H. and Plumpton, B. (2000) *Herding Cats Through Piccadilly Circus: The Critical Role of the Tutor In the Student's On-line Conferencing Experience*, (on-line) available from http://iet.open.ac.uk/pp/r.goodfellow/Lessons/cats/catsAUG00.htm (verified 22 June 2001).

Fung, Y. and Carr, R. (1999) Tutorials in a distance education system, in Carr, R., Jegede, O. J., Wong, T. M. and Yuen, K. S. (eds), *The Asian Distance Learner* (Hong Kong: Open University of Hong Kong Press), p. 151.

Harasim, L. (2001) The future of (e)learning. Keynote Address at CAL 2001, http://www.telelearn.ca/g_access/harasim_presentations/cal2001/sld008.htm, verified 5 July 2001.

Holmberg, B. (1989) *Theory and Practice of Distance Education* (London: Routledge).

Jonassen, D. (1998) Designing constructivist learning environments, in Reigeluth, C. M. (ed.), *Instructional Theories and Models*, 2nd edition (Mahwah, NJ: Lawrence Erlbaum).

Lee, W. O. (1996) The cultural context for Chinese learners: conceptions of learning in the Confucian tradition, in Watkins, D. A. and Biggs, J. R. (eds), *The Chinese Learner: Cultural, Psychological and Contextual Influences* (Hong Kong: CERC and ACER), p. 28.

Lentell, H. (2001) Review of e-moderating: the key to learning and teaching on-line, *Open Learning*, 16, p. 2.

Marton, F., Dall'Alba, G. and Tse, L. K. (1996), Memorising and understanding: the keys to the paradox?, in Watkins, D. A. and Biggs, J. R. (eds), *The Chinese Learner: Cultural, Psychological and Contextual Influences* (Hong Kong: CERC and ACER), pp. 69–83.

Murphy, D. (1999) Still 'Getting the mixture right': increasing interaction on the Internet, in Mills, R. and Tait, A. (eds), *Collected Papers of the 8th Cambridge Conference on Open and Distance Learning*, p. 104.

Nipper, S. (1989) Third generation distance learning and computer conferencing, in Mason, R. and Kaye, A., *Mindweave*, Milton Keynes: Open University, http://www.icdl.open.ac.uk/mindweave/chap5.html, verified 5 July 2001.

Peters, O. (1993) Understanding distance education, in Harry, K., John, M. and Keegan, D. (eds), *Distance Education: New Perspectives* (London: Routledge), p. 15.

Robinson, B. (1999) Asian learners, Western models: some discontinuities and issues for distance educators, in Carr, R., Jegede, O. J., Wong, T. M. and Yuen, K. S. (eds), *The Asian Distance Learner* (Hong Kong: Open University of Hong Kong Press).

Salmon, G. (2000) *E-moderating: The Key to Teaching and Learning On-line* (London: Kogan Page), p. 125.

Tait, A. (2002) Rethinking Learner Support at the Open University UK, paper given at the Conference of the Association of Asian Open Universities (AAOU), February, Delhi, Indira Gandhi National Open University.

Thorpe, M. (2001) Learner support: a new model for on-line teaching and learning (on-line message in MA discussion group) Kaye, H804 Tony's Group 9th June 2001.

Vermeer, R. (1999) On-line identity and learning in the design of a tertiary-level distance education course (MA dissertation, UK Open University).

2 Exploring informal student study groups in a South African teacher education programme

Carol Bertram

Introduction

This chapter focuses on a teacher education degree, the Bachelor of Education Honours which is offered to practising teachers with a four-year qualification. The programme is located within the School of Education, Training and Development at the University of Natal (UN), Pietermaritzburg, KwaZulu-Natal. It is a two-year, part-time programme, and all students are teaching and studying at the same time. The chapter reflects on the nature of the programme's student support strategies and focuses particularly on the *informal* study groups which students set up themselves. We interviewed students to explore the benefits of these groups, and observed them working together to try to understand better the learning processes within the groups. This chapter focuses on the findings of these interviews and observations.

Transformation in higher education in South Africa

South Africa has undergone enormous social and political changes in the past decade, which have had an inevitable impact on higher education, and thus on teacher education. South Africa is not immune to the global pressures facing universities: to increase student numbers and quality of graduates with less government subsidy available, to provide greater access to a much broader range of potential students and to operate in a market-driven environment. According to the White Paper on Higher Education, one of the key goals of transformation in higher education is increased participation with particular focus on a more balanced gender and race demographic, as well as increased recruitment of rural and working class students (Gultig, 2000, p. 41).

Change within the B Ed Hons

The Bachelor of Education Honours was traditionally accessible only to students who had a degree and who lived near to the university campus, as the University of Natal is a face-to-face university. In 1996, due to student demand, it was offered at a satellite campus in Newcastle (some 300 kms north of Pietermaritzburg) and lecturers travelled there at weekends. In 1999, the programme massified further with an enrolment of 2,000 students. It was offered using a mixed mode delivery, which signifies the use of printed course material *and* tutorial sessions. This is in contrast to much distance teacher education in South Africa, which is only by correspondence. Bi-monthly tutorial sessions were offered on Saturdays at twenty-one Learning Centres in five of South Africa's nine provinces.

Clearly changes in delivery have signaled enormous changes in the need for, and the nature of, student support.

What student support systems do we have in place?

One way of understanding the term 'student support' is the range of activities which complement the mass-produced learning materials (Tait, 1995, p. 232). A very broad definition is 'the entire range of methods and strategies employed in the presentation and delivery of courses aimed at assisting and enabling learners to comprehend fully, assimilate and master the skills and knowledge needed to achieve success in their studies' (Mays, 2000, p. 12). Simpson (2000, p. 6) suggests that student support falls into two broad areas: academic (or tutorial) support and non-academic (or counselling) support. In this chapter, I focus on the academic student support within the B Ed Honours programme.

The first step to planning any student support is to know who your students are (Tait, 1995, p. 233). The new National Qualifications Framework allows teachers with a four-year diploma from a teacher training college entry into the B Ed Hons (which had previously been open only to teachers with degrees). A survey done in 2000 of 796 students in KwaZulu-Natal showed that the vast majority of students (84 per cent) do not have a degree, but enter with a four year diploma. Thus, this is the first time they are studying at a university. Seventy-five per cent of the students are women and 66 per cent are primary school teachers. Only 7 per cent have English (which is the medium of instruction) as their home language. Half the students are between the ages of 31 and 40 (Bertram, 2000a).

Institutional support: formal tutorial sessions

Perraton (1995, p.182) states that 'the measures we need to take to raise the quality of a process of distance education all increase interaction between students and tutors or amongst students ...'. With this in mind, as well as an understanding of who our students are, the B Ed Hons programme chose to support students with four formal tutorial sessions per module together with the printed course material. Tutorials take place for six hours on a Saturday.

The programme expects students to have worked through a particular section of the course by doing the in-text tasks, and that they come to the tutorial ready to articulate their learning, and to apply it to different scenarios. Tutors are not expected to lecture the course material, but to facilitate various activities which provide opportunities for students to articulate their understanding and discuss issues with other students. As course developers, we hope that tutorials will enable students to move beyond simply knowing information, to being able to understand and apply the information in different situations.

South African teacher education policy (Department of Education, 2000) highlights the need for teachers to develop practical, foundational and reflexive competences. Foundational competence means knowing and understanding, practical competence means being able to apply this knowledge to practical situations and make informed decisions, and reflexive competence means that a teacher is able to critique her own practice in the light of the knowledge and understanding. The B Ed Hons has a strong focus on applying theoretical concepts to practice and on encouraging teachers to reflect on their own practice. The tutorial sessions aim to sharpen this focus and to give students the opportunity to meet with other students, for encouragement as well as to learn from one another.

Non-institutional support: informal study groups

An end-semester course evaluation which was administered to all students within KwaZulu-Natal in June 2000 (Bertram, 2000a) showed that of the 796 students answering the questionnaire, 70 per cent were part of an informal study group, and of these, 25 per cent met every weekday. Hodgson calls these 'self help groups' (1993, p.110), and I will use the term 'informal study groups'. It became clear that these informal study groups constituted another key area of student support, albeit support not organised by the University.

There is not much literature on student support outside the formal structures of the institution. There are suggestions that there are three sources of support outside the formal structures of the institution: namely from partners, families and friends; from other students and from employers (Simpson, 2000, p.101). In a small scale survey at the Open University, students rated support from partners and friends more highly than support from tutors and other students. In the B Ed Hons programme, the majority of students find support from other students by setting up small informal groups that provide them with academic support (they discuss the course material together) and with moral support and encouragement. The rest of this chapter examines the learning processes that take place within these groups.

Methodology

The data are taken from two sets of interviews with members of informal study groups. We seldom interviewed the whole study group, as some members were not present at the time. Sometimes group members arrived during the interview, or during the learning process we were observing. Thirty students who were members of nine groups were interviewed. The ratio of men to women was 1:3 which is fairly representative of the student cohort as a whole.

The first set of five interviews were conducted in April–May 2000. The purpose of these was to get a more detailed understanding of students' experience of the B Ed Hons programme, with a focus on how the delivery mode aids (or hinders) their learning (see Bertram, 2000b). We interviewed students who were located at different learning centres in the province of KwaZulu-Natal, but found that the data collected did not differ according to where students were located.

The second set of four interviews took place in April 2001, and had a stronger focus on understanding how learning takes place within the informal group. The interviewers were both co-ordinators of modules students were currently studying. After we interviewed students, we observed them working together. Aware that we were taking up students' learning time, we offered to answer questions that they had about the two modules at the end of the session, as a 'payback'. We interviewed the students from Pietermaritzburg at the venues where they usually met.

The informal groups who were interviewed were self-selected. Tutors asked students in their tutorial sessions who were members of an informal study group to volunteer to be interviewed. This means that the students who were interviewed were those who attended the formal tutorial sessions. Usually attendance ranges from 70–95 per cent. While students are not penalised for not attending these tutorials, they are strongly encouraged to do so. A small survey conducted in 2002 indicated that students do not attend due to personal reasons (commitment at family/ work/community functions or illness), rather than because they find the sessions a waste of time (Bertram, 2002).

What learning happens in the informal group?

Moore (1993, p. 20) writes that there are three different learning interactions that occur in distance education. One is *learner–content* interaction – the interaction between the learner and the subject of study, which hopefully results in understanding, and not merely in rote memorisation of text. Another is *learner–teacher* interaction – the interaction between the learner and the 'expert' who prepared the materials, or a person with some expertise who is acting as instructor or tutor. In this situation the teacher stimulates interest and motivation and organises activities which would deepen understanding. Another interaction is *learner–learner* interaction, where students talk to one another about what they are learning. The formal tutorial sessions involve all three interactions, while the informal groups are about learner–learner and learner–content interaction, as there is no 'expert' present.

The type of learning that happens within the group depends very much on the frequency of their meeting. Of the nine informal groups, six groups meet every weekday afternoon for one to three hours, after school and often daily during the school holidays. Three groups meet once or twice a month, with a particular focus on discussing the assignment tasks and on examination preparation.

In three of the informal study groups interviewed, students' first interaction with the material is in their informal study group. They do not read the material on their own first. The individual study that these students do takes place after group discussions, when they go home and write the learning material activities in their own words. Thus there is no initial *learner–content* interaction, or in fact no

Table 2.1 Profile and number of students interviewed

Year	Meeting place of informal group	Number interviewed	Gender	Home language	Observation of groups
2000	St Patrick's School, Kokstad (250 kms)*	3	3 men	2 Xhosa 1 Zulu	No
	Student's home, Pietermaritzburg	2	2 women	2 Zulu	No
	Umlazi library, near Durban (85 kms)	2	2 women	2 Zulu	No
	Thomas Moore School, Pinetown (70 kms)	4	2 men 2 women	4 English	No
	Indhlovana School, Greytown (80 kms)	5	5 women	5 Zulu	No
2001	Lambert Wilson library, Pietermaritzburg	3	3 women	3 Zulu	Yes
	Manaye Adult Centre, Pietermaritzburg	4	2 men 2 women	4 Zulu	Yes
	Mpumalanga township (40 kms)	4	2 men 2 women	4 Zulu	Yes
	Tembalethu Community Hall, Pietermaritzburg	3	2 women 1 man	3 Zulu	No
	TOTAL No. OF GROUPS = 9	**30**	**20 women 10 men**	**2 Xhosa 4 English 24 Zulu**	**3 groups observed**

* The kilometers in brackets indicate the distance from the University in Pietermaritzburg. The venues in Pietermaritzburg lie within 5–10 kms from the University.

'internal didactic conversation' to use Holmberg's term (in Moore, 1993, p. 20). In a sense this adds another dimension to Moore's idea: a learner–learner–content interaction replaces the individual learner–content interaction! This situation contradicts the design rationale of the programme, which expects students to interact with material on their own to gain personal mastery of the concepts. These students are adopting a communal approach to learning which is quite different from the individual model which commonly underpins distance education.

In other groups, members work through the material on their own in preparation for discussion in the informal group. In three of the groups, each member is given a part of the course to prepare and present at the group meeting. In this case a student would only read parts of the course material, and the other parts would be explained to him or her by other group members. Again, this is a communal approach, which subverts the design rationale in that students are not necessarily gaining individual mastery of the course as an integrated whole.

Membership of the groups

Most groups were formed when students met at the formal contact sessions. They recognised colleagues from nearby schools or people who lived in the same place,

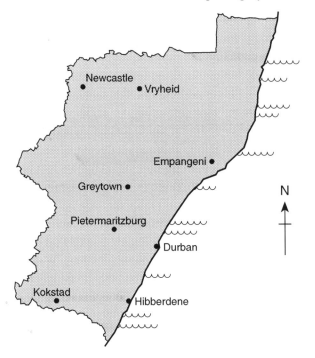

Figure 2.1 Map showing Regional Learning Centres in 2001

and set up groups. There are about 800 students currently on the programme in the province of KwaZulu-Natal, which has eight Learning Centres. Thus it is relatively easy for students to connect up with other teachers on the same programme. One group had been studying together for seven years. They have moved together as a group from studying one qualification to the next at different institutions.

It seems quite common that first year students join a group of students who are in their second year. First year students benefit from the experience of the second years as well as being provided with past exam papers! Although membership does seem to be quite stable, a pre-requisite is that a group is functioning well. One student told us that she left a group that she saw as 'non-functioning' to join her present group. In another group, the pre-requisite for membership is that everyone is committed and is prepared to work hard.

When asked, members said that there was no particular leader of the group, and that everyone took equal responsibility for the group. This did seem to be the case in the smaller groups of three or four members. But in the bigger groups, it was clear that one or two people did take a leadership role. Only one group, at Mpumalanga, admitted that one person was appointed an organisational leader who was responsible for letting everyone know of the time and venue of the meetings.

The benefits of the informal groups

It was clear from all the groups interviewed that the groups offered both academic support and non-academic or moral support.

Academic support

The groups that do all the in-text activities and reading together find it a help to do so in the group. A number of students said that they often did not understand ideas when they read at home, but the group helped them to understand.

> 'Alone you are lost, you are just reading…' (and by implication, not understanding).

> 'We help each other to understand the difficult things.'

> 'We argue about things until we come to a common understanding of a concept.'

One group member mentioned that everyone in the group brought different skills to the group: some could find the facts, some could analyse better.

Students do believe that the informal groups help them to achieve good marks. One teacher from the Greytown group said that she failed her first semester courses because she was working on her own, but passed the second semester because she began working with the study group. A student from Umlazi said that the informal group helped her to pass her exams. The academic records of the students interviewed reveal that most of the students are passing, attaining between 50 per cent and 65 per cent for a module. In only one group, each student had failed two of four modules they had studied so far and had achieved just 50 per cent for the other two modules.

A Pietermaritzburg group mentioned that being in an informal group gave one easy access to past exam papers. It was also mentioned that group members often belong to different formal tutorial groups, and thus can share the ideas that they have learned from different tutors. The study groups also provide self-made deadlines for students which keep them on track with their work.

Non-academic support

For all the informal groups, the benefits of belonging to such a group are that the groups provide encouragement.

> 'Other members motivate you when you want to drop out of the course.'

Members knew that they could not leave the group meeting until they had finished a certain section of work. In some groups, there was also some peer pressure, in that they could see that other students were doing more work than they were, or were achieving better marks.

Together with the academic benefits, one group also mentioned that their study group provided emotional support for one another.

> We meet Monday to Thursday evening from 6–9pm. Our families have to sacrifice. … We are now all friends. If one person has a problem we go to her and help her – we have become friends and family. Just recently one of us lost her brother – we have been there, helping her.
>
> (Grange, Pietermaritzburg group)

A feeling of isolation is one of the reasons for the high drop-out and failure rate of distance courses (Fraser and van Staden, 1996), and obviously the informal groups play a key affective role in making students feel part of a group. This is particularly important for students who may not get support at home (see John, 2000, p. 5).

Learning in formal tutorial groups

Five groups felt that their learning was supported by attending *both* the formal University tutorial sessions and being part of an informal group. They said the formal tutorials were very useful – primarily for clarifying concepts, as well as for sharing ideas with other students. The tutor was seen as the important person who would 'sort out our confusions for us'. They said that the course could not be successful without the tutorial sessions.

> I would struggle if there were no tut session. It makes it more user-friendly when you know that this day I will sit with somebody who has an idea, who will guide us and give direction. Otherwise it would be … just a correspondence course.
>
> (Kokstad group)

One student said that the main thing she had gained from the course was the confidence to talk in English in front of other adults, which was a direct result of the discussions in the formal tutorial sessions.

Some students said that the quality of the formal tutorial depends both on the tutor, and the other members of the group. If other students are not prepared, then the discussions are not fruitful. The complaint from almost all groups about certain tutors is that they do not provide sufficient clarity and direction. When students report back to the whole group on a discussion or task, often the tutor simply accepts all the ideas, even if these ideas are different. This makes students feel frustrated and unclear about the way forward.

This situation arises as a combination of two factors. First, tutors are encouraged to see themselves as facilitators and not lecturers, but some seem to understand their role as being completely non-interventionist! Second, students' own educational experience has favoured a didactic approach, and they are used to being lectured.

Four groups felt that they learned the most in their informal groups. One group said that the informal group was better because

all of us are committed. In the formal tut session, sometimes you are discussing with people who are not prepared. They are blank and they expect you to explain to them. In our [informal study] group, there are no parasites.

(Lambert Wilson Library group)

One group said that tutorial sessions were useful in terms of seeing other people's views and experiences, but academically, the tutorials were not necessary, as the study materials were sufficient.

Observation of the informal study groups in action

Three groups were observed learning together. The first group simply read through a portion of the study material together, clarifying concepts as they went along, and linking ideas to concepts previously encountered in the material. The other two groups we observed were discussing the major assignment task for their module *Assessment in Education*. The first part of the task was to 'discuss what you consider to be the five most important principles of holistic outcomes-based assessment'. The task required students to extrapolate these principles from the material; there was not a predefined list of these principles given by the course author.

One of the groups discussing the assignment task consisted of seven students who initially discussed the assignment topic in twos and threes. The discussion was conducted mostly in Zulu, with key concepts such as 'theories of intelligence', 'characteristics of outcomes-based education' used in English. Everyone was searching through the study material for a heading called 'five principles of holistic outcomes-based assessment'. The group appeared fairly unstructured and there was no sense of things moving forward. After 15 minutes, my colleague (a co-ordinator of the *Assessment* course) intervened and advised students that they would not find a list called 'principles' in the material, but that they needed to extrapolate the key principles from the study material.

The second group we observed, who were also discussing this assignment task, consisted of five students, two of whom did not participate in the discussion. Apparently the last time the group had met, they had agreed that the principles of assessment were the same as the 'five dimensions of assessment' (from Rowntree, 1987) which are listed in the study material. Just as the previous group had done, they were looking for a heading which listed the 'five principles of outcomes-based assessment', and the 'five dimensions' was the closest they could find. One group member had an idea about including the multiple intelligences, but the group held to the idea that they needed to use the 'five dimensions'. In fact his idea was on the right track, had it been explored and taken further. My colleague intervened after about 15 minutes, and explained that they needed to review all the study material and extract the key principles themselves. The students struggled to understand the concept of principles and how these could be drawn from the text as a whole.

A fourth group whom we interviewed after the assignment was due, told us they had spent a whole week looking for the 'principles' in the study material. Eventually they decided to list methods of assessment such as group work, essays, projects, etc. This group was angry at the 'University' for setting an assignment 'so they would fail'. They were not happy about us observing them working together.

Discussion of key themes

Informal study groups seem to epitomise collaborative learning principles and indicate that students are taking responsibility for their learning. Students are convinced about the academic effectiveness and social benefits of studying together, and yet our observations seem to suggest that the groups were *not* helpful in making sense of an assignment topic.

The approaches of 'deep' and 'surface' learning are a useful conceptual tool to make sense of the situation. The deep and surface approach to learning was first introduced by Marton and Säljö in the 1970s. Ramsden (1988, p. 19) explains these two concepts in the following way. The main difference is that a deep approach is characterised by an *intention to understand*, whereas a surface approach is characterised by an *intention to complete the learning task assignments*. Learners who take a deep approach focus on 'what is signified' while those who take a surface approach focus on 'the signs' (or the text). Learners who take a deep approach to learning are able to relate new concepts to everyday experience and to what they already know, and reflectively organise and structure content to make links and associations. On the other hand, learners who take a surface approach focus on discrete elements of new knowledge and memorise new information and procedures for assessment. They do not structure and organise content in ways that make sense to themselves, and associate concepts and facts in unreflective ways. They tend to treat a learning task as an external imposition. This is the other key difference: for deep approach learners, learning has an *internal emphasis*. Through learning they feel that aspects of reality become visible and more intelligible. For surface approach learners, learning has an *external emphasis*. Their focus is on the demands of assessment, and knowledge is cut off from everyday reality.

Using these concepts, I want to suggest that the university privileges and expects the deep learning approach, but that the three groups dealing with the *Assessment in Education* assignment, took a surface approach. The assignment demanded that students go beyond 'the signs', and extrapolate the principles from the material as a whole. Students were unable to do so, and instead looked for the discrete elements. Clearly the numerical cue of 'five' was important for students. Their previous study experiences primed them to look for a list in the material with the number 'five' in it. In particular, the group who ended up listing assessment methods in their assignment, saw the task as an external imposition, with no thought as to how it might improve their own teaching practice.

There are two key reasons that the students used a surface approach to the learning task. The first is their educational background, and the second is their cognitive academic language proficiency (see Cummins, 1984). Many teacher training colleges, where these students initially studied, favoured didactic approaches to assessment which focused on content memorisation. The majority of our students (86 per cent) have studied via distance before, and these learning experiences were probably characterised by print materials designed in a didactic, content-centred manner, with a lack of face-to-face tutorial support for students (Butcher, 1996, p. 10). Thus students' previous learning experience did not demand more than a surface approach. Many students have weakly-developed cognitive academic language proficiency in English, as their own schooling favoured subtractive bilingualism (which means the development of English was favoured over the development of the mother tongue, thus students did not develop strong cognitive academic language proficiency in their mother tongue either). Thus they simply do not have the high level of language competence which is needed for a deep approach.

This is these students' first experience of university study and they have not been initiated into academic discourse which privileges abstractions such as 'principles'. Many students did not see that there was any conceptual difference between 'dimensions' and 'principles'. They have not gained the 'cultural capital' (Morgan, 1995, p. 58) of the university nor the academic discourse (which is abstract, tentative and uncertain) which is necessary to participate in the university academic environment at a deep learning level. Whereas undergraduates have three or four full years to learn the discourse, these students have only two years of part-time study.

It is clear that the informal study groups are vital from an affective perspective: they provide students with motivation and support. From an academic perspective, the groups do seem to help students achieve a certain level of learning: to know the content and, in many instances, to pass the exam. However, as indicated earlier, there is little evidence that the groups support students in developing deep approaches to learning which are advocated by the School of Education. The programme wants students to develop critical thinking, problem-solving and com-munication skills, as well as the ability to reflect on their own practice in the light of what they are learning (Bertram, 1999, p. 2).

Some of the learning that happens in informal study groups may in fact diminish the opportunity for students to develop these skills. There is an indication of 'group think': that the majority view will prevail (even if it is wrong). Vygotsky believed that all higher mental processes are generated through mediation (Gouws, 1998, p. 78). In the groups we observed, none of the students was able to play the mediating role of an 'expert other' in order to move the other students into their zone of proximal development, and they seemed unable to access the learning material in such a way that it could play this role. Thus, in a worst case scenario, students are simply sharing their ignorance and not moving forward at all, although I do not suggest that this happens in all groups.

The study groups may not necessarily be fostering individual responsibility and autonomy. The groups may in fact be hindering students from becoming independent and self reliant learners, particularly when students substitute learning on their own, with learning in their informal group. At worst, the weaker students simply copy the answers to in-text activities from the others, without real understanding. If students do not engage with the material at all as individuals, the possibility of them using their understanding to reflect on their own practice seems remote.

At an assessment level, preparation for assignments in groups may mean that some students have not thought through a problem or idea at all themselves, but are simply writing down what the group decided. This method might usually work well for students (though it did not in the case of the *Assessment in Education* task!), but may not work towards the School of Education's goal of developing an individual's reflective competence. A course co-ordinator tells of students who are amazed that they have failed an assignment because 'everyone else in the group passed, but we wrote the same thing, we did everything together' (N. Mthiyane, pers. comm. 27/05/01).

Conclusion

This chapter has discussed and analysed the data from nine interviews with informal study groups, and three observations of groups learning together. The sheer number of students who are part of informal groups suggests that many are embracing a communal approach to learning, rather than the individual model that usually underpins distance education. The chapter concludes that while the informal groups are widespread and show students' dedication and commitment to the programme, much of this learning time may not be being used very profitably. These informal groups have positive benefits on an affective level, and possibly on a surface learning level, but probably do not encourage a deep learning approach. This may be because the educational experience of most students has not required that they develop a deep learning approach and many do not have the cognitive applied language proficiency which a deep approach requires. It may also be that students and the School of Education have very different understandings of what constitutes 'success' on the programme. For some students, simply getting the qualification is enough, whereas the School has more lofty ideals of developing reflective practitioners and critical thinkers.

One of the issues that has become very clear is the need to provide greater support for students in the demands of the social sciences, such as writing logically, structuring an argument, recognising contrasting opinions, etc. Debates around running separate academic development courses versus embedding these skills into other courses have raged for decades without clear conclusions. As a way forward, the School has decided that all the tutors on the B Ed Hons programme must go through an academic literacy course which highlights these issues. They should become competent and confident to model these concepts to their students in the course of their tutorial sessions.

Acknowledgements

Thanks to Dr Fred Barasa (in 2000) and Ms Nonhlanhla Mthiyane (in 2001) for interviewing students with me, and to colleagues in the School for their comments on this chapter.

An earlier version of this chapter will be published in 2002 in the *South African Journal of Higher Education*, 16 (3), under the title '"Students doing it for themselves": the role of informal study groups in a mixed mode teacher education programme'.

References

Bertram, C. (1999) Delivering a quality B. Ed. – reflecting on a UN/SACTE experience! Paper presented at the First NADEOSA National Conference, August, Pretoria.

Bertram, C. (2000a) Student Evaluation of the UN/SACTE B Ed: June 2000. Unpublished report. School of Education, Training and Development, University of Natal.

Bertram, C. (2000b) A mixed mode distance education model for teacher education: rationale, student experiences and quality. Presented at the second NADEOSA Conference 'Southern African Models of Distance Education', 21–22 August 2000, Pretoria.

Bertram, C. (2002) Why students don't attend tutorial sessions, *Open Learning through Distance Education*, 8 (1).

Butcher, N. (1996) The investigation of teacher education at a distance in South Africa, *Open Learning through Distance Education*, 2 (1).

Cummins, J. (1984) *Bilingualism and Special Education: Issues in Assessment and Pedagogy* (Clevedon: Multilingual Matters).

Department of Education (2000) Norms and standards for educators, *Government Gazette* 4 February 2000, no. 20844 (Pretoria: Government Printer).

Fraser, W. J. and van Staden, C. J. S. (1996) Students' opinions on factors influencing drop out rates and performance at distance education institutions, *South African Journal of Education*, 16 (4).

Gouws, A. (1998) From social interaction to higher levels of thinking, in Kruger, N. and Adams, H. (eds), *Psychology for Teaching and Learning* (Johannesburg: Heinemann).

Gultig, J. (2000) The university in post-apartheid South Africa: new ethos and new divisions, *South African Journal of Higher Education*, 14 (1).

Hodgson, B. (1993) *Key Terms and Issues in Open and Distance Learning* (London: Kogan Page).

John, V. (2000) Learner support needs within the UN/SACTE distance programme: towards broader and more formalised support. Paper presented at the second NADEOSA conference, Pretoria, 21–22 August 2000.

Mays, T. (2000) Learner support: a South African programme perspective, *Open Learning through Distance Education*, 6 (2), July 2000.

Morgan, A. R. (1995) Student learning and students' experiences: research, theory and practice, in Lockwood, F. (ed.), *Open and Distance Learning Today* (London: Routledge).

Moore, M. G. (1993) Three types of interaction, in Harry, K., John, M. and Keegan, D. (eds), *Distance Education: New Perspectives* (London and New York: Routledge).

Perraton, H. D. (1995) Quality in distance education, in *One World, Many Voices: Quality in Open and Distance Learning.* Selected papers from the 17th World Conference of the International Council for Distance Education, Birmingham, United Kingdom, June 1995, ed. D. Stewart (Milton Keynes, UK: The Open University).

Ramsden, P. (1988) *Improving Learning: New Perspectives* (London: Kogan Page).

Rowntree, D. (1987) *Assessing Students: How Shall We Know Them?* (London: Kogan Page).

Simpson, O. (2000) *Supporting Students in Open and Distance Learning* (London: Kogan Page).

Tait, A. (1995) Student support in open and distance learning, in Lockwood, F. (ed.), *Open and Distance Learning Today* (London: Routledge).

3 Supporting the masses?

Learner perceptions of a South African ODL programme

Norma Corry and Tony Lelliott

Introduction

The challenge facing tertiary institutions of accommodating changing educational needs has been in the forefront of discussion in recent years. Much of the discussion has focused on the new demands presented by the increased use of technology in education delivery and the effect this has had on access to study and study method preferences (Tait, 2000; King, 2001). In South Africa and elsewhere, some of the major universities which have customarily only offered face-to-face programmes, are now offering open and distance learning programmes similar to the one that is the focus of this chapter. South African universities are currently in competition not only with each other, but also with foreign universities who have set up campuses in South Africa, and who have the necessary communications link with the mother university. The promise of an international degree through enrolling in these foreign universities is a major incentive for many students who equate quality with Europe or Australia.

Recent trends in support for the open and distance learner

Over the past decade, but particularly since the rise of the World Wide Web, the nature of student support in developed countries has changed considerably. Programmes based on printed materials have traditionally relied on support in various ways, these include regular tutorial sessions, other regular face-to-face contact, telephone tutoring, detailed feedback on Tutor Marked Assignments, formal and informal study groups and support from partners, family and friends (Asbee and Simpson, 1998; Tait, 2000). In the developed 'North', many open and distance learning courses have become available on-line over the past few years, and while some aspects of support may remain constant (such as support from family) others have changed considerably. Evidence shows that the availability of on-line support such as that provided by the UK Open University has resulted in students making considerable use of it (Thorpe, 2001; Phillips *et al.*, 2001). On-line support includes the use of software tools, automated (and tutor marked) feedback on performance, technical support, as well as more traditional supervision by tutors. However, tutors, instead of providing regular (weekly or monthly) face-to-face sessions for their tutor group, are now challenged to provide 'instant' feedback to their tutees, resulting in excessive time demands and 'interaction fatigue' (Mason, 2001). In his paper on planning student support, Tait (2000) analyses the extent of 'take-up' of new technologies by students, and suggests that it depends not only on the location of technology availability (domestic, workplace and social), but also on whether the technology is a replacement of or supplement to the existing support (e.g. face-to-face tutoring). He further suggests that there is 'no universal blueprint for the establishment of student support systems', and that any system will depend on a wide range of variation across the elements that comprise the support.

As will be shown in the next section, the students involved in our study are clearly in the developing 'South'. Perraton (2000), in his review of ODL in the Developing World, maintains that the new technologies are likely 'to narrow rather than widen access' in a variety of ways: learners need to have access to expensive equipment, governments need to provide a power supply and telecommunication links, and there needs to be a service industry to maintain the system. It is likely that only the privileged will be able to access education provided by such a system. Another question raised is to what extent is the service to the learner improved by the new technologies? For example, some institutions, instead of sending out course materials to students by post, have decided to develop them centrally, and distribute them electronically. This has resulted in a shift in the cost from the producer to the user, with the latter eventually receiving an inferior version of the material.

In addition, Perraton also claims that there are considerable increased costs associated with any shift to computer-based learning. For example, a well-developed multimedia CD-ROM is likely to cost up to forty times the equivalent materials in print form (2000, p. 149). Rumble (2001a, 2001b) also indicates that the costs of using technology and on-line support are greater than print media. Therefore the overall costs for the institution providing such technology-based learning and the costs required for connectivity and personal computers owned either by individuals or by some form of 'telecentre' (from which students can access the institution) are going to be prohibitive for most countries in the developing world. Lelliott *et al.* (2000) have suggested that 'the idealized uptake of the idea of the networked society' by such countries is not currently practicable, and they should concentrate on priorities such as the improvement of traditional basic education and the creation of a sustainable civil society.

While the recent literature on learner support emphasises the usefulness of technology-based systems, we consider that for many learners, especially but not exclusively those in developing countries, such support practices are inappropriate, costly and unattainable. Through its description and analysis of student responses to a questionnaire, this chapter aims to show that more traditional methods of support are the most appropriate for the conditions under which our students live and work.

The Bachelor of Education programme at the University of the Witwatersrand

In South Africa, the 'post-graduate' Bachelor of Education (B Ed) degree has traditionally been a one-year full-time or two-year part-time course taken by qualified educators who wish to enhance their academic and professional knowledge and expertise. In 1996, the University of the Witwatersrand (Wits) in Johannesburg introduced a Further Diploma in Education (FDE): a professional development programme for teachers in possession of a three-year teaching diploma (the basic qualification for teaching). The FDE programme is offered on a part-time semi-distance basis, and enables primary and secondary teachers to further develop their educational and content knowledge in the areas of Mathematics, Science or English Language Teaching. As a result of changes in admission policy in line with government guidelines, in 1999 the University allowed entry to its B Ed programme to candidates with either a four-year diploma or a three-year diploma plus FDE. Many applicants came from the University's FDE diplomates, who requested that the B Ed programme be adapted from a face-to-face programme to a semi-distance mode like that of the FDE. As a result, a flexible-learning Bachelor of Education was developed to suit students who live at a distance from Johannesburg.

The Bachelor of Education is taught over two years, and consists of eight modules and a small scale research project. The programme uses a composite of learning materials and contact sessions in the delivery of the B Ed course in a flexible learning mode. During each year three major contact sessions that coincide with school holidays are a compulsory component of the programme. These sessions are designed to evaluate student progress through discussion of concepts and ideas already encountered by students, and to prepare students through lectures and tutorials for the next section of the course. The study materials comprise a course book with activities and a reader containing key readings for the module. The goals of the programme have the three-fold purpose of assisting students to:

* strengthen their academic reading and writing competences;
* develop conceptual and theoretical frameworks that will create understanding and capacity to intervene in practice;
* engage constructively and critically with curriculum innovations.

The materials are thus written with this purpose in mind and the tutorials at contact sessions are a forum in which students can discuss, critique and apply concepts and theories they encounter in the study materials.

The programme provides a variety of support mechanisms to assist the students in their studies. These include face-to-face tutorials and individual counselling during the residential contact sessions; interactive printed course materials which assist the students in understanding course content; detailed feedback on assignments; telephonic contact with the university whereby students can engage with tutors and administrative staff in order to solve academic or other difficulties, and assistance in the formation of study groups.

Student opinion canvassed

Student opinion was canvassed by means of a questionnaire completed at the end of their final year of study. A total of thirty-six students completed the questionnaire, although not all of them completed all questions. The respondents to the questionnaire comprised a moderately representative sample of the first student cohort in terms of gender and employment.

In addition, the majority of respondents (69 per cent) came into the B Ed through the FDE route.

The survey elicited responses to the following broad questions:

- reasons why students chose this course;
- methods of study and students' study environment;
- communication with the university including access to new technologies;
- impact of the programme on students' professional practice.

Our analysis of the student survey will address each of these four areas.

The students in their context

Students who opt for a teacher enhancement programme at degree level in South Africa are usually mature students who bring a wealth of life experience to their studies. While few have a degree, most come with the four-year professional qualification already discussed above. Nearly half of the first cohort of B Ed students at Wits had entered the programme through the FDE route. The majority of students enrolled in the programme were resident in the Limpopo Province, some three to four hours travelling northwards from the University. The second largest group lived in the Gauteng Province, in which Wits University is situated. Gauteng is a largely urbanised province, but many of the schools are under-resourced in numerous ways, as most of them are situated in townships such as Soweto, adjacent to Johannesburg. Many of the students from the Limpopo Province work in a rural or semi-rural situation in resource-poor environments similar to that of the KwaZulu-Natal students described elsewhere (Glennic in Mills and Tait, 1996), that is, environments having inadequate education provision, cramped housing situations and limited public transportation.

A crucial factor in student choice of study mode was the financial benefit to be derived from retaining employment during the years of study. In a time when the

Table 3.1 Student demographics

Male: 53%	Primary education: 42%
Female: 47%	Secondary education: 47%
	Tertiary education: 6%
	Non-governmental organisations: 5%

level of unemployment has risen, mixed-mode programmes are becoming more popular because they increase student access to study opportunities. The majority of the B Ed cohort reported that the programme gave them access to study that they would not normally have. Gordon (2001) reports a similar finding to this in a report on a teacher-upgrading project in a rural area in South Africa.

In terms of the study environment of B Ed students, the primary factors influencing their study patterns were space, opportune times for study and provision of electricity. These factors would obviously be relevant to the resource-poor environments already noted. The majority (80 per cent) of students indicated that they had electricity, but a small percentage of those without electricity reported that this made study difficult. Most students had a private space or room in which to study, while only 46 per cent had regular undisturbed study times. The programme expects students to spend fifteen hours per week in study. Some students achieved this as shown in Figure 3.1.

As would be expected, other commitments of students made demands on their time and attention, work and family pressure being cited as the most common amongst students. These would probably translate into a 'lack of time', which was also referred to in various ways as a difficulty by several respondents. Geographical isolation or lack of a study partner was specified by a small number of participants. Other factors that made study difficult included family problems, noisy neighbours and a lack of understanding of assignment questions.

As has been shown in the research of Bhalalusesa (2001), role conflict is a norm for ODL students. This would apply to both men and women, although Bhalalusesa herself focuses on the difficulties faced by women in such programmes in her home country, Tanzania, and suggests that it is particularly difficult for women in third world countries (2001, p. 158). In this study we have not addressed gender differences in time management problems encountered by students, but the B Ed programme organisers made considerable attempts in the course materials and residential sessions to assist students to organise their own time effectively for study, and to balance time between commitments. When asked what helped them

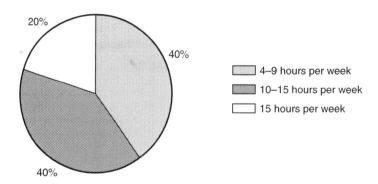

Figure 3.1 Hours per week students spent in study

most, the commonest responses were assistance from their spouse and members of their study groups, and the time allocation suggestions given in the course materials. Students appreciated overall the need for effective personal discipline and time management, although three students stated that nothing assisted them to manage their time effectively.

This finding on what assists students most in their home study environment concurs with research done elsewhere. A survey conducted by Asbee and Simpson (1998) amongst ODL students has shown similar results – the most significant form of support came from partners, family and friends. The type of support would include both practical, in terms of time and space, and emotional support. The Asbee and Simpson survey arose out of research done by Veronica McGiverney in 1996 on drop-out and retention rates in ODL programmes in the UK. McGiverney purports three factors governing retention rates:

- good support from partners, family and friends;
- good contact with the institution;
- good contact and support from other students.

(Cited in Asbee and Simpson 1998, p. 56)

These three factors are useful to us as they encompass some of the questions we asked our students in the questionnaire. The first factor is corroborated by the reports from the B Ed students, who regard it as important. In terms of students supporting each other, the organizers of the Further Diploma in Education programme at Wits have, from its inception, encouraged students to find study partners and to form study cluster groups with other students enrolled on the programme. This has continued in the B Ed, and, given the higher academic demands of this programme, may even be more important than in the FDE. The importance of study groups or 'peer group learning' has been given prominence by other authors, for example Holt (1994), who has carried out a detailed survey of study groups within a distance learning MBA programme. Some of the benefits identified by him are improved students' learning and formal performance, increased student productivity, benchmarking of attainment and an increase in general motivation and support.

Nearly 60 per cent of the B Ed respondents stated that they are a member of a study cluster, and the modal number for such a group is two or three persons (65 per cent of respondents form groups of this size). However, as many as 30 per cent of the students who are members of a study cluster work in groups of six or more persons. There is a relatively large contingent of students from the Limpopo Province (twenty-three out of thirty-six respondents), and it appears that some of these students have formed one large cluster of approximately twelve.

The study clusters usually meet at the students' homes, school, local library or church, and vary in frequency of contact from several times a week to every three months. Most groups appear to meet every two to three weeks, though some groups also contact each other on a regular basis by phone when necessary. Most study group meetings last two to three hours, but the large group in the Limpopo Province referred to above, meets for the whole weekend on occasions, with individual members attending for part of the time. The purpose of such meetings is to discuss aspects of the course materials, often with a focus on assignments.

The students regard the benefits as including understanding ideas as a result of discussion, and the sharing of ideas. One of the theories covered in the B Ed programme is constructivism, with the 'social construction of knowledge' used as an example of one of the ways in which learners learn. The students who form study clusters appear to appreciate that their own learning is enhanced in this manner, in that they refer to peer discussion as a useful tool for learning. In a study of a similar cohort of students elsewhere in South Africa, Bertram (2000) found that students perceived study group discussion to be valuable for learning. The students who have not joined study clusters cite distance as being the main reason why they have not formed a study group. Logistical transport difficulties and financial constraints also contribute to a lack of peer group learning among a minority of students. Holt (1994) and Tait (1996) suggest that in the case of geographically isolated students, the use of Information and Communications Technology (ICT) may assist in enabling interaction. However, as we discussed above, this is not likely to be feasible for rural South African teachers. We turn now to the second factor in McGiverney's list of support, namely, contact with the institution.

Student opinion on their experience of contact with the University was canvassed in terms of contact sessions at the university and after their return to their home environment. Students were asked what worked best for them.

As shown in Table 3.2, the majority reported that tutorial help through telephonic contact worked best for them, in addition to the help received in the form of feedback on written assignments. The programme has implemented a policy of maintaining contact with distance students and this means in effect that tutors often phone students, either on their own initiative or in response to messages left on voice mail facilities. The prevalence of mobile telephones has increased accessibility of the University to students, especially in remote rural areas having no formal telephone infrastructure. The use of the telephone as a means of contact for students in isolated areas has been investigated by Maher and Rewt (2001), who found that over 80 per cent of lecturers in the Open University in Scotland supported their students in one-to-one telephone tutorial sessions. However, even

Table 3.2 What worked best for students in terms of their contact with the University

78%	75%	67%	40%	3%

Note: Some students chose more than one category.

though telephone contact is regarded by students as worthwhile it is, as reported by Gordon, costly to maintain for students in rural areas, both in terms of time and money (2001, p.12). Over the past two years such costs are decreasing, as the use of Short Message Service (SMS) has become more prevalent, and this may be a realistic use of technology for the future. It is important to stress that rural South African students are here being pragmatic in their use of a technology that is relatively old (telephone tutoring has long been a feature of many open and distance learning programmes), but has enabled greater access in its new format (mobile voice and messaging).

Meeting with staff was important for 67 per cent of respondents. Many students emphasised in individual comments that they found the accessibility of staff and their interest in student progress, coupled with the emotional support offered, to be of most help. Conversely when asked what did not work well for them some students reported that tutors were not always accessible and did not always give sufficient feedback on assignments.

Over one third of students indicated that they made use of library services during contact sessions. Less than 15 per cent of students also reported benefit from other types of support set up for them during contact sessions, such as a counselling service, and a study skills programme. Individual criticisms from students were few and included a slow postal service, failure to receive feedback in time for examination work, difficulty in engaging with a particular module, time spent travelling to the institution and isolation from other students in their home context.

From the outset of the B Ed the programme organisers made a decision *not* to include the use of ICTs as a core component of the courses. This decision was based on an assumption that, from our experience with students enrolled on the FDE programme, few had access to computers or the Internet. It was suggested that any requirement for teachers to interact with each other or with the University by (for example) email, would heighten the disparities between the more- and less-resourced students. There was evidence from research carried out on the FDE programme (Adler *et al.*, 1998) that issues of differential resource provision between the rural and urban-based teachers were a source of potential friction. We also considered Mansell and Wehn's proposition that ICT applications for education in developing countries have three serious weaknesses: they are unsuited to the technological and organisational infrastructure of the countries concerned, their technological sophistication requires constant expensive updating and they are insufficiently focused on the problem-solving environment (Mansell and Wehn, 1998).

In the survey, nine teachers (25 per cent of respondents) reported that they have access to a computer that they can use in their studies. The majority of these have access at home or at school, and six of the nine have email and Internet access. While this is an encouraging figure when compared to the assumption described above, it does reflect that only 17 per cent of students would be able to interact with each other or the University using email or a web-based programme.

Unsurprisingly, twenty-one teachers (over 90 per cent of respondents of this part of the survey) would favour having email and web-based learning integrated into the programme, the main reasons cited being easier access to information, that it is important to be computer literate, and that we live in a technological world. Notwithstanding the resource constraints, we intend to conduct a pilot study to investigate the possible use of study centres, Internet cafés and similar sites through which technology-enhanced learning might be achieved.

Intervention in professional practice

A considerable portion of the questionnaire given to students was designed to gauge their opinion on how they perceived the programme to have made a difference to their professional practice. This included their use of print-based materials. As one of the goals of the programme is to assist students to develop their capacity to intervene in practice, we expected some positive response from students in this regard. Of course in this type of qualitative survey we can only report what students claim about any significant change.

In all the responses to the questionnaire, students recorded that the B Ed programme had had a significant impact on their professional practice. This was perceived by students to occur in two ways:

- it assisted them to relate theory to practice (64 per cent).
- it gave them a new confidence to take on a more prominent role in their educational context (36 per cent).

Several students indicated a direct relation between study and classroom practice. They claimed an increased ability to think more critically and reflectively, and also a new perspective to teaching approaches in their specific subject. The majority claimed a greater competence in developing new strategies and approaches to teaching and learning and several claimed improved relations with learners. One student alleged there had been a radical change to his classroom practice. In terms of cross-curricular application, at least three students said that they were better able to integrate their subject area with other subject areas. Other claims included an improved ability to recognise and resolve issues and problems within the school community. The way in which the programme informed them of new issues in curriculum empowered students to take a leading role in curriculum development in their context. Three students attributed their promotion in school directly to their B Ed studies.

Perhaps the following response from a student sums up student perception of the impact of the programme on their practice:

'I started to see education and my career in a new way.'

Student perception about what specifically initiated change in their professional practice was attributed to:

- working with the course materials (70 per cent);
- interaction with academic staff (30 per cent).

Students found that the course materials were relevant to their context, and also challenged them to think more critically. Materials were user-friendly, provided a good introduction to topics, and assisted them in understanding new concepts and ideas. The way in which the modules had been written encouraged reflection and application. Many students stated that they had acquired new skills – academic, leadership and communication, time management – through engagement with the course materials.

Less than 10 per cent of responses were critical of the materials. Though one module was considered by some students to be 'too theoretical', the same students nevertheless felt that it also challenged them to think critically and understand new concepts. Another criticism concerned the number of activities set for students. Generally it was felt that, with the exception of two, each module had too many activities set for students. Students were divided in opinion regarding the style of writing of two particular modules, but felt that these modules nevertheless assisted them in progressing their understanding of concepts and new ideas and in thinking more critically about issues.

'Lecturers who are willing to assist', 'the approach of lecturers', 'the influence of lecturers' and 'contact with lecturers during contact sessions' are examples of the comments given by students. One student felt that she could not be certain what instigated change but stated 'I found myself changing as I went through the course and that was demonstrated in practice'.

Therefore, in summary, student perception of how the programme impacted on their classroom practice was perceived by them to be a result of how they interacted with the course materials in their context, and with the academic staff from the university. The benefit to students included a new awareness of themselves in relation to their context, and the acquisition of new skills, both academic and professional, which empowered them to contribute meaningfully to educational change in their context.

Development of ODL students, academically, personally and professionally, and the role of learner support in this growth, has been the subject of debate over the last three decades at least, if not longer. Whereas in the early days of ODL, teaching and learning were seen in terms of passive transmission models in which the teacher transmits knowledge – through contact and course materials – the movement in more recent years has been to a constructivist model in which teaching and learning is located in a social context with active role players (Young and Marks-Maran, 1998). We have already noted that students felt that sharing in discussions with peers in study groups assisted them in learning. It has been the policy of the programme organisers from the beginning to ensure that more interactive models of teaching and learning are included in course provision. The materials developed for the B Ed programme were done so cognisant of the learner and the learners' context. The writers endeavoured to include interactive and personal reflection type exercises relating to the work experience of the student.

This is a move away from mass-produced and pre-packaged course materials that are questionable in terms of their support of individual learners in flexible learning programmes (Tait, 1996).

The importance of the relationship between theory and practice for professional growth is emphasised by Leach, who maintains that learning in the broad sense of being a lifelong exercise should have central place in learner support (1996, p. 104). Leach concludes in her discussion that learner support is more of a 'process' that enhances learning than a 'provision to be managed' (1996, p. 123).

The value and importance of personalised communication in flexible learning programmes through both horizontal and vertical relationships, has been raised by Tait (1996), who points out the dangers of losing the personalised community face of a programme in favour of a more managerial approach, which minimises interaction between learner and tutor (1996, p. 66–7). Much of what is being debated about the personal nature of learner support is owed to Holmberg (1981) who developed the notion of 'guided didactic conversation' as an approach to distance education. He argues that students need to be directed through their study by good 'conversations' or interactions with tutors that includes emotional and academic support, and through accessible and supportive course materials.

It is important for our programme that the feedback from students favours the more traditional approaches to learner support.

Conclusion

Clearly a mixed-mode flexible learning programme of this type suits both urban and rural teachers in South Africa, given that they can develop their professional competence while still earning a salary. Even though many students come from resource-poor environments there is an interest in the use of Information and Communications Technology on the part of the learners. This is becoming a changing context for our learners who are increasingly being exposed to new technologies. We do not want to make a case for entirely ignoring the recent trends and advantages in using modern technologies for teaching on open and distance learning programmes in developing countries. Where such technologies are appropriate and financially feasible, as in the case of the use of mobile telephones to assist with tutoring, we recommend that they be used and encouraged. We do, however, maintain that development of conventional learner support activities such as face-to-face tutorials, counselling, interactive printed course material, detailed feedback on assignments, telephonic contact with the university, assistance in the formation of study groups, and support from partners, family and friends are more important for the majority of students in the 'South', who are still yet to benefit from the technological revolutions taking place in the developed world.

We consider that we are some way towards meeting the goals of our programme in that we have assisted students to move away from the passive models of teaching and learning and become independent learners and critical thinkers who can engage constructively with course materials. The fact that students' academic growth appears to derive most benefit from a more personalised interaction with staff in face-to-face sessions and through the reflective style of the course materials, indicates that the more conventional support described above appears to be better suited to the context of a developing country.

While there is constant change in the field of open and distance learning support, it is vital that not all programmes make a change to technology-driven support without considering all its implications. In the case of the 'South', policy makers and programme developers need first to determine what is most appropriate to the context of their learners before developing what could be costly and entirely unsuitable developments.

References

Adler, J., Lelliott, T., Reed, Y., Bapoo, A., Brodie, K., Dikgomo, P., Nyabanyaba, T., Roman, A., Setati, M., Slonimsky, L., Davis, H. and De Wet, H. (1998) *Mixed-mode FDE's and their Effects: A Study of the Classroom Practices of Primary and Secondary Mathematics, Science and English Language Teachers Enrolled in the Wits Further Diplomas in Education Programme*. Interim Report, University of the Witwatersrand, South Africa.

Asbee, S. and Simpson, O. (1998) Partners, family friends: student support of the closest kind, *Open Learning* 13 (3), pp. 56–9.

Bertram, C. (2000) A mixed mode distance education model for teacher education: rationale, student experiences and quality. Paper presented at the 2nd NADEOSA Conference, Pretoria, South Africa.

Bhalalusesa, E. (2001) Supporting women distance learners in Tanzania, *Open Learning* 16 (2), pp. 155–68.

Gordon, A. (2001) SAIDE's rural education research project: the Jozini case study, *Open Learning Through Distance Education*, 7 (1), pp. 10–12.

Holmberg, B. (1981) *Status and Trends of Distance Education*, New York: Nichols.

Holt, D. (1994) Peer group learning in open and distance education, *Teaching and Learning in Open and Distance Education* 2: Study Guide Section 2. University of South Australia.

King, B. (2001) Managing the changing nature of distance and open education at institutional level, *Open Learning* 13, (3), pp. 56–9.

Leach, J. (1996) Learning in practice: support for professional development, in Mills, R. and Tait, A. (eds), *Supporting Learners in Open and Distance Learning*, London: Pitman, pp. 101–26.

Lelliott, A. D., Pendlebury, S. and Enslin, P. A. (2000) Promises of access and inclusion: on-line education in Africa, *J. Philos. Education*, 34 (1), pp. 41–52.

Maher, P. and Rewt, P. (2001) Using the telephone to support isolated learners. Paper presented at the 20th World Conference of the International Council for Open and Distance Education, Düsseldorf, Germany.

Mansell, R. and Wehn, U. (eds) (1998) *Knowledge Societies: Information Technology for Sustainable Development*, Oxford: Oxford University Press for the United Nations.

Mason, R. (2001) Effective facilitation of on-line learning: the Open University experience, in Stephenson, J. (ed.), *Teaching and Learning On-line*, London: Kogan Page.

Mills, R. and Tait, A. (eds) (1996) *Supporting Learners in Open and Distance Learning*, London: Pitman.

Perraton, H. (2000) *Open and Distance Learning in the Developing World*, London: Routledge.

Phillips, A., Phillips, M. and Christmas, D. (2001) Student services on the Web: towards in integrated approach, in *Student Services at the UK Open University*. Papers presented to the 20th World Conference of the International Council for Open and Distance Education, April 2001.

Rumble, G. (2001a) E-education – whose benefits, whose costs? On-line at http://www.iec.ac.uk/resources/e_education_costs.pdf.

Rumble, G. (2001b) The costs of providing on-line student support services, in *Student Services at the UK Open University*. Papers presented to the 20th World Conference of the International Council for Open and Distance Education, April 2001.

Tait, A. (1996). Conversation and community: student support in open and distance learning, in Mills, R. and Tait, A. (eds), *Supporting Learners in Open and Distance Learning*, London: Pitman, pp. 59–72.

Tait, A. (2000) Planning Student Support for Open and Distance Learning, *Open Learning*, 15 (3), pp. 287–99.

Thorpe, M. (2001) *Learner Support: A New Model For On-line Teaching and Learning*, in *Student Services at the UK Open University*. Papers presented to the 20th World Conference of the International Council for Open and Distance Education, April 2001.

Young, G. and Marks-Maran, D. (1998) Using constructivism to develop a quality framework for learner support: a case study, *Open Learning*, 13 (2), pp. 30–7.

4 Addressing the learning skills needs of students at a distance

A dual medium approach

Margaret Johnson and Clive Barrett

In this chapter we look at a particular project, set up within the Open University UK, to produce generic learning skills materials that would support a large and diverse student body. The project aimed to develop, simultaneously, both paper- and web-based resources which would be available to all our students free of charge and on request.

Background

When the Open University UK Charter was awarded in 1967, its aim, through a managed open entry system, was to offer higher education to all those who sought it, regardless of educational, social or cultural background. Initially it offered an undergraduate degree programme only, but since then has expanded to include postgraduate and vocational courses as well. This openness has remained, and the University's strategic plan for 2002–12 still states in its mission that it is: 'open to people; open as to places; open as to methods and open to ideas' (OU, 2002). Over the last thirty years the means to achieving this openness may have changed, but the over-riding ethos and vision of the organisation have not. If we examine these core values, we can see that they have both contributed to stability and also led to change. These changes have been due to both internal and external factors.

What then has remained the same? The system of Supported Open Learning has been enhanced over the years, but at the core it is as it was in its first pioneering days. The Open University has always been open in that it does not require previous educational qualifications to gain entry to its undergraduate courses. In fact this 'openness' has been extended by changes to regulations, permitting students to start their studies on any course of their choice. Although guidance material encourages students to start on a level one course (equivalent to first year university study) a student who wishes to enter at a second or even third level (equivalent to honours level or third year undergraduate study at a conventional university) is not refused. This means that course choice is a critical process for the student and much of the Open University's advice and guidance is geared to helping students make the right choice. The consequence of such choice, however, means that not all students choose appropriately and sometimes find themselves on courses for which they do not have the prerequisite knowledge and skills. The Open University therefore provides preparatory advice and activities and a good deal of on course support in order to help students develop the necessary skills.

The notion of learner support has been fundamental to the Open University and its systems. This support comprises a mixture of written materials, access to help and advice via the telephone (or latterly electronic means) and the opportunity for face-to-face meetings. Although the course materials are written and produced at the University's headquarters in Milton Keynes, each student is allocated to one of thirteen regional centres for support, according to where they live. These regional centres are responsible for allocating a tutor (a part-time academic) to a student, for organising academic support and for providing advice and guidance. Additionally, at Milton Keynes, there is a central Student Services unit which provides further administrative and other services.

The crucial relationship for the student is that with their tutor who is there as an academic guide throughout the course. The tutor marks the student's assignments; offers correspondence teaching on the script as well as assessment; offers help and support by telephone and correspondence both written and electronic; and runs face-to-face group tutorials, which students are encouraged, but not compelled, to attend. Behind the tutor there is a raft of staff who give academic, personal and administrative support, again by telephone, correspondence, email or via face-to-face meetings. Support materials and events, like learning skills workshops, are available and students are encouraged to make use of them. This support system has been in place from the start, but has been developed so as to be delivered by an increasing range of methods and technologies.

Openness and student centredness have been in place from the start of the Open University but so, also, have the needs of the learner. It has always been understood that students need access not only to high quality course materials, but also to a wide range of support materials and strategies to enable them to become successful independent learners in an increasingly complex system of open and distance education.

If the core of learner needs and support has remained much the same, then the methods of addressing these needs and delivering support has not. In order to provide, maintain and develop a quality service, the University has had to change and adapt in response to both internal and external drivers.

The sheer volume of the delivery of support has greatly expanded. Numbers of students have increased from approximately 25,000 in 1971 to more than 200,000 in 2002. With this volume has come increasing complexity. Where there were four courses on offer in 1971, there are now more than 300. At the start there was only one qualification: the BA degree. Now there are many qualifications and awards that students can obtain at sub-degree, undergraduate and post-graduate degree level. Changes in regulations have also allowed students more flexibility and choice over their studies. This increasing scope and complexity has meant that the University has had to devise appropriate information and management systems.

Over the years, technology has seen considerable advances and the Open University has seized on this not only as a means of dealing with increased volume and complexity but also for maintaining the cutting edge in the field of distance education. Sir John Daniel, former Vice Chancellor, stated that:

> The continuing development and extension of information and communication technology (ICT) will substantially change the modus of approach of The Open University over the next ten years. The Open University must engage with the use of ICT in a proactive and deliberate way so as to give our students the benefits of these developments and retain our leadership in the large-scale application of technology to higher education.
>
> (Daniel, 2000)

Plans for Change (2002) states that 'nearly 40 per cent of the UK population and 89 per cent of Open University students have access to a PC at work or home, 19 per cent of people in the UK used the Internet in 2000, and every day world-wide 80,000 people log on to the Internet for the first time.' The Open University's Learning and Teaching Strategy (OU, 2001) states its aim is 'to establish the critical baseline of IT elements for all courses and programmes by 2002; build IT elements into courses to achieve compulsory IT elements for all University degrees by 2005; to increase web-focused course to at least 20 by 2002'. In the Open University Student Services the potential of web-based advice and guidance is also being realised with the development of the Learner's Guide – a web site covering all aspects of student advice and guidance, with course choice, induction, learning skills and services for disabled students (NTSS, 2002). Technological innovation and change is vital if we are to compete with other higher education providers.

The Open University's share of the part-time higher education market in the UK has held steady despite the growth in competition: 35 per cent of all part-time undergraduate students in the UK currently study with the Open University (*Plans for Change*, p. 12). However, many of the traditional universities are now offering both part-time and distance education. They are also attracting an increasing number of mature students who are the traditional Open University market. It is important therefore that the Open University retains not only its distinctiveness, but is also seen to be using current technologies in its deliveries.

Accountability both within and outside the Open University is becoming increasingly important. With the new funding regime whereby funding is attached to students who complete courses, retention is a crucial issue. The Open University has recently undertaken a university-wide retention project and is at present implementing many of its recommendations. Notable amongst these is the student value chain which shows the importance of 'value added' services at all stages of the student's career from registration to completion of an award. Quality assurance is increasingly important and the University is setting quality standards for all its services. Externally, the quality review scheme set up by the Higher Education Funding Council for England has been an important driver and the University has had to respond by making transparent its quality assurance processes.

The student too is becoming more discerning and demanding high quality materials and services. In a world where rights are given prominence and litigation a common feature, the University cannot afford to drop its standards and must listen to what the student wants. The Open University has developed a Student Charter which sets out both the University's and student's responsibilities. It has also recently set up a Student Complaints Office. The student is central to the organisation and if we are to be responsive and truly student centred then we must listen to what they say.

The Student Toolkit Project

It is against this background that the Open University Student Toolkit Project was set up in response to the perceived need for generic learning skills material. We could no longer be sure that students entering at a variety of levels had the necessary learning skills to tackle university study. Learning skills are generally integrated into level one courses, but less so at higher level. The project recognised that tutors had varying degrees of expertise in developing their students' learning skills, and most were pressed for time and had other priorities for valuable tutorial time. Excellent learning-skills work had been available in the regions via workshops and materials; these materials, however, varied in standard and were developed according to enthusiasm and expertise with no overall co-ordination. The intention of the project was to produce professionally printed materials, with an agreed content, overseen by a small steering group comprising members of central and regional staff drawn from across the OU and having a wide range of academic perspectives. They all were, or had been, tutors and so had direct knowledge of students' needs in this area.

The Student Toolkit Project was funded as a three-year pilot under the auspices of the Pro Vice Chancellor (Students, Quality and Standards) and approved by the main policy board for student support. It was charged with producing a limited print run of nine paper-based toolkits over the period 1998–2001, each focused on a particular generic study skills area and designed to complement work undertaken by regional learning skills teams, as well as the approaches taken to learning skills by Faculty Course Teams. The toolkits were aimed at meeting the needs of students who had a particular gap in their study skills, and titles were planned over the life of the pilot according to need. They include the following titles: *The Effective Use of English, Revision and Examinations*; *Working with Charts, Graphs and Tables, Reading and Note-taking*; *Essay and Report Writing Skills*; *More Charts, Graphs and Tables*; *Maths for Science and Technology*; *Learning How to Learn*; *Extending and Developing Your Critical Thinking Skills*. Each booklet is between 24–40 pages long, begins with a reflective exercise for students to gauge their current skills, is designed for active learning and contains both tips and practice exercises. Each toolkit is aimed to be a starting point rather than a 'magic wand' and gives suggestions for further reading and study. As this was a pilot project, the toolkits were advertised to regional staff and tutors rather than directly to students, with the intention that they were sent only to those with a clearly established need. Later, this policy was reviewed and the toolkits were advertised directly to students through regional mailings and an article in Sesame, the student newspaper. The original proposal had also included the development of web-based toolkits in parallel with the paper-based ones, but in the event web development lagged behind production of the booklets since it proved more challenging than anticipated.

Evaluation of project

The booklets have been evaluated in several ways in conjunction with the Open University's Institute of Educational Technology (IET) in order to get feedback from both students and regional staff. This feedback has been valuable for two reasons: first, to collate evidence to support the case for permanently funding toolkits and second, to inform the development of the Student Toolkit series.

Evaluation carried out included:

- postal survey by questionnaire of a sample of students receiving the toolkit booklets;
- telephone survey of a sub-set of the students responding to the postal survey in order to obtain qualitative data;
- database survey to identify the 'profile' of students who have been sent the toolkits;
- survey of regional policy, practices and distribution.

The first postal survey (Allen and Woodley, 2000) consisted of analysis of 356 questionnaires from students who had received one or more of *The Effective Use of English*, *Revision and Examinations*, and *Working with Charts, Graphs and Tables*. The survey suggested that there are some clear differences between the characteristics of those recipients of Student Toolkits who responded to the questionnaire and the overall profile of OU undergraduate students. Respondents were more likely to be female (68 per cent compared to 54 per cent), disabled (18 per cent compared to 4 per cent) and older (47 per cent were 45 or older compared to 26 per cent). Respondents were also more likely to have low qualifications upon entry, i.e. lower than university entrance requirements (53 per cent compared to 37 per cent).

Feedback was very largely positive about the value of the toolkits. Ninety-eight per cent of respondents thought that the ideas were clearly or very clearly presented, and 86 per cent judged the length of the toolkits to be appropriate. Eighty-seven per cent thought that the materials were pitched at the right level, while 10 per cent regarded them as being pitched too low. However, it is worth noting that 29 per cent of respondents have high entry qualifications and may have less need of study skills support than less well qualified students. Seventy-one per cent found the activities helpful or very helpful while only 3 per cent reported them to be unhelpful. The toolkits were rated as being easy to relate to course material by 45 per cent of respondents while 10 per cent found it difficult to do so. Fifty-nine per cent thought that the toolkits met their needs well or very well while only 5 per cent thought it unlikely that they would recommend the toolkits to other students.

The survey results implied that the strategy of targeting the provision of Student Toolkits to students with established study skills needs was well founded. It also indicated that while there are some limits to the effectiveness of generic study skills materials, there are nonetheless clear benefits in providing them, in order to help those students who do not obtain sufficient support from within their course materials.

The telephone survey consisted of sixty semi-structured telephone interviews carried out in September and October 2000, just prior to students' course completion and examination. The sample was drawn from students who had responded to the postal survey and had indicated a willingness to participate in further research. Nearly all interview participants had given favourable ratings to the toolkits in the quantitative study. The survey covered the first three toolkits and was carried out by an independent consultant.

Students receiving *The Effective Use of English* toolkit were usually studying at level one, despite the intended market group being those on levels two or three. Respondents indicated that their grades had improved after receiving the toolkit, e.g. one student who was told by her tutor that she was losing marks because of her essay writing and punctuation, felt that she had benefited by using the toolkit:

> I was extremely enthusiastic to do the course, but my enthusiasm waned when I didn't get the marks I expected and didn't realise what was wrong. It was my tutor who told me about the toolkit and now I'm doing better (science student).

Others commented

> … they are not suitable for everyone, but I think it was good for me and my needs.

> I needed the toolkit to help me in my studies because I had not studied for years.

However, a few students felt the toolkit was pitched too low and not really what they were looking for: 'Book too simple for my needs'. Although there were a lot of exercises in the toolkit, the message was clearly that students didn't complete the exercises as paper exercises, but 'did them in my head'. The tendency was not to read it from cover to cover, but it was felt that:

> the format was good and easy to understand, interesting. I just glanced through it the first time and now I just dip into it. Useful to dip into.

Similar comments were made by respondents about the toolkit *Revision and Examinations*, but the student profile was different and included those on a range of level one, two and three courses and also included a number of experienced students, i.e. seven or eight years into study. Many had requested the booklet because they were anxious, and a high proportion were taking a re-sit examination. This group, among others, responded that the main reason they had not completed all the exercises was due to time pressure. There was considerable interest in the revision techniques offered and students thought that there were a lot of good tips and ideas, particularly around the theme that revision is active and not passive. The respondents also suggested a need for wider publicity.

As can be expected, *Working with Charts, Graphs and Tables* was requested by students whose courses had a significant numerical component. This sample was smaller since the toolkit had not long been available at the time of the survey. The toolkit was felt to be useful:

> For me it was most useful and especially for anyone coming back to study.

Once again students did not always complete the activities and exercises due to a lack of time, and pressure in studying the work. Other students found it pitched too low for their needs:

> I found the book more for people who are frightened of numbers.

In her report conclusions the interviewer stated:

> that the interviews conveyed how important and valuable the toolkits were to individual students. They appreciated the value and aims of the toolkits. They have found them a confidence boost and students are reassured by the toolkits. However, activities are only completed where there is enough time. Therefore the activities are marginalised in favour of using the toolkit as a resource. This is not a negative comment, rather it is a strategic use of the resource. Students commented that the toolkits let them know that they were on 'the right lines' and felt that the style of writing was simple and easy to understand, although at times took too long to get to the point.
>
> (Jelfs, 2000)

The survey of regional staff revealed that they too found the paper toolkits a valuable resource. They were publicised and distributed through a variety of means, such as sending to students who attended learning skills workshops, and advertising in student guides or leaflets. All regions advertised the toolkits to course tutors by in various ways and used them for staff development purposes. They were distributed to students by advisory and other student services staff on request from students or referral from tutors. Many regions regularly used them in their learning skills workshops. All regions said they were useful as a resource, as a back-up to tutors and advisory staff. Comments made included:

> They are a fantastic resource – much underfunded and so underused.

> Help such as this is long overdue and should definitely be continued.

It bridges a gap in a sensible manner.

They should be sent out to every student rather than on a request-only basis where relevant to their course.

The toolkits are very good at instilling confidence in the students.

The toolkits should become mainstream.

The toolkits were useful for filling in the gaps in knowledge and skills for those changing direction within their degrees.

Development of web versions of the toolkits

The original project outline stated the intention of putting the toolkits on the web at the same time as developing the paper booklets. In the event, web development followed the production of the paper versions of the toolkits and only the first two, *The Effective Use of English* and *Revision and Examinations*, were developed during the pilot project. This change was due to difficulties of production rather than any change in strategic thinking. During the evaluation of the booklets, the student interviews were also used to gauge views about making materials available on the Internet prior to the start up of that part of the project.

Rather surprisingly, not all responses were as enthusiastic as we had expected:

I didn't want the toolkits on the Internet. I prefer study in my hands but I could access the Internet.

By putting it on the Internet it would be environmentally friendly and save money.

It's alright for some people, but not for me.

I would print off only those parts I thought were relevant.

I like a book in my hand.

Nice to have a book to travel with. In the course I am doing I use the Internet and CD-ROM a lot and it makes a nice change to have something to flick through.

I am on the computer all day and in the evenings I don't want to start on it again.

The interviewer noted:

When questioned about Internet use, many students who were enthusiastic IT and Internet users would like to be able to print off only those activities of the toolkits which they needed. However there are still a number of students who don't want to read on-line material. Students have different learning styles and apply these different styles as and when they feel appropriate

(Mumford, 1987) therefore they need to have a variety of methods available to them either on-line or paper based.

(Jelfs, 2000)

This part of the project was implemented in cooperation with the Learning Support Technology Unit (LSTU) which is based in the University's North Region, some 250 miles from the main campus. The Open University is committed to moving forward with web-based learning as part of its strategic aim to maintain leadership in the application of educational technology. Its mission statement (OU, 2002) states that it be:

> ... open as to methods – using and developing the most effective media and technologies for learning, teaching and assessment.

The process of putting the toolkits on the web was, however, not an easy one and took much longer than expected. The task of adapting written materials for the web involves various dimensions: process, content, pedagogy and technology. The combined knowledge and skills of the team straddled all these areas, but the range of expertise was not within the grasp of any one individual; nor could it be. For all concerned, what transpired was a long, sometimes painful and sometimes exhilarating, journey into the largely unknown territory of web-based learning without a commonly understood 'map'. The various areas of expertise resided in different people with many different roles, most of whom were based several hundred miles apart. It was possible to communicate electronically, but this did, on occasions, lead to misunderstandings and slowed down the whole process. It did not always compensate for the face-to-face meeting where ideas could be thrashed out, common understandings reached, ideas and experiences shared. If possible, a team such as this should be in close contact throughout the whole of the development process.

When the work began in 1998, there were few precedents within the OU. There was no recognised development process as there was for the production of written materials. In the latter case, there is a clear line of communication from content author, to editor, to critical reader, to designer, to publisher, all overseen by persons who have expertise in their particular area and whose job it is to get such things done. There was no such process or team of people in place when work was started on the web-based toolkits. Robinson (2001) reminds us that:

> Changes in teaching and learning methods, or the adoption of new learning technologies, are not simply technical changes, confined to a single department, but involves changes in other departments and the wider culture too.

Some time after the project began, the New Technology for Student Services (NTSS) Team was established which does combine expertise within the same team. They have been responsible for the setting up of the Learner's Guide – a comprehensive advice and guidance web site for enquirers and students. Towards the end of the Student Toolkit project NTSS managed the quality assurance process for the toolkits, and it is now in the Learning Skills section of this site that the toolkits are located.

The authors of the first toolkit were clear from the start that the booklet could not simply be put on the web as it was largely text based. A major reversioning was needed: the text had to be structured and broken up; more examples were needed; there had to be interactive exercises with immediate feedback. Oliver *et al.* (2001) have suggested that 'Interactivity is the Holy Grail of Multimedia'. Above all, the web version of the toolkit had to be presented in such a way that the student could interact with the material rather than just read: an approach that provides a constructivist rather than an instructivist model of learning (Reeves and Reeves, 1997).

It was important that research into the pedagogy of web-based learning should inform the adaptation of materials. The pedagogy of the written materials with the need for student reflection and self-development was well understood, but the authors were unsure whether the pedagogical underpinning of web-based materials was the same; current research suggested not. After a trawl of web sites in June 1999, it seemed that most of the learning-skills sites put up by other universities, both in Britain and the USA, seemed not to have got it right: too much text, too little interaction and visually rather dull. It was therefore difficult to find a model to emulate. It was intended that the learning outcomes of both paper-based and web-based toolkits were the same, but the methods of achieving this clearly differed. The authors wanted to develop learning skills in an active and reflective way, not simply put up didactic or reference material: an example of e-learning rather than e-library approach (Stefik and Cerf, 1997).

The initial approach involved some degree of development of the web materials by trial and error, seeing what worked and what did not. The authors adapted the materials; the technical team said what they could or could not do; together they experimented to see what worked (Johnson *et al.*, 2000). The LSTU team were also on a learning curve as it was the first time they had worked on student learning materials although they had developed a number of student web-sites. They therefore had to check with the authors that what they did technically, effectively implemented the pedagogic methods and outcomes that the authors intended; while the authors developed their web awareness skills in order that their pedagogic ideas could be implemented with the currently available technology. The web building team were learning new techniques, for instance the use of JavaScript, Macromedia Flash and Java technologies that were incorporated as the pages were developed. The site that went live looked very different, therefore, from the first version produced, and the second web-based toolkit *Revision and Examinations*, used more advanced technology than the first.

The current site includes a questionnaire which incorporates questions about style and content as well as ease of navigation. This feedback form largely consists of tick boxes, but some of the comments put in the 'open' box at the bottom have been:

Great idea. Glad I found it on the web site.

I have found this site very useful in getting my ideas together.

I would like to see some more information about exams ... but all in all excellent. Well done OU.

Usability testing has also been carried out on *The Effective Use Of English* site with student volunteers to make sure that both the design and pedagogy is effective. The following aspects were tested: navigation, usability of interaction, look and feel of the site, level of difficulty of exercises, focus and learning experience.

The general feedback was positive in that they found it a useful resource. There were, however, some difficulties with navigation and with the ease of doing some of the interactive exercises, which will be addressed in any redevelopment of the site.

How successful was the project?

The project was widely considered to be a success and subsequently mainstream funding has been secured for both the maintenance and the development of the printed toolkits. Updating and reprinting of the current toolkits are planned as well as development of new toolkits. *Computer Mediated Communication* and *Presentation Skills* are in development and it is hoped to produce at least one new title a year.

The web-based toolkits now sit firmly within the Learner's Guide and are being updated in the light of user feedback. As an interim measure the remaining toolkits are available electronically in pdf format on the Learning Skills area of the Learner's Guide, with clear guidance to students about how to use this resource and how to request a paper booklet from their regional centre.

An exciting development, leading from this project, has been made possible with funding from a HEFCE National Teaching Fellowship awarded to the first author. This will enable the contextualisation of the web version of *The Effective Use of English* for students entering their first level course in the School of Health and Social Welfare: Understanding Health and Social Care (K100). This is an open entry course: approximately half of its students have educational qualifications below normal university entry level and large numbers are from ethnic minority backgrounds. In partnership with NTSS and the School of Health and Social Welfare, the materials will be adapted using the techniques afforded by Extensible Markup Language (XML) and Reusable Learning Objects (RLO). Students on that course will be presented with a customised version of the web toolkit. From this project it is intended to create a model that can be used to adapt other learning skills materials for specific courses.

During the usability testing on the existing site, students comments indicated that they would have preferred it if it had been directly related to their course:

I would be learning to use the right words for the situation within the course. Otherwise it is out of context.

The researchers noted in their conclusion:

Throughout the site, the participants seemed more likely to claim that they would not have the time to do an exercise if they felt it was both irrelevant to what they were studying and would divert their attention. Participants repeatedly made the point that they would prefer examples of text relating to their course.

(Johnson and Doye, 2002)

Another strand of development is to explore the viability of a student 'picking and mixing' various selections of web-based learning materials according to their particular needs which are determined by self-audit. At present, a Learning Skills site that corresponds to student needs is being developed on the Learner's Guide. Once students have identified their skills gap, they will be linked to a range of resources.

Alongside these developments it is important to continue reviewing and researching both the technology and the pedagogy. Oliver and McLaughlin (2001) reinforce this:

These new technologies and the growth of Internet-based teaching and learning signal new directions for teachers, and require the creation of new forms of learner-centred pedagogy, supported by technology.

Usability testing should be continued in order to investigate how students learn from the web and what is best taught this way and what is not. It cannot be assumed that this is the best method for all students or for all kinds of teaching: 'Delivering educational content using the web will not altogether improve learning' (Bostock, 1997); rather it has to be used in such a way as to enhance the learning process. It is essential that the skills associated with learning to learn are developed in the student and that this element is incorporated into any design of web-based learning. Web-based learning offers an enormous opportunity but should be treated with caution, otherwise the danger is that it will be used in an inappropriate way: 'if the web is to live up to its promise, we must strive to understand the basic dimensions that the web can (and cannot) accommodate' (Reeves and Reeves, 1997). Any design of web-based learning should be based on sound learning theories, be culturally sensitive and flexible enough to appeal to students with different learning styles. Repeated evaluation, reflection and refinement will contribute to our understanding of the web as a learning medium so that we are best placed to grasp its full potential.

So, how successful was the project in meeting the learning skills needs of Open University students? The evaluation suggests that both students and staff found the paper-based toolkits a valuable resource. They are now firmly embedded within student services and are used as a resource for individual students and as a basis for running regional skills workshops.

The Learners' Guide is getting as many as 120,000 hits a week, while the Learning Skills site has received more than 42,000 at the time of writing. The questionnaire feedback on both live sites and the usability testing carried out on *The Effective Use of English* site showed that students valued the support offered and that it made a difference to their learning.

What the project has demonstrated particularly well is that there is a need for generic study skills materials and that it is possible to make them relevant to a large and varied student body without forfeiting quality. While to some extent learning skills support is embedded in courses themselves, it is not practical – or indeed desirable – for all courses to carry the overhead that would be necessary to meet the needs of all students, especially at higher level. Thus, extra support will always be necessary and new media offers an easily adaptable and cost-effective alternative to the printed word. These two media should not be seen in competition but as complementary. Students will choose between them according to purpose and learning style and may well move between the two. It is important therefore that when addressing the learning skills needs of students at a distance we do not privilege one over the other. The two devices should not only inform and support each other but also the student for whom they are intended.

References

Allen, T. and Woodley, A. (2000) *Postal Survey of Student Toolkit Users* (Open University Internal Report).

Bostock, S. J. (1997) Designing web-based instruction for active learning, in Khan, B. H. (ed.), *Web-Based Instruction* (Englewood Cliffs, NJ: Educational Technology Publications).

Daniel, J. S. (2000) *The e-University Investment* (Open University Internal Paper)

Jelfs, A. (2000) *Student Services Toolkit Report* (Open University Internal Report).

Johnson, M., Barrett, C. and Hogg, R. (2000) Putting Learning Materials on the Web, paper presented at the Open University Student Services Millennium Conference, Durham.

Johnson, M. and Doye, Z. (2002) *The Contextualisation of Web-based Learning Skills Material: Usability Testing the Effective Use of English Web Site* (Open University Internal Report).

Mumford, A. (1987) Learning styles and learning, *Personnel Review*, 16, pp. 20–3.

NTSS (2002) *The Learner's Guide*, available from: http://www.open.ac.uk/learners-guide/

Oliver, R. and McLoughlin, C. (2001) Using networking tools to support on-line learning, in Lockwood, F. and Gooley, A. (eds), *Innovation in Open and Distance Learning* (London: Kogan Page).

Oliver, R., Towers, S., Skippington, P., Brunetto, Y., Farr-Wharton, R. and Gooley, A. (2001) Flexible toolboxes: a solution for developing on-line resources?, in Lockwood, F. and Gooley, A. (eds), *Innovation in Open and Distance Learning* (London: Kogan Page).

Open University (2001) *Learning and Teaching Strategy*, available at http://www2.open.ac.uk/ltto/LTstrategy/ltstrategy.htm

Open University (2002) *Plans for Change: the University's Strategic and Development Plans 2002–2012* (Milton Keynes: The Open University).

Reeves, T. C. and Reeves, P. M. (1997) Effective dimensions of interactive learning on the World Wide Web, in Khan, B. H. (ed.), *Web-Based Instruction* (Englewood Cliffs, NJ: Educational Technology Publications).

Robinson, B. (2001) Innovation in open and distance learning: some lessons from experience in experience and research, in Lockwood, F. and Gooley, A. (eds), *Innovation in Open and Distance Learning* (London: Kogan Page).

Stefik, M. J. and Cerf, V. G. (1997) *Internet Dreams: Archetypes, Myths, and Metaphors* (Cambridge, MA: MIT Press).

Appendix

Student toolkit titles and authors

Student Toolkit 1:   *The Effective Use of English*
Johnson, M. and Goodwin, V.

Student Toolkit 2:   *Revision and Examinations*
Goodwin, V. and Bishop, J.

Student Toolkit 3:   *Working with Charts, Graphs and Tables*
Gilmartin, K. and Rex, K.

Student Toolkit 4:   *Reading and Note-taking*
Bates, D.

Student Toolkit 5:   *Essay and Report Writing Skills*
Manning, E. and Houston, M.

Student Toolkit 6:   *More Charts, Graphs and Tables*
Gilmartin, K. and Rex, K.

Student Toolkit 7:   *Maths for Science and Technology*
Gilmartin, K., Laird, H. and Rex, K.

Student Toolkit 8:   *Learning How to Learn*
Coats, M.

Student Toolkit 9:   *Extending and Developing Your Critical Thinking Skills*
Talley, J.

5   Supporting the student in new teaching and learning environments

Brian Kenworthy

Introduction

Over the past decade higher education, in both developed and to a lesser extent in some developing countries, has undergone and is still undergoing significant change. Most of these changes are based upon the increasing availability and sophistication of information and communication technologies (ICTs) and the way in which these technologies are not only impacting upon the delivery of educational programmes, but also upon the support systems being made available to learners. The expectations of a more sophisticated, more demanding student body and the growing trend towards life-long learning has also contributed to the need for institutions to plan for this changing educational environment. One result of this has been a growing trend to perceive potential students as clients or customers, and higher education as a commodity which can be packaged, marketed and sold like any other product. The Report of the National Committee of Inquiry into Higher Education in the UK – the Dearing Report (1997, ch.13.7) in commenting on this trend had this to say:

> over the next decade, higher educational services will become an international tradable commodity within an increasingly competitive global market ... within the UK, by the end of the first decade of the next century, a 'knowledge economy' will have developed in which institutions collaborate in the production and transmission of educational programmes and learning materials on a 'make or buy' basis.

In relating this trend to open and distance learning (ODL), Tait (2000, p. 288) describes a dimension of change as a result of the ICT revolution as:

> the marketisation of education, where the student in ODL, as in other educational fields, is being constructed as 'customer'. This derives from pressures on institutions both to drive their costs down and to find ways of out-competing others, while more widespread external changes in consumer culture lead to the demand for services to individuals to be speeded up. Indeed, the experience of contemporary ODL is being assessed as a guide to how education more generally will be structured in the future.

Similarly, Alan Gilbert, Vice Chancellor of Melbourne University and the prime mover for the consortium of universities known as Universitas 21, supports the notion of students as customers. In an interview on the ABC radio programme Background Briefing (2000) he suggested that:

> we should at least treat them as well as other enterprises treat their customers, and we don't always do that, education is very much a supply side business, and the empowerment of customers is something that I am afraid is going to happen, whether we like it or not.

Tait's other point about the expertise and experience of ODL being utilised more widely in the educational community is supported by King (2001, p. 51):

> … the infrastructure of distance education in dual mode universities – expertise in planning and scheduling, facilities for production of learning resources, experience in non-traditional delivery, appreciation of the administrative and support needs of students not on campus and the provision of systemic response to these, and professional development programs for academic staff – can be deployed to better support *all* students.

This chapter therefore will attempt to outline the student support systems and services traditionally provided by the distance education institutions and how, through the utlisation of ICTs, these services can be enhanced and expanded to include all students. It will also attempt to describe the ever increasing competition for the provision of on-line higher education and question whether the new providers entering the field will be ready and able to provide the various support services which will be expected by a more customer-focused and demanding student market.

The growth of new services

The growth of on-line or virtual providers of higher education courses and services is the clearest manifestation of the changes and forecasts outlined by these commentators and many others. However, the rapidly changing educational landscape makes it difficult to keep abreast of these new developments and the participants in a field which was formerly the domain of a small number of specialist providers. These new services fit into a number of loose categories: the existing universities which have already been involved in distance education or have recently commenced such provision; the virtual universities; and the consortia or networks of education provision. A good example of the first of these categories is the Open University (UK) which according to Daniel (2000) is now 'the world's largest on-line learning community in higher education.' At an address at the Open University of Hong Kong in December 2000 Daniel further stated that 'at present we have 110,000 of our degree-credit students who work with us on-line from home and another 105,000 elementary and secondary school teachers, also on-line, who are doing our Learning Schools programme.' At the other end of the scale, in terms of student numbers, is the University of Southern Queensland, a dual mode university, which has been involved with traditional print-based distance education for the past twenty-five years, but has now entered into a contract with a corporate on-line provider, NextEd, to develop 'USQOn-line' as its vehicle for providing on-line learning services to its distance education students. At the moment these students make up 75 per cent of total enrolment and are situated in more than sixty countries. Most of the former dual mode universities in Australia, and many that were not categorised as such, are now providing courses on-line and attempting to capture a share of the new 'e-learning' market.

There are numerous examples of the second category, the so-called 'virtual universities'. Some of the better known are the University of Phoenix On-line, one of the pioneers of operating on-line education successfully as a business; Jones International University founded in 1987 was the first accredited, fully on-line university; Western Governor's University is a virtual institution that offers courses created by about forty colleges and universities from twenty states in the US, plus one in Canada; Cardean University has been established as an e-university by a US company, Unext, and adapts teaching materials from Columbia University, Stanford University, Carnegie Mellon University and the London School of Economics; the UK e-University is an ambitious project of the UK government which has given the Higher Education Funding Council a mandate for creating an e-university with a budget of £400 million pounds. Shares in the venture will be made available to all UK universities.

The Global University Alliance (GUA), which is a consortium of nine Australian, Canadian, New Zealand, British and United States universities, typifies the third category, consortia or networks. Together with a corporate partner, NextEd, the GUA is now on-line with an initial portfolio of postgraduate programmes targeting major Asian markets. Others in this category include Universitas 21 with about eighteen member universities located in Australia, Britain, Canada, China, Germany, New Zealand, Singapore, Sweden and the United States. The prime force behind this initiative is Melbourne University, which has drawn together prestigious institutions from the countries identified above. Universitas 21 also has a corporate partner in Thompson Learning which will provide on-line course design, content development, testing and assessment. The Canadian Virtual University, Scottish Knowledge and the US-based DL Alliance are just a few of the other educational providers which have entered into consortia type arrangements.

The role of student support

These new initiatives, although many are still in the embryonic stage, demonstrate that distance education is now certainly undergoing substantial change and that a whole new competitive industry is developing around the provision of university level programmes through various forms of on-line delivery. This begs the question of where and how student support, an integral part of successful traditional distance education provision, fits into this new scenario. As Rumble (2000, p. 217) points out 'when it comes to articulating what we mean by student services, distance educators are way ahead of their colleagues in conventional universities.' He further states that:

> it is surprising how little attention universities in general have paid at a theoretical level to the definition of the services they offer students. Distance education institutions tend to be the exception to this rule. Distance educators seem to have a clear understanding that student support services are integral to the overall working of their systems.
>
> (Rumble, 2000, p. 232–3)

There is no doubt that the dual mode system, which operated in Australian universities for a number of years, provided institutions with the basis for understanding the necessity for developing well supported student services. In order to determine how provision will be made for such services by those now entering the market, it may be useful to determine how they can be described or categorised. Rumble (2000) analyses three different approaches to how these services can be defined by looking at the work of Reid (1995), Tait (2000) and Simpson (2000). He makes a distinction between 'compensatory services', that is services which are designed to overcome students' learning difficulties, and 'comprehensive services' which are integral or built into the programme being delivered. He makes the point that:

> compensatory services tend to be reactive, activated only when the institution feels they have to be. If you want to control the use made of a service, or run it down, you will make it reactive. Comprehensive services, on the other hand, tend to be more expensive because services are available even for those who do not want or need them.
>
> (Rumble, 2000, p. 223)

Tait (2000, p. 289) in a recent paper in Open Learning, divides the primary functions of student support into three categories:

1 cognitive: supporting and developing learning through the mediation of the standard and uniform elements of course materials and learning resources for individual students;
2 affective: providing an environment which supports students, creates commitment, and enhances self esteem; and
3 systemic: establishing administrative processes and information management systems which are effective, transparent and overall student-friendly.

He also identifies some of the typical services that are employed to meet the demands of these functions:

1 enquiry, admission and pre-study advisory services;
2 tutoring;

3   guidance and counselling services;
4   assessment of prior learning and credit transfer;
5   study and examination centres;
6   residential schools;
7   library services;
8   individualised correspondence teaching, including in some cases continuous assessment;
9   record keeping, information management and other administrative systems;
10 differentiated services for students with special needs of one sort or another, e.g. disability, geographical remoteness, prisoners; and
11 materials which support the development of study skills, programme planning or career development   (Tait, 2000, p. 289–90).

It is interesting to note that all these services were, and still are, a feature of the distance education programmes provided by the dual-mode universities in Australia, the former national Distance Education Centres (DECs). The one exception being 'residential schools', which apart from one or two institutions was never a major requirement. These services, apart from the residential component, are also currently provided, in some form or another, by Open Learning Australia to support the approximately 10,000 student enrolments it receives each year, with more and more of these services being provided on-line.

Student support in a changing educational environment

A number of issues or questions arise from this. First of all the application of ICTs will enable many of these services to be delivered in different ways and in some cases services may be greatly enhanced and more accessible. Both Tait (2000) and Rumble (2000) have commented upon this situation. 'ICTs are also enabling more established providers to rethink and re-engineer the nature of their student services. The UK Open University is involved in just such a process as part of a strategy to position the University as a global player' (Rumble, 2000, p. 227). The University of South Australia has also developed a range of on-line student services, which can be accessed by all students whether they are campus based, studying by traditional distance education or on-line. These services developed because of a long-standing commitment and awareness of the needs of distance-education students within the university, the realisation that such services should be available to all students and a change in focus from teaching to learning.

The change in focus from teaching to learning is illustrated by new applications of technology in on-line learning. Here transmission models of teaching are replaced. Learner control of navigation, resource use, and interaction become central issues. An on-line learning environment also encompasses the administration of courses and subjects (registry functions); accessing of resources (commercial textbook suppliers, links to libraries, Internet service providers); interactions within the delivery of courses and subjects (virtual tutorial groups, broadcasts, one-to-one communications between students and between student and teacher); and accessing student support (learning support about and through the on-line environment).

(Nunan et al., 2000, p. 91)

This student-centred, e-learning environment at the University of South Australia (UniSA) relies totally on the student support systems that have been developed and implemented over the past five years. The Flexible Learning Centre (previously Distance Education Centre) has been the major catalyst in providing these on-line services. Staff from this centre have developed about thirty interactive study support workshops and more than twenty learning guides are available to support students around the clock. In addition each student is provided with a copy of *Get Connected*, a CD-ROM which provides simple access to information about the University's on-line environment, on-line learning resources to assist students with their learning, and downloadable software to enable students to connect to all on-line services. Although all these services are available from the University's web site, this provides an additional avenue for students wishing to access services when web access may be difficult or not possible. The Flexible Learning Centre has also developed on-line tools which can be used for assignment submission, course evaluation, and staff and student surveys. A personalise and customisable student portal called *LookUP* enables students secure on-line access to programme and course enrolments, fees, results and a range of other information related to students' activities at the University. University-designed software, called *transcript2* enables students to record their study, personal and work achievements against the graduate qualities that have been developed and implemented to determine what sort of person is a graduate of the University. Students are able to link these records with an on-line careers centre, *Experiencebank*, a unique on-line career community where staff, students, recent graduates and employers are able to access a number of services related to recruitment and employment. The library at UniSA has a long history of providing a library service to distance-education students both within Australia and overseas. With the shift to a more flexible teaching and learning environment within the University the library has introduced a Flexible Delivery Service to all students and staff of the University, which provides access to the collections and information resources regardless of physical or institutional boundaries. The library also provides a flexible, on-line service to all students enrolled in Open Learning Australia academic programmes and for the Global University Alliance (GUA).

As has already been pointed out these services have been developed and implemented because UniSA has had a long standing commitment to serving the needs of students who for a variety of reasons choose not to study on campus. However, many of the institutions, corporations and consortiums identified earlier in this chapter have had little or no prior experience in distance education. As Tait (2000), Rumble (2000) and many other commentators have noted, the emphasis that distance-education institutions have historically placed on student support is quite an unusual feature within higher education. To a large extent 'distance and open education practitioners have led the field in higher education both in terms of the student-centredness of their teaching approaches and the sophistication of the support services students receive' (King, 2001, p. 57). Given that this is the case, it will be interesting to see what level and kinds of support these 'new players' into the field of ODL will provide. On the one hand the commercial nature of most of these new ventures will be 'customer focused' and so the very nature of the technology should enable students better access to the services which they require. As Rumble (2000, p. 227) has pointed out:

> self-help and self-service concepts have revolutionized banks, restaurants and petrol stations. Similarly, the provision of on-line services with access to information, advice and guidance, or to automatic enrolment and billing facilities, will enable students to do far more for themselves in the future. This hands them greater control of the relevant process by *enabling* the customer, and it also helps to reduce costs.

However, will these customer-focused services include those categorised by Tait as being in the affective and cognitive areas? These are the very features which, together with better design of learning materials, enabled traditional distance education to move from a correspondence model with very high drop-out rates and a bad image to a more successful, and academically respectable alternative to traditional university study. There is a danger here that the commercial nature of many of these new ventures, even though they may employ 'customer focused' services, will lead to a situation, which actually disadvantages students.

> One result is likely to be that new articulations of customer care, e.g. through Web sites supported by Call Centres, replace existing understandings of student support. Whether greater student success will be the result is not, yet, however known. One fear is that the real human cost of educational failure will be replaced by the diminished notion of the disappointed or even worse inadequate customer, returning ODL to the earlier culture of correspondence education.
> (Tait, 2000, p. 298)

A third issue arises from the very nature of the on-line teaching and learning experience. Because of the interactive capacity and the immediacy of the on-line environment, the potential for supporting students, particularly in the 'cognitive' and 'affective' functions identified by Tait, would seem to be greatly enhanced. However, for this to occur two conditions need to be met.

First of all teachers need to learn or acquire new skills in facilitating learning on-line. As Salmon (2000, p. viii) points out:

> Successful on-line learning depends on teachers and trainers acquiring new competencies, on their becoming aware of its potential and on their inspiring the learners, rather than mastering the technology.

The new roles which lecturers/tutors will be called upon to fulfil as facilitators or e-moderators are obviously crucial to the success of the on-line learning experience.

By constructing dynamic learning activities, encouraging participation and interaction and by continually assessing students' capabilities and involvement, they may not only provide such a learning experience, but also support students in some of the 'cognitive' and 'affective' areas.

Second, the students themselves, many for the first time, are now 'faced with a new learning environment and the expectation that they will have independent learning skills and the capacity to engage in activities that require self direction and self management of learning' (McLoughlin and Marshall, 2000, p. 1). It can of course be argued that tertiary level students should already have these attributes. However, those of us with experience with tertiary students can probably attest that this belief may be somewhat naïve and that learner support systems, particularly for novice users learning on-line, are essential for successful learning outcomes. As McLoughlin and Marshall further state:

> support systems are essential for learners to engage in the processes of learning and need to be developed in response to needs. It is also imperative that a range of support systems be put in place to enable learners to become competent in learning on-line, and to learn to interact in a virtual environment.

On the surface this may suggest that students may require different kinds of support services than those formerly provided by ODL. This may indeed prove to be the case, but it can be argued that the principles of independent learning, self direction and self management of time and learning activities will basically remain unchanged. The challenge for those now involved in the development of new delivery systems is to recognise, first of all, the value of services which are designed to support these principles, and then determine how they can best use the technology to provide access to them.

Conclusion

The very nature of distance education is being changed and challenged by the introduction of new technologies. King (2001, p. 47) has argued that 'the closing years of the twentieth century saw enormous technological changes, with the potential to remove any claim to distinctive delivery by open and distance education practitioners.' The result of this has been that the traditional providers of ODL have now been joined by a host of new providers from traditional educational institutions, consortia and corporations. On-line education is now being aggressively marketed on a global basis in an attempt to capture market share of an estimated global market for e-learning of US$300 billion which is expected to grow to US$365 billion by 2003 (Moe and Blodgett, 2000, p. 189). Many of these new providers will develop and deliver on-line services for students, which attempt to replicate the 'customer care' services provided by other service industries. However, experience in those institutions involved in ODL over a long period of time has shown that the kinds of support which students require go much further than technical support (an on-line help facility) and other administrative arrangements. There is no doubt that these other forms of support particularly related to the development of successful learning outcomes, can be provided to students on-line. This has been already demonstrated at a number of institutions, including those described earlier in this chapter through the University of South Australia's on-line learning and support environment. The question is whether the commercial imperative of the new providers, particularly those from the corporate sector, will recognise the need for such services and be in a position to provide them.

References

Daniel, J. (2000) Inventing the On-line University, paper presented on the occasion of the opening of the Open University of Hong Kong Learning Centre.

Gilbert, A. (2000) Interview on ABCs Radio national's weekly investigative documentary: Background briefing, 16 July 2000.

King, B. (2001) Managing the changing nature of distance and open education at institutional level, *Open Learning*, 16 (1), pp. 47–60.

McCloughlin, C. and Marshall, L. (2000) Scaffolding: a model for learner support in an on-line teaching environment, in Herrmann, A. and Kulski, M. M. (eds), *Flexible Futures in Tertiary Teaching*. Proceedings of the 9th Annual Teaching Learning Forum, 2–4 February 2000. Perth: Curtain University of Technology.

Moe, M. and Blodgett, H. (2000) *The Knowledge Web* (San Francisco, Merrill Lynch & Co).

The National Committee of Inquiry into Higher Education (1997) Higher education in the learning society: the report of the national committee of inquiry into higher education in the United Kingdom (The Dearing Report).

Nunan, T., George, R. and McCausland, H. (2000) Rethinking the ways in which teaching and learning are supported: the flexible learning centre at the University of South Australia, *Journal of Higher Education Policy and Management*, 22 (1), pp. 85–98.

Rumble, G. (2000) Student support in distance education in the 21st century: learning from service management, *Distance Education*, 21 (2), pp. 216–35.

Salmon, G. (2000) *E-moderating: The Key to Teaching and Learning On-line* (London: Kogan Page).

Tait, A. (2000) Planning student support for open and distance learning, *Open Learning*, 15 (3), pp. 287–99.

6 The importance of the tutor in open and distance learning

Helen Lentell

Introduction

Tutors in distance education have always been undervalued. This is a result of many factors. But the underlying explanation, I believe, resides in the belief that 'teaching' was the preserve of the study materials thus making the 'teacher' redundant – at best an unfortunate necessity for the remedial student. (I have always had a suspicion that this is what has made distance education so attractive to many policy makers! The appeal of reducing the numbers of expensive personnel rather than the appeal of access and equity implicit in the value systems of many distance educators.) The provenance of the tutor in distance education literature has invariably been confined to 'marker' and 'giver of feedback'. In addition, in much distance education provision the tutor has invariably been the provider of 'learner support'. Learner support is frequently but, mistakenly in my view, narrowly conceived as the range of services that guide the student through the administrative maze of off-campus study – this is often conceptualised as a counselling/mentoring type activity – not an educational, and certainly not an academic one. Thus distance education provision, despite the existence of Open Universities with missions to democratise educational provision, have unknowingly replicated the hierarchies of the academy. These hierarchies favour and admire the academic role over all others.

The tutors' role, I have argued elsewhere (Lentell, 1994), is little understood both by managers of distance education provision and by writers in the field of distance education. But the practice of distance education is changing. Partly these changes arise out of evolutionary processes internal to distance education – we are now in, or entering, what Taylor (1999) has called 'the intelligent flexible learning model' phase. But I consider the more powerful drivers of change are external pressures bearing down on education in general and distance education in particular. The tentative conclusion I draw from this is that at last the tutor is being recognised as key to success in distance education provision, and is also being written into the distance education script. This chapter seeks to identify why tutoring has been a devalued activity. It establishes core activities tutors conventionally and typically carry out. It explores some key external factors that are driving distance education to change and thereby to (belatedly) recognise the pivotal role of the tutor. And, finally, it describes one example of distance education provision that is placing the tutor centre stage.

The background

In the 1990s the distance education community debated the Fordist nature of distance education. This was a discussion that was rooted in Peters' work (1983), which had characterised distance education as an industrialised process of education with a clearly defined division of labour. On the whole, colleagues writing in this field saw industrialisation as a 'bad' thing – leading to an increase in administrative and management control, de-skilling, and sequential rather than integrated 'product' development and production (see, e.g. Campion and Renner,1992; Raggatt, 1993). Concerns over deskilling were invariably expressions of disquiet over the position of central faculty in universities like the OUUK who were characterised as losing autonomy. The ability to freely initiate, define and guide the academic and educational processes was, it was argued, being eroded. The position of other staff, equally important in the process of course production and presentation, was ignored.

Rumble has critiqued the Fordist argument both from within the theoretical framework that defined Fordism, as well as from the empirical world of distance education's institutional practice. However he conceded that there may well be deskilling for those academics, e.g. tutors, employed as temporary, part time or contract staff. 'There seems little doubt that the work undertaken by peripheral workers within distance education – and particularly those who tutor and counsel students, or mark their assignments and examination scripts – involves less skill than a traditional academic job' (Rumble, 1995).

It is a highly questionable assumption whether the role of tutor is being 'deskilled', although it is true that there has been little sustained attention given to tutoring by ODL theorists. Tait has recently pointed out, that 'whilst there is a substantial literature on methodologies relating to the production of course materials and resources in open and distance learning (ODL), relatively little has been written about the planning and management of student support' (Tait, 2000). Tait is however referring to the range of services and activities that can broadly be termed student services – tutoring he identifies as a subset of these. Broadly this is the approach taken by the contributors to the collection of papers presented at the ICDE 20th World Conference by the OU UK Student Services division (The Open University, 2001). Here student services are seen as the processes that have to be in place to ensure that the service is delivered efficiently and effectively (Ryan, 2001). And if little has been written about planning and managing student services, even less has been written about tutoring. As with conventional classroom teaching, the voice of the teacher is mute (Schratz, 1993). Perhaps this is because tutors in ODL define their professional and academic home as their academic and subject discipline, and not the group of people concerned with wider student support and delivery systems. This would not be surprising if, as Rumble suggests, their work as tutors is viewed as low status and routine rather than central to student learning. In the OU UK the relationship a tutor has with a faculty is cemented by line management responsibilities: tutors report to staff tutors who are faculty staff and it is they who recruit them. Student support systems cover the wider services of, e.g. enquiry, guidance, course choice, registration, fee payments, etc. and are located in the operational unit: Student Services Division.

Tutoring is an undervalued activity in distance education. In most distance education provision tutors occupy a second class position and are on the periphery of the academy, and this is true even when they may be prestigious academics elsewhere. This lowly status stems from the lack of significance attributed to teaching and supporting learning by academic staff in universities: research counts for much more. The employment position of tutors in most distance education provision – part time and paid on some form of piece-work system – gives them the precarious status of casual sessional staff. Inevitably the university committees and decision-making processes privileges those with permanent, full-time status. Moreover, the literature on 'deskilling' as it applies to distance education is imbued with elitism in that it values those who author study-materials over all others in the collective endeavour of distance education. This is the case even when the final study materials may, due to the input of other professionals – e.g. educational developers, instructional designers, those with expertise in assessment, editors, even tutors, have changed the original 'academic' submission beyond recognition. It has always seemed to me that a fundamental weakness in distance education's understanding of itself is its failure to grasp the centrality of the tutor, among the many others, involved in distance education provision (Lentell, 1994). Within the OU UK the tutor falls between two monoliths: the academic faculty on the one hand and student services – operations and customer services – on the other. The effect of this is that exploring what tutors do to aid their students' learning, and the institutional understanding of how student learning develops and progresses and is affected by, e.g. course design and assessment, is no-one's meaningful responsibility.

Otto Peters' (1983) characterisation of some kinds of distance education seems fundamentally right. Distance education involves an increased division of labour, and therefore managing educational processes does become essential. However, it is misguided to assume that because the distance education tutor is not supreme that this represents some form of deskilling and managerialism, and all this is 'a bad thing'(Lentell, 1999). Indeed for many employed in universities the professional bureaucracy of the conventional academic organisational structure is equally managerial (Mintzberg, 1983). But neither does it follow that the so-called managers of distance education will necessarily have a holistic view of their practice. Few will appreciate what the tutor does, and fewer still will understand that the tutor more than the course materials – however well designed – underpins learning.

What do tutors do in distance education?

If we were to accept that tutors in distance education are merely 'markers' of their students' work, it would be to fundamentally misunderstand what good tutors do. It is not the assigning of a mark that matters but the marking and the giving of personalised feedback to each individual student. In distance education effective learning takes place when students process the material they have studied, and completion of assignments and assimilation of the tutors' responses to them is an essential part of this learning. This is feedback and is a student-led exchange, in which the teaching starts with the student's work: it is individual tuition in the form of a dialogue between a single student and the tutor. Each student presents particular challenges and thus the tutor–student dialogue has to focus on different things accordingly – for instance understanding the course, lack of appropriate skills required to demonstrate understanding, lack of presentational skills, etc. In 'Making a Mark' Marni Jackson writing in the *Globe and Mail* captured the essence of giving feedback (she is quoting a Toronto teacher): 'You don't really know where your students are until you read their papers. Getting inside their sentences is how you find out what's missing in their skills, and what to focus on …'.

Jackson goes on to comment, 'Careful reading of student work is the core of teaching – the place where gentle reinforcement and tough, practical criticism can have an effect'. And quoting the Toronto teacher again, 'what's important is to pay attention. They don't care unless you demonstrate that you care. And if students realise that you are paying close attention to their work, they feel a responsibility to pay attention to you' (Jackson, 2001).

Tutors facilitate and guide the learning of their students so that the students gain knowledge and understanding. To achieve this, tutors develop and practice a multitude of skills and strategies. It is arguable that these skills are no different to those employed by teachers in contiguous environments, and this may well be true. But distance educators have been far more learner-focused than typically is the case of their colleagues in conventional academic institutions (Keegan, 1996).

The typical duties of a distance education tutor can be drawn from tutor handbooks and guides. One handbook notes that the main role of the subject tutor is to:

- ensure students gain a thorough grounding in the subject;
- provide students with academic support in the subject;
- help students explore the links between this module and other modules;
- help students integrate practical work experience with academic knowledge.

Subject tutors are not required to deliver the curriculum – this is the task of the study guides – but to facilitate students' learning. This is done through:

- sensitive and full commentaries/feedback on students' assignments;
- being available on the phone or via email so that students can contact tutors for advice;
- introducing the key learning points of the module at the two residential schools associated with the module, and devising group and individual sessions to assist understanding of the module;
- maintaining necessary contact with your students' tutor mentors.

This list of tasks and responsibilities requires that tutors are multi-skilled. It does not suggest 'deskilling'. Tutors need to understand their subject and to communicate it effectively, be totally committed to their students' learning, and to be effective teachers (Burge *et al.*, 1991).

The changing environment

Thus far I have tried to establish that tutors have always been central to distance-education students' successful learning, but they have largely gone unrecognised in the literature on distance education. However, over the last few years I have begun to notice a change: tutoring is becoming more prominent in the distance education discourse and the design and delivery of distance education provision. This change appears to have been driven chiefly, but not exclusively, by factors external to distance education. Broadly these factors are:

Quality assurance

Quality assurance processes imposed externally on providers by government and funders seeking at one and the same time efficiency and effectiveness. For example, in the UK, the Quality Assurance Agency's core business is to review the quality and standards of higher education in universities and colleges. It does this by auditing institutional arrangements for managing quality and standards, including arrangements for assessing the quality and standards of teaching and learning at subject level. These activities result in reports that are available to the public both as printed publications as well as on the Agency's web site. The Agency's mission is to promote public confidence that quality of provision and standards of awards in higher education are being safeguarded and enhanced. It achieves this in a number of ways, one of which is to provide, it says, 'clear and accurate information to students, employers and others about the quality and standards of higher education' (Quality Assurance Agency). Whilst much has been written about the workings of QAA – both negative and positive – no provider can afford to ignore it. Poor subject-review affects business. An inspection (or subject review) has put in the spotlight the work of tutors and all the processes that are put in place to brief, support and monitor them.

Commercialisation

The growing commercialisation of distance education whereby education becomes just another consumer good has focused providers' attention on students as customers of services (teaching and learning support) as well as the product (study and course materials). Indeed the quality of customer service is, in the highly competitive distance learning market, frequently the distinguishing feature between providers. Thus, an aspect of the quality assurance processes in distance education is the system that monitors and ensures customer satisfaction. This again means providers cannot ignore the work of the staff who have direct contact with students and who mediate the relationship between students (customers) and the institution. We have seen this in recent years in, for example, the benchmarking of student support (including tutor support), the development of customer complaints procedures, training and staff development for staff who handle enquiries and applicants as well as the tutoring staff.

Clearly the generality of student services is important in keeping the student-customer satisfied: pre-enrolment advice, enrolment administrative processes, speed and efficiency of programme delivery, etc. If these services collapse or do not adequately satisfy the student's needs, then an issue of service competency and fulfilment are raised for the student-customer. But in essence these are back-office concerns, and students are only aware of them when they fail in some way. Of far more immediate import is their tutor. The tutor is their ongoing contact point and may be the same person who offered pre-enrolment guidance. The tutor is the one who helps them learn what they actually signed up to and purchased. It is the tutor who individualises and mediates the mass produced product (the course) of distance education. It is only to the tutor that the distance education learner exists as an individual. Market-sensitive providers recognise this crucial aspect of service provision and have addressed the service standards (quality of tuition) this raises.

Information and communication technologies

A new worldwide engagement with distance education is taking place fuelled by the development of Information and Communication Technologies (ICT). There has been an enormous proliferation of e-courses, which can be studied at a distance. These range from one end of the scale with small initiatives run on the enthusiasms of individual lecturers and teachers, to major developments funded by huge corporate financial investments. Dhanarajan (2001) has pointed out that there is a naïve faith that the new technologies will solve the problems of educational deprivation around the world, and he rightly points out the challenges the techno-logy poses. These challenges are not about the potential of the technology but include, among others, the issue of lack of skills in using the technology for teaching and learning.

Many recent educational and training developments launched themselves on assumptions that investment in technology would reduce costs, especially the costs of expensive human resource – teachers/tutors. Scepticism about the claims being made for the technology was heresy. Now, bloodied by reality and experience, educational providers know that technology is not a quick and cheap fix. It requires tremendous, sustained effort on the part of providers and makes huge demands on critical resources. Experience has demonstrated a far more complex relationship between technology and educational processes, and the tutor, far from being redundant, is in fact vital. The power of the new technology (aside from informa-tional and administrative power) is its capacity to support dialogue through computer mediated communications (CMC) and Asynchronous Learning Networks (ALN). In a recent lecture John Daniel, drawing lessons from his experience as Vice Chancellor at the OU UK, noted that 'the main conclusion I draw from observing Open University students on-line is that they use the technology more for activities associated with their studies rather than the mainline work of studying course content. They make it clear, for instance, that they prefer to read books as books, not as downloaded computer files' (Daniel, 2001). Daniel went on to identify the strengths of ICT in learning; and a critical strength he identifies is the communicative aspects of the media. 'Asynchronous group discussion is a powerful learning tool, although to be really effective it needs a human moderator'(Daniel, 2001). He concluded by referring to an earlier debate in distance education – independence and interactivity (Daniel and Marquis, 1979) – with which he had been associated and which remains a seminal paper in distance education. Interactivity, Daniel notes, is 'one of the slippery words in the educational vocabulary. I use it to mean a situation where an action by the student evokes a response from another human being, who may be a teacher, a tutor or another student. The response is tailored specifically to the student's action' (Daniel, 2001). ICT can do many things except replace teachers. As Peck and Dorricott affirm:

> Some things only teachers can do. Teachers can build strong, productive relationships with students. Technologies can't. Teachers can motivate students to love learning. Technologies can't. Teachers can identify and meet student's emotional needs. Technologies can't. Technology based solutions in education can, and must free the teachers to do the important work that requires human interaction, continuous evaluation, and improvements of the learning environment.
>
> (cited in Berge, 1996)

The issue of student motivation is captured by Laurence Herbert, who, in a summary of the 2001 meeting of the European Association of Distance Learning, wrote,

> I was particularly struck at the importance attached to the tutor/mentor role, by Joaquim Daurella in his case study of e-learning provision for SMEs in Barcelona. He defined the tutor's role as a combination of being dynamic and motivational; proactive, available and speedily responsive; and, of course, pedagogically supportive. He had no hesitation in attributing the high success and completion rates of his students to the tutor support they enjoyed during their studies.
>
> (Herbert, 2001)

This appraisal of the technology, grounded in experience, is beginning to be reflected in the publications around the educational use of ICT. No longer are these limited to technical wizardry, but rather they are exploring pedagogical skills (Burge, 2000; National Extension College, 2001; Salmon, 2000; Murphey *et al.*, 2001).

New organisational forms

Herbert also draws attention to another set of developments that are changing the context – the dramatic increase of new organisational forms in education –

particularly at the post-secondary level and in the area of company staff training. These new organisational forms are often between businesses and educational institutions or are joint venture initiatives between educational institutions in partnerships or consortia, they involve both for profit and not for profit organisations. These partnerships are developing for a number of reasons: to gain market share in the global educational market, to take advantage of value added opportunities such arrangements enable, to reduce cost and to benefit from the burgeoning demand for life-long learning. These new organisational forms are stripping out the 'non-essentials' in the university package – counselling, careers, student affairs, varsity life in general – and concentrating on the high-quality product and the high quality service supporting that product. The capacity of distance education, undoubtedly enhanced by the potential offered by ICT (Taylor's intelligent flexible learning model) to deliver 'on demand' access to information and skills and 'just in time learning', at home or in the workplace, during convenient hours – preferably 24/7 – situates distance education well to respond to the new niche markets, e.g. educational and training programmes for companies, and the SMEs (small and medium-sized enterprises) reported on by Herbert.

Funding

But whilst the technology might be the means to achieving niche provision, and the new organisational forms the means of delivering that provision, a critical ingredient is cost and cost-effectiveness. And critical questions are: What are customers and/or governments or funding agencies prepared to pay for? What element of costs can be recovered from learners and/or funders?

Budgetary discipline, with an eye on the bottom line, has encouraged simplistic managerial solutions: cut out and/or reduce expensive items such as tutors. This is a folly if providers are concerned with the quality of service provision and take note of market information regarding what learners value. Moreover, experience of working in partnerships setting up and delivering distance education undergraduate programmes and postgraduate training for large international corporations (Coca Cola Enterprises and Cadbury), who are ruthlessly focused on cost efficiency (mistakenly often assumed by many to be the same as cost reduction), has taught that when the focus is on learning/training outcomes, these companies are not interested in cutting tutor provision so long as they are persuaded that tutors are delivering effective support to students. Thus they are rigorous monitors of tutor performance.

Another important factor is the change in public sector funding. For instance in the UK the relationship between government and universities and colleges has been transformed. Higher education is no longer dependent on the state for funding. Indeed the state is no longer a monolithic entity with a single purpose. There are numerous departments with their own particular agendas using access to funding to realise these agendas. Moreover, there are other agencies with trans-national remits, e.g. agencies within the European Union. Most of these bodies establish contractual relationships with providers. Thus we have experienced major changes to the ways in which state and public funds are allocated. To obtain funding, institutions must demonstrate that they can meet the policy objectives of the government or agency. They are required to bid, to set targets, to audit, as opposed to receiving grant. These are contractual as opposed to fiduciary relationships, with tighter political control with the establishment of formal audit and assessment systems.

Through these funding mechanisms agencies can target which group of the population is to benefit from education and training opportunities. These groups may not have participated in educational provision previously, nor would they have been catered for either because it was too difficult and/or expensive to do so, or because traditionally higher educational provision has been provider led. The availability of funding that is targeted has allowed institutions and individuals within them, often in partnership with others, to bid for resources that have enabled them to work with excluded groups. However, the funding is allocated on the clear contractual understanding that providers deliver on performance and outcome.

For many in distance education these funding arrangements have enabled the use of ODL methodology – indeed to adapt and to refine it – for student groups that would not in the past have given the student volume to make such provision economically feasible; or whose 'special needs' and the tailored provision required would have placed economic demands on institutions that could not be met within their budgets. (Much of this 'new' funding is short term and administratively burdensome which makes sustainability an issue, but that is not the issue here.) In this environment student activity and completion become critical. Providers have to think of models of delivery that will provide some level of comfort that the contract targets can be assured. The best assurance is the tutor who, as we have demonstrated, is concerned with the student as an individual learner.

These five factors external to ODL – quality assurance, commercialisation, ICT, new organisational forms and funding – provide a new focus on the role and importance of tutors in distance education to come into their own. An illustration of this is the focus of the remaining section of this chapter.

The tutor: coach and mentor

In 1998 APU (Anglia Polytechnic University) and the NEC (National Extension College) successfully bid to the European Social Fund (ESF) for funding to develop accessible and relevant higher education learning opportunities for the owners, managers and employees of small and medium-sized businesses (SMEs). A second tranche of funding was secured in 2001, when the partnership was joined by the national training organisation for small business (SFEDI). A dynamic small business community was seen as crucial (being 96 per cent of all UK business and employing some 80 per cent of the working population) in ensuring that the UK became a more enterprising nation. SMEs had not typically participated in training. It was assumed that this was because SMEs did not recognise or have the resources to invest in training. Until the advent of ESF funding, the specific training needs of SMEs had been largely ignored, or there had been a (misguided) assumption that their needs were the same as those of the corporate sector.

In planning what the Sesame (Small Enterprise Sensitive Accessible Management Education) programme should be, a number of key underpinning principles were established.

- All learning should start with the learning needs of the students. That is within each module the students would individually define what their learning problems were and what they wanted to be able to do or know by the end of the module of study. This would be established through extensive discussions with their tutor and would lead not only to drawing up a learning contract, but would also establish the process of study.
- The learning materials would not be linear – there would be no curriculum defined from beginning to end. Students would be able, with the guidance of their tutor, to concentrate on some units, or none of them, according to their learning needs. Thus the modules would be supplemented and added to by tutor guidance.
- The learning experiences would create opportunities for students to relate their learning experiences to the workplace, so the extensive use of case studies and exemplars were developed and tutors were actively encouraged to add their own examples to these. Moreover, tutors were required to get to know in some detail the work situation of each of their students.
- Both formative and summative assessment must reflect the work-based learning of the programme, and demonstrate the learning that had occurred. It would be learning journal and project based. Assessment would not be compulsory, although we would strongly encourage students to use the formative assignments. (In adopting this approach we were greatly assisted by the funding in that what we were required to report on was student activity and not simply student completion.)
- Accreditation should be available for those who want it so a diploma of credit in small business management was negotiated through the university and will be awarded on the completion of three modules (sixty credits). There must be clear progression routes into other programmes.
- Everything would be done at a distance through email and telephone contact – there were no organised tutorials or residential schools, thus enabling students to study according to their own requirements. The only requirement was that students completed each module in fifteen weeks, subsequently extended to twenty weeks. This was to ensure that we fitted into the funding time scale.

The implication for the tutor role of this approach was very significant. It is very intensive and personal to each student. We expected tutors to be proactive rather than reactive and they were contracted to contact each student on their list weekly. They had to be able to help the student articulate their learning needs and help them acquire the skills of reflection. They had to have a deep conceptual understanding of the subject area in order to appropriately and confidentially guide student learning. In this sense they were a knowledge resource equal to the study materials. Tutors had to be able to help students translate real world problems experienced at work into a form from which they could learn. The problems identified on the first presentation ranged from deciding which altar candles to burn – a significant issue for a Roman Catholic priest (Harris, 2001) on the financial management course – to guiding a student through the process of working out how he might diversify his business. In this case the student's micro business had been solely based on supplying a large multinational with components but the multinational was about to withdraw from the country and our student's business looked like going down with it. This student was registered on a strategic management course. In this way tutors were also key in setting the assessment – although the learning journal and project had frameworks to guide students and tutors.

With such a personal, active and direct role tutors could only handle a small number of students – no more than twelve in the first presentation. Thus there could be no economy of scale for these tutors – a possibility when all students are submitting for marking the same assignment at the same time. With Sesame each student is completely different. This made it exceedingly difficult to work out how to pay tutors and to determine the basis for this, given that some students did the assignments, and others did not but still had weekly contact with their tutor. This meant that we had to move away from a simplistic piece work rate and find some more appropriate and professional form of remunerating tutors to take into account the role they were playing and not to exploit them. This role also includes regular feedback to the programme administrators and managers in order that the programme can be effectively monitored and adapted if necessary. Tutors also maintain regular contact with each other through email, providing learning support for each other.

Clearly in a simple market situation the Sesame programme may not be viable although Empire State College, State University of New York, has operated a similar approach for many years. The set up and presentation costs have been very high, but the programme is viable because of the ESF funding and the positive government steer to work in this area. The project management team are exploring the cost implications of offering the programme without this funding and the position, at the time of writing, is looking positive.

The Sesame programme, and indeed more and more accounts of on-line tuition, are showing that the tutor is indispensable. Tutors need to have knowledge and a broad conceptual understanding of their field. They have to be effective listeners and communicators, to be a coach, facilitator, mentor, supporter and resource. They have to listen, to shape, to give feedback, to motivate, to direct, to appreciate – broadly to be developmental and problem solving. This is not deskilling.

Concluding remarks

The role of the tutor in the Sesame programme goes beyond the conventional understanding of the tutor in distance education. I have argued that the conventional understanding of the role of tutor has seriously underestimated the significance of the tutor in distance education historically. I suggest that this may not continue, because a number of external factors are forcing change. However, one needs to proceed with caution when making any generalisation. Some view the signs differently – commodification and commercialisation would lead to the standardisation of courses and programmes, tutors would be more exploited as providers sought to drive down costs, and the behaviour of for-profit and not-for-profit providers would be similar. One can never be confident predicting the future – but one can seek to shape it.

References

Berge, Z. (1996) http://www.emoderators.com/zberge.shtml

Burge, E. J., Howard, J. L. and Ironside, D. J. (1991) *Mediation in Distance Learning: An Investigation of the Role of Tutoring* (Ontario: Institute for Studies in Education).

Burge, E. J. (ed.) (2000) *The Strategic Use of Learning Technologies* (San Francisco: Jossey-Bass).

Campion, M. and Renner, W. (1992) The supposed demise of Fordism: implications for distance education and higher education, *Distance Education*, 13 (1), pp. 7–28.

Daniel, J. S. and Marquis, C. (1979) Independence and interaction: getting the mixture right, *Teaching at a Distance*, 14, pp. 29–44.

Daniel, J. (2001) http://www.unescobkk.org/news/speech/0201raja_roy_singh-prn.htm

Dhanarajan, G. (2001) Distance education: promise, performance and potential. *Open Learning*, 16 (1).

Harris, P. *The Guardian*, Tuesday, 5 June 2001. http://education.guardian.co.uk/further/story/0,5500,501156,00.html

Herbert, L. (2001) The ten commandments, EADL internal report (the National Extension College).

Jackson, M. (2001) Making a mark, *The Globe and Mail*, 23 June 2001.

Keegan, D. (1996) *Foundations of Distance Education*, 3rd edition (London: Routledge).

Lentell, H. M. (1994) Why is it so hard to hear the tutor in distance education?, *Open Learning*, 9 (3), pp. 49–52.

Lentell, H. M. (1999) Quality assurance of distance education – management seriously matters, *Open Praxis*, vol. 2.

Mintzberg, H. (1983) *Structure in Fives: Designing Effective Organisations* (London: Prentice-Hall).

Murphey, D., Walker R. and Webb, G. (eds) (2001) *On-line Learning and Teaching with Technology: Case Studies, Experience and Practice* (London: Kogan Page).

National Extension College (2000) *Frontline Tutor Handbook*.

National Extension College (2001) *Tutoring On-line*.

Open University, Student Services (2001) *Student Services at the UK Open University*. Papers presented at the 20th ICDE Conference on Open Learning and Distance Education, Düsseldorf, Germany.

Peters, O. (1983) Distance teaching and industrial production: a comparative interpretation, in Sewart, D. and Keegan, D. (eds), *Distance Education: International Perspectives* (London: Routledge).

Quality Assurance Agency, www.qaa.ac.uk.

Raggatt, P. (1993) Post Fordism and distance education – a flexible strategy for change, *Open Learning*, 8.

Rumble, G. (1995) Labour market theories and distance education 11: how Fordist is distance education?, *Open Learning*, 10 (2), pp. 12–29.

Ryan, Y. (2001) The provision of learner support services on-line, in Farrell, G. M. (ed.), *The Changing Faces of Virtual Education* (Vancouver: The Commonwealth of Learning).

Salmon, G. (2000) *E-Moderating* (London: Kogan Page).

Schratz, M. (ed.) (1993) *Qualitative Voices in Educational Research* (London: Falmer Press).

Tait, A. (2000) Planning student support for open and distance learning, *Open Learning*, 15 (3), p. 287.

Taylor, J. C. (1999) Distance education: the fifth generation. Paper presented at the 19th ICDE Conference on Learning and Distance Education, Vienna, 20–24 June.

7 Remembering our common work

Institutional support for open learning

Alan Mandell and Lee Herman

The institutional context of open learning

Non-traditional or 'open' universities and colleges have been around long enough to become traditional. Many are regional, national and even global in the reach they seek and access they offer. And while many of these are still innovative, particularly in applying digital and distance technologies to the delivery of learning, open learning institutions have become large, complex, formal organisations. Perhaps inevitably, the structures and the imperatives of systems – the infra-structural means of education – have become distinct from and even predominant over the principles or ends of education which those systems were originally created to serve. Roles are separated and specialised. Policies, procedures, programmes and standards are created with emphasis on efficiency, uniformity and appeal to large, supposedly homogeneous markets. And authority is concentrated in the hands of administrators pre-occupied with systems functions.

Because of the great success and growth of systems of distance and open learning, it is too easily forgotten that our universities and colleges ought to be first and foremost *communities* of educators and learners. Administrators, faculty and students work, teach and learn in academic institutions which ought to express, in *all* the details of their structures and practices, the intellectual and political values of the 'open-ness' they were created to nurture in the larger society. That is, our institutions should both reflect and distribute the 'primary goods' of a just society (Rawls, 1971). They should serve as 'facilitating environments' in which the learning they claim to teach is actually lived (Nussbaum, 2001). It is in this sense that we shall explore here what a 'supportive' open learning institution ought to be. Such an institution, we shall argue, is one in which all practices, both administrative and academic, are integrated and animated by the basic principles (or 'maxims', as we shall call them) of good education.

We work as a faculty of a college in a large, public university, the State University of New York. Our college, Empire State College, was founded in 1971 to provide 'student-centred' or open learning. Most of our students are adults already busy with careers, families and community commitments. Our faculty are formally called 'mentors': we work with our students, primarily one at time, in distance learning and face-to-face tutorials; we advise them on designing each of their studies and their entire curricula or degree programmes to suit their purposes; we arrange for their experiential learning to be evaluated and integrated into their academic learning; we connect them with other faculty and with community tutors suited to their needs; and we help our students learn to manage the opportunities and demands of open and independent learning. Our college, through most of its history, has supported these open learning activities with very flexible policies and procedures. These accommodate and encourage improvisation in the pace, the organisation and the content of learning. However, like similar institutions, ours has become increasingly systematised, complex and rigid. Thus, our effort to explore in this chapter structures and processes of open learning is also an effort to remember the work all of us in our institution and others like it should have in common. We begin, as we do each day, with our students.

Two cases: a beginning

Alex walks nervously into my office to learn how our college works and to plan a first independent study with me. Now in his mid-twenties and living on his own since he was 15, he had never graduated secondary school, but managed to pass an exam which secured him a diploma. Alex then enrolled in several required liberal arts courses at another college. He did poorly in all of them, even though, as he tells me while sweating and fidgeting in his chair, he's interested in psychology, philosophy and writing. Alex wants to continue reading in and writing about those subjects, which he has done on his own for some years while working as a labourer at a local steel mill. His schedule of rotating 12-hour shifts made it all but impossible for him to meet the attendance requirements of any college he'd found so far. And, on top of that, although Alex clearly loves learning, he simply hated school.

Alex did have clusters of time during which he could follow his intellect. I asked him what he'd been reading, what he'd been thinking about, and what kind of writing he liked to do. He offered me a short list. It included Freud and Goethe; he also wrote poems and meditations in his journal. I could easily feel his eagerness as well as his anxiety. He seemed to want to learn everything all at once. However, Alex also feared that he just wasn't smart enough for college and, perhaps even more, that another school experience would twist and squash the learning he deeply cared about.

He and I struggled to find focus and organisation for a first tutorial. We searched for a question, a theme, a topic that would both engage his expansive interests and offer him a manageable frame within which to pursue them. This fascinating problem was difficult enough, but two additional worries hovered over our discussion. First, Alex's company was only willing to pay for studies that were 'work-related'. Second, Alex and I had to face a set of course requirements, which my college had recently imposed upon all its students. These courses, as many as ten, are 'general education' studies. Some people might think them necessary for any well educated citizen. But the imposition of this claim on all students is precisely the kind of 'school' demand that would drive someone like Alex away.

Doris is quite proud of what she has accomplished. After completing high school, she found a secretarial job, married, raised three children, whilst devoting herself to her church and its community activities. With the full encouragement of her company, she became more and more adept with computers and at supervising a small staff, to the point where she had mastered the skills, though she lacked the title, of IT manager.

During our initial conversations, I understood as well as Doris did that she was professionally stuck without a college degree. With twenty-five years of experience, Doris could, I was sure, earn substantial credits for the skills and knowledge she'd acquired along the way. Her apparent competencies in technology, in administration, and in effectively dealing with people will nicely support and get her very close to her life's goal of managing a church-based service agency. But she had no degree.

Doris had never been to college and worried that her age and her lack of a formal academic background would impede her success. I knew that her enthusiasm, her religious values, and her experiential learning would all but ensure her success and would open all kinds of possibilities for simultaneously planning her undergraduate degree and her professional career. And when I then discovered that Doris loves to see films and is looking forward to learning more about them, I was yet again struck by the power and expanse of her inquisitiveness. I'm sure she can make it.

But, we are not operating in a vacuum. Her company will fund her college education only to the extent that her degree focuses on business. Her very busy life – filled with work, family and church – conspires against the pattern and pace of any typical academic calendar. In so many ways, Doris has been a dutiful learner. She learned how to be a spouse and parent; she learned what her company asked of her; and she learned the traditions and the theology of her faith. But now, at this time in her life, she has found her own path. She knows what she wants to learn and why she wants to learn it. This knowledge is based on the rich 'general education' of her life, and Doris, no less than Alex, for her own good reasons, does not want to adhere to a set of academic requirements which will obstruct her learning.

Principles and practices

The principles from which our academic practices flow are often neglected in our discussions of educational policy and administration. That is, the link between sound education and a suitable organisation for it is broken. This problem can be, to some extent, attributed to an overemphasis in universities, especially large and 'mega-universities', on cost, access and quality (see Aronowitz, 2000). As a result, those normal criteria of administrative decisions have been deformed. They have become obsessions: with cost as maximum yield of measurable product for minimum investment; with access as market penetration into the broadest groups with the greatest ability to pay; and with quality as the transformation of learning into homogeneous course requirements and standardised outcomes. These distortions, however damaging to learning, support the fantasy of a literally Global University (the GU). In this global system every student learns the same things in the same way according to the same tests and for the same costs. The rules governing these matters are set by those few who presume to know what is best for everyone.

Our purposes in this chapter are to set out a few 'maxims' of good teaching and learning, and then to apply those maxims to the forms and routines in which we work and our students learn. We shall suppose that these maxims really do, to some degree, still govern and can still transform our institutions.

To be sure, our maxims are debatable. In fact, we use the word 'maxims' here not because we believe them to be immutable and self evidently true, but simply to indicate that within this context we are using them as starting points. Our maxims have emerged through our years as teachers, advisors and administrators (see Mandell and Herman, 1996; Herman and Mandell, 1999).

This chapter, we hope, will serve as a reminder of a rather simple point: principles are important. But the point needs minding now because all of us are working during a time of frenzied institution-building and because the power of those regional, national and truly global academies is unprecedented. Without taking principled care, we may find that, quite contrary to our intent, we exacerbate social injustices and systematise plainly poor learning.

Five 'maxims' of good education

1) Authority and uncertainty: act so that what you believe you know is only provisionally true

This is the most fundamental maxim of the five. We take it from the Socratic effort to learn wisdom, which is to claim to know only that one does not yet know (Plato, 1961). Institutions of learning gain their power because they are repositories of knowledge and expertise. However, they gain their legitimate authority because they are places of inquiry where knowledge claims are questioned and expertise is uncertain. Inevitably, faculty and administrators exercise power over each other and over students. But, in keeping with the provisionality of knowing, administrators are responsible for making rules that are not absolute and that preserve openings for interpretation and change. And, by the same token, faculty are responsible for being as critical of their own knowledge claims as they are of their students' opinions. In this way, administrators guard the academy from the deadening consequences of power propelled by fashionable ideas; and teachers inspire their students to become makers of ideas by respecting the lure of truth.

2) Diversity of curriculum: people learn best when they learn what draws their curiosity

Standardised curricula rest on the supposition that experts can judge what knowledge is most worth having. However, scholars of learning know that what is known and its value vary with cultures, with time, with status, and with the interests and abilities of individuals (Minnich, 1990). Even so, faculty and administrators influence what students will learn and how they will do so. However, with a self-critical eye on their own influence, administrators are responsible for preserving the ability of faculty and students to decide what valuable educations will be. And, in the same spirit, faculty are responsible for respecting and sustaining the wonder of each one of their students. An authoritarian curriculum suppresses wonder. An indefinite diversity of learning opportunities invites people to turn their curiosities into inquiries that work and last.

3) Communication and collaboration: continue the inquiry until all the participants fully offer their opinions, including the reasons for them

Universities deserve prestige because they are communities of scholarship. They are due respect because they are communities in which intellectual freedom holds full sway. This freedom is essential if the tension between the provisionality of knowledge claims and the search for truth is to thrive. Administrators ought to be leaders of a community in which rules and structures support collaborative decisions and do not mystify or abort communication. Faculty ought to guide discussions so they and their students gain practice in a polity in which people are free to say what they think. Students ought to be heard, and to be responsible for considering the implications of their ideas.

4) Integration of functions and roles: treat all participants to an inquiry as whole persons

Like all complex organisations, universities work efficiently through the division of labour and responsibility. Similarly, the strength of the intellectual expertise housed in universities depends upon divisions of knowledge into specialties. But without integration and permeability among specialties, ideas become trivial and intellectual authority becomes officious. Help that truly nurtures and education that lasts care little for such constrictions. Such learning addresses the lives of people in all their aspects, their capacities and their concerns. In an integrated university, administrators and their staff must be teachers and learners. Faculty must teach by attending to the connections between their expertise and other areas of learning, as well as to the range of their students' experiences and commitments. In this way, administrators and faculty become effective and caring counsellors, advocates, facilitators and teachers. Moreover, administrators, faculty and students too will see each other, not just as components of a system, but as members of a human community.

5) Diversity of outcomes and quality control: assume predictable outcomes and standards of evaluation, like all other knowledge claims, are incomplete

Every organisation, including the academy, is expected to guarantee its product; thus, every organisation tests. But schools carry a special evaluative burden. They are responsible for conserving the knowledge and meanings of a dominant,

relatively homogeneous culture. However, schools also are responsible for recognising new knowledge and meanings. Thus, not only must they use reasonable
and fair criteria for judging learning and awarding degrees, schools must also
remain true to the understanding that knowledge claims are unpredictably diverse
and inherently provisional. Administrators must not reduce standards of admission,
achievement and graduation to what can be unequivocally measured. And faculty
must devise criteria for and ways of evaluating learning, which appreciate the
diversity of student purposes, abilities and academic entry points. Rather than
testing for correctness and certifying closure, evaluators should inspire learning
and reflection, including their own.

Applying the maxims to the cases

How should we respond to Alex and Doris according to these maxims?

Both of these students need university degrees. A sufficiently convenient curriculum
and schedule, combined with a welcoming and encouraging staff could help them
succeed in an otherwise conventional academic system. Modern and savvy
universities now offer night and weekend classes, courses on the web, and firm
but supportive counselling that is sensitive to the exigencies of the lives of adult
students. In all but the most exclusive institutions, these kinds of services are
taken for granted. Today's university will allow Alex to take a course on Freud or
Goethe, and to take a course on creative writing once he has fulfilled the general
requirements and committed himself to a programme of professional studies that
his company will fund. After appropriate testing, Doris would probably be placed
on more advanced information technology courses. Moreover, she would be
allowed to choose among a variety of offerings on religion and on film, once she
too has completed the set of general education requirements. In effect, both Alex
and Doris would be free to indulge their individual interests as long as they were
willing, in the main, to do what was expected of them. Access results from quite a
simple deal, a bargain made between the student and the academic organisation:
the university retains control of curriculum and standards, and it conforms to the
surrounding system of values and power. Students acquire degrees, marketable
career training, a version of liberal arts education, and some freedom to choose
what they really want to learn.

But, there is a tension. The rich and inquisitive minds of Alex and Doris will
chafe against enormously powerful academic conventions that simply do not
recognise who they are. Moreover, the authority of those conventions rests upon
the presumption that the university, as a community of scholars and as a gatekeeper
institution, knows what is best to learn, how it should be learned, and when it
should be learned. The elaborate rules, procedures and vocabulary Alex and Doris
must follow will admit only a small portion of the learning they already have and
will strictly regulate the flow of curiosity that animates them.

Nonetheless, these two students prudentially looking at their options in light of
their goals might well adapt. They will accept the bargain and learn as they are

told. They will decide to believe what they are told is best for them. However, if they retain the spirit and energy of their inquisitiveness, they will also remember the difference between their desire to learn and their pragmatic acceptance of learned authority. *That* lesson will stick.

Alex and Doris will no doubt also believe that the tension stimulated by this memory is their fault. But, fundamentally, this tension grows from an organisational culture housing two opposing principles. First, the university presents itself as the arbiter of a society's legitimate knowledge. Yet, second, as the protector of learning, the university must also nurture unlimited inquiry. The first principle allows the university to tell Alex and Doris what is best for them. The second principle requires the university to doubt its own authority and, giving Alex and Doris the benefit of that doubt, to help them learn as their curiosity and questions lead.

Our first maxim of education gives precedence to the second principle. No person or institution, however learned, can claim the truth. If we are wise, the best we can do is offer the beliefs and skills we've acquired through our intellectual efforts and the certainty that our best ideas must be opened and changed as we continue to learn. Administrators must protect Alex and Doris from the imposition of a required curriculum, no matter how imperiously currently celebrated cultural authorities make demands on one (Hirsch, 1987, and his many successors). Faculty must place all their own abilities as learners in the service of helping Alex articulate an idea or question he cherishes and which he can use as a clear line of inquiry through his many interests. And faculty must help Doris create a satisfying and workable mixture of studies, which accommodates the many demands of her life, takes advantage of her technological expertise, and which responds to her ultimate professional and spiritual goals.

Since, as our second maxim stipulates, people learn best from what draws their curiosity, faculty and administrators should expect that curricula will emerge with unpredictable diversity. This means that faculty must listen for and learn about what their students want to learn. Administrators must promote that kind of dialogue within the institution, as well as advertise its integrity and value to the outside world.

In order to plan his initial study, Alex and his faculty mentor have several long conversations. It became clear that he needed to be reassured that his interests and questions could become topics of legitimate academic inquiry. Alex and his mentor began to focus on the conflict he was experiencing between conventional learning demands and the integrity of his real learning interests. Having become familiar with Alex's interests in psychology and philosophy, his mentor suggested that he explore this conflict over what is to be learned and how by reading Vivian Paley's *You Can't Say, You Can't Play*, and Plato's *Apology*. Then, to examine the same conflict between the individual and convention in terms of modern debates about curriculum, Alex, also at his mentor's suggestion, read works by John Dewey and E. D. Hirsch.

Unlike Alex, Doris has no trouble specifically saying what she wants to learn. However, she does have trouble imagining how her seemingly disparate interests will cohere within a single undergraduate curriculum that also suits her professional goal. As Alex's mentor did, Doris's mentor suggests that they make her 'trouble' into a topic of academic inquiry. This inquiry would result in Doris constructing an appropriate interdisciplinary degree plan – an individualised curriculum. They therefore create a study through which Doris can discover and investigate themes touching upon her several interests, which include technology, communication, helping people and spirituality. At her mentor's suggestion, she uses writings by Marshall McLuhan, Neil Postman and Riane Eisler, among others. These authors are meant to provide a context of ideas that she can turn to as she makes decisions about her degree plan.

It is clear that neither Doris nor Alex is beginning to study in the conventional way. A curriculum is not handed to them, and they are not starting out with the traditional 'survey' of the academic disciplines. It is therefore necessary that an institutional structure of both policy and procedure must allow these departures from convention. Such a flexible structure is necessarily an administrative creation, and it must be maintained by administrators who understand and value this kind of inquiry and the diversity of learning which results from it. Equally important, this commitment must extend through all levels of the organisation. Whether senior managers or public relations professionals, all must take pride in this particular educational endeavour and be well prepared and forthright in advertising its integrity beyond the institution.

The third maxim stipulates a truly collaborative and communicatively open polity of learning. As any study develops, three moments of shifting authority usually occur. At first, faculty mentors listen closely and check that they are hearing their students accurately. Then, faculty make some specific suggestions about readings and organising the inquiry. But, once the study is well under way, in a third moment, the authority shifts toward the students, who will often propose their own ideas about how to continue.

For example, after beginning with the four books and the study focus proposed by his mentor, Alex said that he wanted to alter the focus a bit to include some work on the dynamics of social convention. He proposed reading Freud's *Civilization and its Discontents* and something by Marx. His mentor agreed and as they discussed these new materials, they realised that the 'course' truly belonged to both of them. Similarly, Doris's readings helped her articulate more and more clearly the questions and topics which really engaged her. Her responses helped both mentor and student see how her interests could cohere into an academically strong programme of study. This vision of the whole emerged over time; it could only have come about through their collaboration.

To permit this approach to creating individual studies and entire degree programmes, an administrative structure is necessary which is not only flexible but is open to multiple and unpredictable improvisations. Nonetheless, learning must be documented. The fluidity of the inquiry process must be orderly and equitable; colleagues have to be able to tell what students have learned; and the public to which the institution is beholden, must have some means of being informed about the legitimacy of the learning which occurs. Administrators thus have to design and maintain a records system, an institutional memory, which suits the suppleness of the learning process. The system should be operated simply, and should be clearly intelligible to everyone – to students, to faculty, to managers and to the public. In this way, the institution is demystified both to the community of scholars and to the community at large.

A modern university that supports collaborative education will inevitably be a complex organisation with an elaborate division of labour. However, mirroring the actual learning process, this collaboration, as the fourth maxim requires, must occur at the interstices between each role and every other. As we have already suggested, administrators need to deeply understand and involve themselves in the teaching/learning process. The flexibility of schedule, curriculum and planning, which Alex and Doris require in order to follow their inquiries, demands closely attended and rapid adjustments. Only administrators who themselves are very involved with students will likely be this responsive. Indeed, they very likely should remain teachers, ones who are still eager to learn how to make things work for their students. Similarly, in order for faculty to maintain the institution's elasticity, they must thoroughly understand and participate fluently in managing the administrative system. Every role ought to be permeable.

In conventional universities, academic freedom is acquired through distance from management. Faculty exercise the freedom to teach and do research as they see fit by remaining relatively uninvolved in administrative decision-making. Administrators exercise their power by not meddling very much in the details of faculty work, but focus instead on organisational, budgetary and 'programmatic' matters. Of course, this separation is more real than apparent, because the decisions administrators make, 'systems' decisions, inevitably will govern academic life: the range and content of curricular offerings, class size, selection and retention of academic personnel and research opportunities. But in a genuinely collaborative learning community, freedom requires engagement – and not only with administrators and administrative systems. Faculty mentors have to engage with their students across a very broad range of concerns. Alex's faculty mentor was able to help him design a carefully focused study on the conflict between the individual and society by appreciating how Alex's initially vague but passionate concern with that issue grew out of his particular life history. In the same way, Doris's faculty mentor had to listen to and 'mirror' the complex aggregation of her life goals so as to be able to recommend readings which could help her pull together her interests into an academically sound and personally satisfying degree programme. It should be evident that faculty in this community are no longer merely professing. They are simultaneously counselling, advising, manipulating an administrative system, structuring independent studies that follow ideas across disciplines, questioning and tutoring, suggesting learning activities to their students and taking suggestions from them.

Administrators teach; teachers administrate and counsel; administrators and teachers learn. This integration of roles in all its fine elaboration can only hold if the student is at the centre. In fact, students themselves, like administrators and teachers, must take on a new role. Doris has to articulate what she wants from her education, and she has to tell her mentor what she believes she's already learned –

from database management to church liturgy. Alex needs to explain the connection between his abstract interests and his life history. Further, he must show his mentor what sort of academic arrangement will work for him. Like good administrators, Alex and Doris take responsibility for managing their education. Like good teachers, they have to make sure official teachers understand them. In the society implied by the fourth maxim, members are not fixed to functions in a system. Their common work as administrators, teachers and students expresses their wholeness. In order to do their work, they have to see each other as members of a human community.

The fifth maxim requires that Alex and Doris, their mentors and their university's administrators be responsible to several communities: the university itself, the larger world of higher learning and the vocational or professional communities which these students hope to join. Accountability to standards of learning – quality control – is necessary. But how then will Alex and Doris be evaluated? What criteria will be used to honour the diverse individuality of their learning? And how will those criteria clearly accord with standards that are both common and fair?

Just as knowledge claims are provisional, so the exact outcomes of Alex and Doris's learning activities should not be specified in advance. It would be convenient for Alex's mentor to stipulate at the beginning just what he should learn about Freud, Plato or Vivian Paley. To use a standardised test to evaluate what he has learned would be seemingly fair but inaccurate. For, at the heart of Alex's learning project is the exploration of a theme, the tension between individuality and society. He is trying to uncover its meanings, particularly to understand himself better. Alex does not know what he will find in the contact he makes with those readings. Though having a greater knowledge of the texts than Alex does, his mentor cannot know what Alex will or should discover for himself.

Doris's mentor can certainly construct an academically strong curriculum, even one that touches on most of what her mentor understands to be her interests. But the mentor's plan of study will not serve as a meaningful template for judging what Doris says she wants to learn. The mentor's curriculum can never be her education. Like Alex's mentor, Doris's cannot know in advance just what will suit her. And even Doris cannot know in advance just what she will discover she needs to learn.

But from the start, Alex, Doris and their mentors do share some common learning expectations: that the students will become clearer, more precise with, and more informed about their own discoveries, whatever they are; and that they will be able to apply those ideas to their lives and to shaping the learning they plan to do. Alex's future learning will be about whatever questions or themes he raises as a result of the reading and reflection he is doing now. Doris, however, will soon be building an entire degree programme plan, which will specify her remaining studies. The work of both students will be assessed by them and by their mentors in part by these 'products', which they will have created from the discoveries they make. They will have had to read accurately, analyse carefully, credibly defend their own interpretations, and make reasonable connections both among the texts and with their own experiences and purposes. These intellectual skills and the products Alex and Doris create with them can serve as the points of reference for making judgements about the learning they have achieved. When Alex and Doris's mentors prepare evaluations of their learning, or better yet, when student and mentor collaborate in evaluating the learning, they will have to describe how the studies progressed according to those standards. These evaluative criteria are roomy enough to be adapted by faculty to individual and diverse inquiries. But they are also easily understood and are consistent with quite ordinary academic expectations. And it is the responsibility of administrators to explain this consistency to their external constituencies.

The current rage for outcomes assessment and quality control in education is driven by a passion for certainty. If the desire to know were replaced by the fantasy of certainty, then learning could indeed be reduced to a perfect system of measurement. The learning Alex and Doris really achieved would disappear and so would the possibility of noticing the discoveries each made. In such a world, surprise is forbidden and wonder killed.

The real world

The five maxims do not describe the real world, except in so far as our non-traditional, experimental and open universities still preserve some gripping memories of their birthrights. Universities, like all institutions, forget and ossify. And thus, even institutions of 'open and distance learning', however different they claim to be, mimic that which they were created to transform. Roles are specialised and authority is hierarchical and undemocratic. Students learn, teachers teach, advisors advise, and managers administer. This division of labour suits the global regime of huge, complex, formal organisations. That is, most socially valued human activity, including higher learning, occurs within arrangements of power that distribute opportunity and reward according to a basic economic criterion: cheaply acquired inputs are worked upon with highly specialised techniques, by replaceable labourers, to produce maximum outputs of stable things and services. This rule is applied everywhere, from the manufacture of pins to the education of students.

Critics lament that this dehumanising system is malevolently, ineptly and/or complacently administered. This criticism appropriately applies to many specific situations. However, at the level of regional, national and international systems, the fact is, no-one and no group is in charge of anything. As Anthony Giddens says, we live in a 'runaway world' (2000). Today, organisations are huge, complex and omnipresent. Both internally and among themselves, they operate with nearly unrestricted power as a semi-autonomous system of systems. Thus, whether an Open University or a General Electric, and no matter how elegant and systemically logical their edifice of official control might be, institutions present to us a chaos of rationalisation, nearly beyond comprehension and human control. No one person or group, however well-intentioned, can change a policy without creating unmanageable consequences. Neither CEOs nor university chancellors, no more than professors, can be drastically deviant without driving away their 'customers', alienating their workers, losing their market, and, finally, sacrificing their jobs.

So, what is to be done? How do students, teachers and administrators, guided by maxims of sound education, find the freedom and the wherewithal to change and humanise their universities?

First, every institution must attend to the reasons it exists, and part of the mission of every university, even the most conventional one, is to create ideas which are taken seriously. It would violate the essential identity of any educator to simply dismiss principles of good education, like our five maxims, as unrealistic. However faint, the memory of principle must still inform educational practice. Without this attentiveness, the language through which open learning universities understand, legitimate and market themselves will inevitably lose its meaning and credibility. Thus, the hope of institutional reform today requires that all participants in the educational enterprise – students, teachers, administrators – be careful and critical collaborators.

Second, the jumble of every large organisation breeds openings for change. Our maxims, particularly the fourth, point to a community in which identities are not reified. Administrators, faculty and even students are all teachers, learners and managers. Thanks to the ironic and unintended flexibilities of any system driving toward total rationalisation and control, these role transgressions can occur quite easily and often safely. Teachers can manage administrative mechanisms; administrators can devote themselves to the practices and principles of teaching; and students can become experienced collaborators in determining what and how they learn.

These transgressions are not hypothetical. In various ways, opportunities for admirably transformative deviance present themselves everyday. Sometimes, perhaps with difficulty, we act on them. This is how we remember our common work. When we do, we learn democracy and we want to practice it everywhere. We teach and learn citizenship – the heart of an education which might animate the academy and beyond. Fortunately, Doris and Alex are real.

References

Aronowitz, S. (2000) *The Knowledge Factory: Dismantling the Corporate University and Creating True Higher Learning* (Boston: Beacon Press).

Giddens, A. (2000) *Runaway World: How Globalization is Shaping Our Lives* (New York: Routledge).

Herman, L. and Mandell, A. (1999) On access: towards opening the lifeworld within adult higher education systems, in Tait, A. and Mills, R. (eds), *The Convergence of Distance and Conventional Education: Patterns of Flexibility for the Individual Learner* (New York: Routledge).

Hirsch, E. D. (1987) *Cultural Literacy: What Every American Needs to Know* (New York: Houghton Mifflin).

Mandell, A. and Herman, L. (1996) From teachers to mentors: acknowledging openings in the faculty role, in Mills, R. and Tait, A. (eds), *Supporting the Learning in Open and Distance Learning* (London: Pitman Publishing).

Minnich, E. (1990) *Transforming Knowledge* (Philadelphia: Temple University Press).

Nussbaum, M. (2001) *Upheavals of Thought: The Intelligence of Emotions* (Cambridge, UK: Cambridge University Press).

Paley, V. G. (1992) *You Can't Say You Can't Play* (Cambridge, MA: Harvard University Press).

Plato (1961) *Apology*, in Hamilton, E. and Cairns, H. (eds), *The Collected Dialogues of Plato* (Princeton, NJ: Princeton University Press).

Rawls, J. (1971) *A Theory of Justice* (Cambridge, MA: Harvard University Press).

8 On-line learning and supporting students

New possibilities

Robin Mason

The changing student context

Most people who attended university before the 1970s will have experienced the *in loco parentis* approach to university life: e.g. locked residences after 11 o'clock, and other examples of the university controlling the activities of the student. This kind of authority is, of course, completely out of fashion now. What is 'in fashion' now, is student support.

Since the 1970s, the Open University (OU) has pioneered the concept of supported open learning in which adult students are provided with a range of systems and supports to help them overcome the loneliness of studying at a distance. Examples include: face-to-face tutorials, regional centres, counselling services, pre-course packs and study skills advice and training.

However, the advent of on-line courses and virtual institutions since the 1990s raises the question all over again, about the responsibilities of universities towards their students. Just as controlling the bedtime of university students would be considered preposterous nowadays, will the kind of support services that many open and flexible institutions currently consider essential to a quality distance education experience, be seen as unnecessary hand-holding and outmoded for a lifelong learning generation who take charge of their own learning needs and choose courses which fit the requirements of their lifestyle?

If so, or even if only partially so, perhaps it is time for us to re-consider our role as educational provider and plan for a future which may make quite different demands from today. This changing context for learning is most apparent at the moment in on-line and adult education, although the campus-based 18 to 22-year-old environment is also undergoing significant change. To put the issue into familiar polemical form: is it the concern of an on-line university that many people will sign up for a course but drop out without completing because they don't have the time to study, or some crisis arises at work or home, or they have got what they wanted from the first weeks of the course? Is an on-line university in the business of selling high quality products which people are prepared to buy? Or is it still the business of any university to ensure that learning happens?

In this chapter I will concentrate on just one aspect of this very extensive debate: supporting students through the tutoring provision.

Students' attitudes to face-to-face tutorials

Studies of OU students going back over nearly thirty years continue to show that students value face-to-face tutorials, request more of them whenever they are asked, object to on-line tutoring being considered a substitute for face-to-face meetings, choose face-to-face as the preferred method of interacting with their tutor, and generally consider face-to-face tutorials an important part of the course. A study from the Indira Gandhi National Open University comments:

> It is becoming more and more clear that distance learners require much more than distance tuition and self instructional materials. In spite of the high quality of self instructional materials most distance learners generally seem to need human support at some stage during their academic pursuits.
>
> (Manjulika *et al.*, 1996, p. 19)

One in-depth study of OU students reports that:

> The estimation of the worth of tutorials was generally very high. ... Usually they expressed the sentiment that contact with one's tutor helped confirm your own understanding – that you had got the right end of the stick as it were – or that it helped sustain or rebuild confidence after a low grade, or some difficulty with the course material. As one student put it, tutorials 'are a big help in getting the attitudes of the Block', by which he meant gaining a strategic perspective on it. Another wrote that for her, tutorials were good 'for making sure you are on the right track'. Yet another studying a Mathematics course, attended regularly because she benefited from the tutor 'going over the problems in the units'.
>
> Similar comments were made by most members of the group in relation to day schools, gallery visits and other forms of face-to-face interaction. Essentially any contact with tutors seemed to help build confidence and motivation, and its regularity acted as a sort of routine check whereby they could reassure themselves they were still pointing in the right direction.
>
> (Rickwood and Goodwin, 1997, p. 62)

Early studies before the advent of on-line tutoring are categorical in their support of the value of face-to-face tutorials:

> Field (1993) found that when students were surveyed about what they would like to be added to their study support, 'more tutorials' was the first demand. Jelfs (1998) found that for new students entering at second level, the tutor was perceived to be the principal contact and supporter during their course. This result has been repeated throughout the history of the Open University – in 1986, research completed by Thorpe *et al.* concluded that without the tutor/ tutor counsellors, the University would fail and that students wanted more contact with tutors and more tutorials.
>
> (Castles, 1999, p. 15)

Despite this apparent enthusiasm for face-to-face contact, there is also evidence that the responses students repeatedly give at interviews and on questionnaires is not always borne out by reality: namely, their actual attendance at tutorials. There is considerable variation in the attendance rate of OU students according to subject, year of study, level of the course, etc. but 50 per cent is roughly accurate with upper level courses below this and first year courses above it.

A 1977 study by Gallagher (1977) of OU students found that, while 69 per cent of respondents had attended tutorials at least once, only 29 per cent rated them as very helpful.

Furthermore, the two courses which have attracted the largest number of students in the OU's history (the 2000 presentation of the new Social Sciences Foundation course and the Technology course, 'You, Your Computer and the Internet') have both made a feature of reducing the face-to-face contact. The former course has removed the compulsory one week attendance at summer school and the latter has no face-to-face tutorials at all – a first for an OU foundation level course. Feedback from the evaluation study of this latter course shows that on-line tutoring and particularly collaborative group work did substitute reasonably well for the lack of face-to-face tuition (Mason and Weller, 2000). There is also anecdotal evidence that many students chose these courses precisely because there was no summer school or face-to-face tutoring respectively.

Various distance educators in other parts of the world also present evidence that face-to-face tutoring is not the 'be all and end all' for students. For example, Holmberg and Bakshi (1992, p. 36) provide support for the case that good pre-design can make face-to-face sessions unnecessary, and also note that students' uncoordinated personal study schedules limit the usefulness of tutorials. An Australian study focused on the actual content of tutorials:

> meetings are more likely to be attended if they focus on learning difficulties or problems encountered in interpreting the learning package.
>
> (Kember and Dekkers, 1987, p. 4)

Agboola writing in the *Indian Journal of Distance Education* notes:

> A number of distance teaching institutions share the view that education cannot be given without some face-to-face contact sessions. … However, the overall contribution of contact sessions to distance learning appears to be of limited value. Reports on attendance have been rather discouraging. … An assessment of what takes place at the contact session also reveals a mixture of desirable and undesirable trends. … The advantages of the contact sessions give meaning and an identity to distance education, although at some substantial costs. Thus contact sessions are both an asset as well as a burden which distance teaching institutions have to cope with in order to achieve desirable educational goals.
>
> (Agboola, 1993, p. 17–21)

Other studies investigate the variable quality of tutorials around the world and note that the training of tutors, both in the course content as well as in facilitative tutoring skills, is critical to the effectiveness of face-to-face contact sessions (Burt, 1997, p.107).

There are a number of databases on the web which list on-line courses and one of these, called TeleCampus, has more than 40,000 listings. To qualify for entry on this database, the course must be delivered entirely on-line and require no face-to-face contact. Seemingly there are a lot of students managing without contact.

Studies on the acceptability of computer interaction between students and tutors have shown from the very early days of the medium, that graduate students (who are more motivated, more self-directed in their learning and more mature in their study habits) are able to take advantage of conferencing as a learning vehicle much more readily than undergraduates, younger learners or less confident and less motivated students. Similarly, OU studies show that younger age groups (under age 30) tend to have a lower retention and performance rate than older age groups (Ashby, 1995). This leads to the conclusion that face-to-face tutoring is less necessary the more advanced the learner, but also that the most vulnerable students – least confident or motivated – will benefit from face-to-face provision in terms of increased persistence and higher pass rates. Burt (1997, p. 118) describes a range of studies from around the world which aimed to find a positive relation between various kinds of face-to-face support and reduced drop-out and/or improved pass rate. While some studies did find such a correlation, others did not.

So to summarise this discussion of students' attitudes to face-to-face tutorials, we are faced with conflicting evidence. On the one hand, there is indisputable evidence of their value to many students both as a learning medium and even more importantly as a motivator and steer for keeping on track. However, questions have been raised about whether the educational benefits are commensurate with the costs and about how to improve the quality of the sessions which tend to be very variable. More interestingly perhaps, there is some evidence, though less robust and with nothing like the long standing pedigree of the former, that some students may be voting with their feet. That is, they are choosing flexibility over hand-holding, and the convenience of on-line tutoring over the multi-sensorial impact of face-to-face contact.

Could this be an indication that the kinds of students who will choose on-line courses in the future are the pioneers of a new consumer-centred approach to learning provision?

Responding to the challenge of the changing context

Critics will suggest that the consumer-centred approach to higher education is merely synonymous with poor quality. In this sense, virtual universities are in the same position now regarding on-line education, as the Open University was thirty years ago: challenged with the task of demonstrating that distance education need not be third rate. My own view is that on-line course providers and virtual universities should respond to this challenge by proving that on-line education can be exciting, interactive and high quality as well as being flexible and adaptable to individual learner requirements without replicating traditional tutoring support systems.

There are three critical elements to on-line tutorial provision that I want to examine in the light of this changing context:

- individualisation or personalisation of courses;
- quality and quality assurance of the tutorial provision;
- cost effective tutorial support system.

These three elements always exist in tension with each other: extremes in any one of the three produces an unworkable system. Finding the golden mean which maintains quality, provides individual support, but does not lead to higher costs, is the continuing challenge.

Personalisation of course provision

The concept of personalised courses usually involves the customisation of the on-line environment in which the content is delivered. For example, students studying courses at Royal Roads University can opt to have their course material presented according to their personal learning style preference (Shank, 2000).

Another aspect of personalisation relates to the flexibility of the options for studying the course. Applied to the tutoring system, flexibility could be seen to encompass the following:

- that courses could be designed to include any level of tutor support from considerable to none;
- that students could have the option of tutor support or not, and the price of the course would vary accordingly;
- that some courses might demand considerable group collaborative work and others might be stand-alone or involve individual email exchanges between the student and tutor;
- that some courses would be based on a cohort of students beginning and ending the course together, while other courses or other options for the same course would be available on a rolling intake basis;
- that students should be able to 'audit' courses for a reduced fee, if they do not want to submit assignments or obtain accreditation;
- that for tutor-intensive courses the student/tutor ratio might be as low as 10/1, while on other, self-study courses, the ratio might be as high as 50/1.

All of these options are desirable in theory in order to maximise the tailorability of on-line education to a wide range of potential 'customers' and to attract and continue to attract learners with varying styles and propensities for studying. However, the administrative overhead of managing all of these options and the quality assurance procedures required to monitor them are daunting, even if the costs could be justified.

Quality and quality assurance

The procedures that would be needed to monitor the tutor feedback for both individuals and cohorts, and to assure the fairness of assignment marks across both options, would be complex. The quality assurance would also have to develop standards of good practice for the whole range of tutorial provision from 'a lot' to 'a little'.

Clearly the easiest provision to assure is the least complex and most standard: all courses are of type A and provide tutorial support of type B and have an assessment system of type C. However, the days of 'one size fits all' are gone, or to be more accurate, customers are no longer prepared to accept only one size.

A critical aspect of the quality of the tutorial support is the selection and management of the tutors, and their involvement with the courses and their commitment to the students they tutor. The greater the dissociation of the course providers and the course tutors, the greater the potential for the tutors to be, and to be perceived to be, little more than 'hired hacks'. For the purposes of quality of provision and commitment of tutors, it seems obvious that tutors need training, support, mentoring, monitoring and affiliation with the institution, the course and the course developers. However, this brings us right back to the 'supported open learning model' both for students *and* tutors. OU tutors have been enculturated to expect a high degree of institutional support and 'caring', just as they in turn expect to provide for students. This situation begs the question, 'can a more streamlined support for tutors co-exist with top quality support for students?' If we see signs that 'the new student' wants more flexibility and less hand-holding, can we restructure the tutoring role to reflect this? What does high quality, low hand-holding as a tutoring system actually look like?

I think we have to assume that the new breed of learner has neither the time nor the inclination for extended interactions and institutional affiliations – rather, ease of access, quality of information and tailorability of access are the key concerns. These learners have reasonably good learning skills, focused motivation and less concern for certification than for appropriate, effective learning opportunities. Furthermore, these learners are usually not socially or intellectually isolated, and have opportunities in their personal and workplace contexts to discuss or apply course concepts.

A high quality, 'tutor-lite' model, therefore, should focus on the following:

- personalised feedback to individual students on their assessed work;
- facilitation of on-line small group collaborative activities;
- options for various levels of tutoring at differing fees;
- streamlined support systems for both tutors and students.

Cost-effective use of tutors

If there is one thing which researchers and practitioners of on-line teaching agree about, it is that interacting with students in this medium is more time-consuming than traditional campus lecture courses or print-based distance education tutoring. Anyone with experience of tutoring on-line will be considerably more familiar with the over-demanding, emotionally needy, or endlessly chatty student, than with any picture I have conjured up of confident, efficient, focused learners.

Can we anticipate that the social, emotional and administrative interactions of students on on-line courses, which account for so much work for tutors, are a temporary blip in the history of on-line learning? As an etiquette of on-line learning develops, will much of this exchange either cease or be re-directed to other channels? Will expertise in the design of on-line courses and the structuring of conferences help to alleviate the overload? Personally I think this problem will subside in time, and it will be accelerated by the changing student context which calls for streamlined support systems.

One of the rationales for the tutor-intensive approach to tutorial support is that it improves student retention rates. Another, perhaps more significant rationale is a moral one – that educators have a duty to support students in the process of learning. However, there is no simple relationship between the amount of support provided and the rate of student drop-out. Retention is more complex than that unfortunately, and a whole range of personal and employment related issues play a large part in students' reasons for withdrawing from courses. It is interesting to note that in a survey of OU students, 'partner or spouse' was rated more highly than 'tutor' as a source of help and support on the course. The question remains, 'How much resource is necessary or desirable to devote to retaining students?'

In line with this emergence of a new type of e-learner, perhaps it is appropriate to reconsider the question of retention. In a telephone survey I conducted with some of my on-line students taking a professional development course, it emerged that students who were not taking part in the intensive on-line interactions, were nevertheless quite satisfied with what they were getting from the course. Perhaps it is time to acknowledge that there are many ways of learning, of benefiting from learning opportunities than the obvious signs of on-line interaction and retention to the end of the course. Why should dropping out or withdrawing from participation be considered a failure either by the institution or the student? Many will argue that this is a supermarket approach to teaching in which consumers take products down from the shelves and put them back if they don't appeal. However, to believe that educators know best what is good for students, is no longer a mindset with much currency.

Towards a streamlined tutorial provision

I do not have any illusions about how difficult it will be to evolve an appropriate tutoring system for 'the new learner', if or when they start appearing in any numbers. What follows are merely observations about the issues I have raised so far.

Reducing the burden on tutors

There is evidence from in-depth OU studies that effective arrangements for a whole array of administrivia can go a very long way to making students feel they are receiving a personalised service without involving the tutor:

> It is interesting how much goodwill was secured through what we might think were quite trivial procedures like changing a student's tutor without fuss, authorising special sessions and coursework extensions, or facilitating summer school attendance by adjusting living accommodation. One student said the OU reminded her of the slogan once used in a credit card advertisement, about 'your flexible friend', because its monolithicity was tempered by a quality of personal care and attention that gave it a responsive edge.
>
> (Rickwood and Goodwin, 1997, p. 58)

Providing a 'human face' at local level, even if that face isn't a tutor, goes a long way to compensating for the lack of face-to-face tutoring.

Another possibility is the use of self-help groups arranged at a local level to facilitate students meeting, or alternatively in small virtual groups where location would be irrelevant. As with so much of distance education, one man's meat is another man's poison, and self-help groups will not appeal to all or even the majority of students. But for some, they can be a lifeline and can function at both a social and motivational level.

Another version of the notion of self-help groups is that of learning partnerships in which students are paired for the duration of the course and act alternatively as listener and teacher to put the ideas of the course into practice. The on-line version of this method has been developed by Stathakos and Davie (2000).

Small group tutorials through webcasting are even more cost effective in terms of tutor time and arguably for learning effectiveness as well. Many on-line courses are experimenting with this kind of contact at the moment and while global timezones provide something of a challenge, they are not insurmountable. The global web-based Masters Degree in Open and Distance Education offered by the OU, ran four realtime tutorials in 24 hours to cover both the number of students and the variety of timezones.

A trawl through the virtual course offerings on the web at the moment shows that most practitioners are using models of course delivery which combine elements of synchronous interaction (either through periods of face-to-face study or through videoconferencing or webcasting, or even realtime text-based chat) with large amounts of asynchronous interaction through delivery of content via print, web pages, CD-ROM materials or set books (Mason, 1998). There are also examples of virtual courses which provide little or no tutorial support or contact at all, whether synchronous or asynchronous. This kind of provision may have its place (e.g. professional qualifications or updating; short just-in-time learning objects), but on the whole, it is taken for granted that a high quality teaching environment involves human tuition. A mix of realtime and asynchronous opportunities for interaction is increasingly also assumed in best practice guidelines for on-line delivery.

The OU places considerable importance on correspondence tutoring, and views the extensive commenting on students' assignments as part of the learning provision of the course. Consequently, it invests much time and resource in training new staff how to do this and in setting up mentoring and monitoring schemes to ensure high quality provision.

> Tutors are asked to give constructive and full feedback, as they would do in a face-to-face situation. It is recognised that students are sensitive to the tutor's comments and grading, and adverse criticism or negative remarks may discourage students from continuing with their courses. Staff development for written feedback is an on-going concern at the University.
>
> (Castles, 1999, p. 15)

While much development is taking place in the area of automated web-based assignments, and they may have a place in the on-line university, the tutor's individual comments on student assignments are certainly one of the most significant ways in which the course is personalised.

Small group collaborative work has opened a whole new opportunity for distance educators moving to the on-line environment. There is growing expertise and fascination with this alternative to face-to-face tutoring. Many programmes and courses are experimenting with joint projects, group assignments, on-line debates, small group activities, all conducted asynchronously and usually moderated by the tutor or in some cases by the students themselves. While most practitioners experience the usual problems of all groups (some people not getting on together) and some additional problems in applying this approach on-line (difficulties of coming to closure in an asynchronous environment), there is general enthusiasm for the educational benefits of on-line collaborative work (see, for example, papers at http://collaborate.shef.ac.uk/research.htm).

While this form of tutorial facilitation is demanding and costly, the quality of student learning which can result makes it potentially cost effective.

Alternatives to 'the course'

It could be argued that the discussion so far applies only or particularly to long courses (OU courses typically last from February to October) or sustained programmes of study over several years. For distance learners to maintain motivation and concentration over such long periods may require the kind of support that only human tutors and local systems can provide. But perhaps this new consumer-oriented market will not really be looking for such 'old fashioned' offerings as degrees, sustained programmes or even formal courses. Perhaps they will want much shorter learning opportunities which fit more closely with problems, gaps, or activities in their working or leisure concerns. In which case, the carefully scaffolded learning environment crafted by the OU over many years may not be necessary and the new concern will be entirely on 'fitness for purpose' of the learning materials offered by the virtual university.

One factor seems at the moment to be virtually indisputable: the learners will have very little time to spend on their studies and hence the effectiveness of the learning material will be measured by how efficiently students can access and master the ideas and skills being taught.

Lack of time to study is the single greatest cause of dropout in distance education, and increasingly there is less interest in 'just-in-case' learning. It has also been shown time and time again that overloading courses leads to surface-level learning, higher drop-out rates and general dissatisfaction of students. If we are moving to a just-in-time approach with minimal levels of support structures, then it is critical that the offerings also be just-the-right-amount.

One of the often cited problems with the consumer-driven model of higher education, is that the consumer is not in the best position to know what content is appropriate. There is considerable evidence within the OU to show that when students were no longer required to begin with Foundation Level courses, many chose to enter at higher levels of study than they were really capable of mastering. Of course the consumerist response is 'buyer beware!'

Finally, multimedia on the web – in the form of simulations, video and audio clips, graphics, etc. – help to focus students' learning on the course content, rather than on the tutor. For example, learning segments which talk the learner through a diagram, a problem, or a painting, can lend an air of intimacy and immediacy which has some of the same effect as a live lecture. Furthermore, interactive activities in the course materials can provide increasingly tailored and responsive feedback, and can demand a high level of active and interactive skill from the learner. The development of this kind of learning material can be expensive, time consuming and labour intensive; however, with judicious use, it provides a high quality learning environment which does not over-burden the tutor.

Yet another approach would focus on the notion of short learning modules (anything from several hours' worth of work up to say a few weeks' work). This model *could* be completely tutor free and if assessment were appropriate, it could be computer-generated and marked. Learning advisors – rather like a personal fitness trainer – could advise students on appropriate choices and combinations of learning modules. This concept is of course a very long way from what most people still see as the role of a university.

Conclusions

The traditional OU model of distance education still places considerable importance on face-to-face tutoring and local support systems – despite the fact that many students do not attend and on-line tutoring is increasing in use and popularity. This traditional model is embedded in a caring, supportive 'big daddy' approach to higher education – even for adults.

There are signs that this model may not be necessary or appropriate in the future; but especially for courses which are on-line, it is aimed at a global market to attract primarily a learner wanting continuing professional development or lifelong learning for future employability. If a more consumerist attitude is the order of the day, there are many ways in which on-line courses could pioneer the development of high quality on-line education.

Just as we have witnessed the extraordinary degree to which mobile phones have changed communication patterns over a very short period, so it may not be too far fetched to speculate that supported open learning will become as outdated as student curfews and locked gates. As the technologies develop, virtual contact will cease to have the somewhat pejorative association it currently has *vis-à-vis* face-to-face contact. Personalised learning opportunities may become the new Holy Grail and on-line learning would be well placed to exploit this trend.

References

Agboola, R. (1993) Contact session in distance education: an asset as well as a burden, *Indian Journal of Distance Education*, 2 (1), pp. 17–22.

Ashby, A. (1995) *Equal Opportunities – Statistical Digest*, The Institute of Educational Technology, Student Research Centre.

Burt, G. (1997) *Face to Face with Distance Education* (Milton Keynes: Open and Distance Education Statistics).

Castles, J. (1999) *Characteristics of Adult Learners: A Review of the Literature*, Institute of Educational Technology, Student Research Centre Report No. 165.

Field, J. (1993) *End-of-Year Comments on 18 Courses in 1992 – Undergraduate and Associate Students from Annual Survey of New Courses*, Institute of Educational Technology, Student Research Centre Report No. 75.

Gallagher, M. (1977) *Broadcasting and the Open University Student*, IET papers on Broadcasting No. 88. The Open University.

Holmberg, R. and Bakshi, T. (1992) Post mortem on a distance education course: successes and failures, *The American Journal of Distance Education*, 6 (1), pp. 27–39.

Jelfs, A. (1998) *Second Level Entry Students*, Institute of Educational Technology, Student Research Centre Report No. 136.

Kember, D. and Dekkers, J. (1987) The role of study centres for academic support in distance education, *Distance Education*, 8 (1), pp. 4–14.

Manjulika, S., Reddy, V. and Fulzele (1996) Student opinion of counselling: the experience of Indira Gandhi National Open University, *Indian Journal of Open Learning*, 5 (2), pp. 19–29.

Mason, R. (1998) *Globalising Education. Trends and Applications* (London: Routledge).

Mason, R. and Weller, M. (2000) Factors affecting students' satisfaction on a Web course, *Australian Journal of Educational Technology*, 16 (2), pp. 173–200. http://cleo.murdoch.edu.au/ajet/ajet16/mason.html

Rickwood, P. and Goodwin, V. (1997) *A Year at the Front. A Consideration of the Experience of a Group of Students During their First Year of Study with the Open University*. The Open University West Midlands Region.

Shank, P. (2000) Personalization, anyone?, available at: http://www.ittrain.com/new/nov00/humble.htm

Stathakos, J. and Davie, L. (2000) Learning partnerships in the on-line classroom: a collaborative design model. Paper presented at the TCC2000 Conference, April 2000. Available at: http://fcis.oise.utoronto.ca/~ldavie/papers/tconn.html

Thorpe, M. *et al.*, (n.d.) *Adult Learning: Constructing Knowledge Through Texts and Experience*, Institute of Educational Technology, Student Research Centre Report No. 1.

9 The centrality of learner support in open and distance learning

A paradigm shift in thinking

Roger Mills

Introduction

It can be argued that in almost all educational institutions student, or learner support, whether it is academic, administrative or personal, is regarded as less central and more peripheral than the provision of teaching. The terms teaching (and learning) and student/learner support undoubtedly overlap. The broad hypothesis of this article however, is that, perhaps especially in the context of open and distance education, teaching (i.e. the production of learning materials) tends to take precedence over learning and student support.

This chapter argues that we need a new approach to thinking about student support which will place it at the centre of a distance education system alongside the production of teaching materials. In order to encourage this change of approach we must move away from the notion that whilst producing courses generates income for an institution, student support is a cost. With an increasing emphasis on student retention, in the context of widening participation and expectations of high quality customer service those involved in the provision of student support need to demonstrate more clearly than hitherto how it adds value to the institution, and how financial models might be developed which convince institutional managers and external funders of its importance.

The literature dealing with the costs of student/learner support is quite limited. Partly, one suspects, this is because definitions are not clear and also because institutional managers have focused on materials production, relegating learner support to a non-essential element and therefore of less concern to institutional resource planning. One of the latest and detailed examinations of costs in distance education, a handbook produced by Hülsmann (2000), deals primarily with the comparative costs, across a number of institutions, of different ways of the production of learning materials (print, audio, audio-visual and computer). Even where, in part two of this handbook, the costs of student support are examined it is a restricted view of student support, dealing only with correspondence tuition and face-to-face teaching (Hülsmann, 2000, pp. 88–9). There is no mention for example of the costs of providing admissions advice or careers guidance.

Rumble (1994) makes the point that the relatively little support provided for students in a distance learning system compared with a conventional system means that the direct cost per student is lower. He notes that much management and academic effort in institutions is put into 'the development and maintenance of educational materials and the administrative systems for the control of distance students'. In reality, not much attention is paid in the literature to the costs and benefits of student or learner support, and in particular there is little analysis of how learner support can contribute positively to an institutions balance sheet. Paul (1988) put the issue characteristically clearly: 'If student services are so important then why are we cutting them back?' There is a good deal of rhetoric about student support, but when the chips are down the production of learning materials tends to be protected on the grounds that we need the 'products' to attract the students (and therefore the income).

An example from the OU UK gives a flavour of the relative importance of the elements in distance education. Resources are generated from government and from student fees (and from other places e.g. research and other grants/entre-preneurial income). The system used in the OU UK known as the Inter-Unit Planning and Contracting model is based on a flow of resource through the institution. Although the model is just that, a model and not a resource allocation tool, nevertheless the psychology of the process is interesting. Resource first goes to the academic faculties broadly on the basis of their student numbers and the income they generate, and then flows through to the support units such as student services, management services, the library and computing services. It would be very interesting to examine the impact of a theoretical model, for example, in the context of the OU UK, which was based on resource flowing directly from student fees to the regions, with the regions paying the materials producers for the courses which students studied. Such modelling would illustrate what it might look like in institutional terms if learner support is given a more central role, and it might also encourage the use of learning materials produced by other institutions.

How do we change the institutional thinking so that student support is regarded as an income-generating element of the system rather than a spending ministry? The benefits to learners are well documented (e.g. Mills and Tait, 1996). This chapter begins to put together some of the arguments and suggests that now is the opportunity for those involved in learner support to be more assertive and more focused in setting out the clear institutional benefits of this element of distance education.

Definitions

It is important to be clear about what is meant by student/learner support in distance education. The literature offers a range of definitions including student support, academic support, personal/emotional and administration support. It also describes the process by which such support is provided for by letter, email and telephone for individuals or groups; and who provides such support, e.g. the institution, family and friends, other students in, for example, self help group situations and employers (see Simpson, 2000). Sometimes a distinction is made between learner support and student support, with the former referring to tutoring and the latter to administrative and personal support.

For the purposes of the argument here, the widest definition of learner support will be used. This is the totality of the provision by an institution to support the learner, other than generic teaching materials produced by instructional designers/ course producers. To be absolutely clear, where learning materials are produced for numbers of students (e.g. TV and radio programmes, print on-line teaching materials), this is regarded as the academic teaching and is considered to be outside the framework of learner support. Learner support is designed to help the individual student learn from the teaching materials, may be academic, administrative, or personal, can be provided through a range of media and by a range of people. It can also be individualised or generic. A good example of generic materials-based learner support is that designed to help students plan their study time, to choose their next course, or to develop examination skills. It is also the case that the distinction between individualised and generic support is diminishing. For example, the on-line *Learner's'Guide* provides access to generic information and advice including the use of frequently asked questions, but enables the student to email for individualised advice and guidance as required (see Phillips elsewhere in this volume). Similar examples can be found in many other institutions including Athabasca University, and at California State University, Monterey Bay, which interestingly is using the OU UK model for its *Calteach* initial teacher training programme.

The added value of learner support

The core of the argument here is that by planning learner support as an integral part of a teaching and learning programme, rather than an afterthought which can be excised when times get difficult, institutions can demonstrate a recognition of the link between income generation and learner support.

The core elements of the teaching and learning system to which learner support can contribute directly are recruitment and retention, especially in the context of widening participation. Closely linked to this core are market research, the development of a learner- rather than a provider-led curriculum, and expectations of customer service of a level commonly experienced in organisations outside the educational field. These different aspects will now be examined in more detail.

Learner support, recruitment, retention and widening participation

How can learner support contribute to the three key and interlinked issues of widening participation, recruitment and retention?

As far as recruitment is concerned, most institutions in the UK are committed to expansion to meet the UK government target of 50 per cent participation in England in higher education by 2010. In order to meet expansion targets institutions are spending an increasing amount of their resource on advertising. In the OU UK in 2001, some £8 million was spent on generating 600,000 enquiries of whom only 32,000 registered and of whom only 14,000 or so were still studying with the institution some three months into their second year.

Learner support can help with recruitment in a number of ways. Systems have to be in place to deal with the enquiries mass advertising campaigns generate, students have to be guided onto the most suitable course and the enquiries made of an institution need to be systematically collected and analysed to take note of consumer demand.

But the story is not so simple. Attracting non-traditional groups of learners has always been a major concern of governments. Widening participation is the current term used by the UK government. In the 1990s this was described as Access. Whatever the terminology the intention is clear. There is pressure on institutions to recruit from a broader band of the population. It is both an altruistic aim and an economic one. Lifelong learning is now regarded by most governments as an essential element of economic growth and success. However, Yapp used the annual external lecture at Cambridge Regional College to reflect on the additional importance of life-wide and life-deep learning, and described the values of continuing education which relate to personal growth and growth of the importance of community and environmental understanding as well as the economic advantages of lifelong learning (Yapp, 2002).

The challenge is that an increasing number of students who have not taken part in anything other than the most basic education will be participating in education in the future. Distance learning has a major role to play here. In particular the need to mediate the learning resources (no matter how they are delivered to the learner) to the individual student will become increasingly critical.

Inexperienced, uncertain, poor, unsure and perhaps lonely learners will need more and more support. If people are to put their toe in the water of learning they need careful nurturing and support. Not all this need be face-to-face and in groups – a number of studies by Norquay (1986) have demonstrated that learning on one's own can be a safer way of starting out. Given this scenario we must find ways of providing learner support which are more focused on the individual and their needs whilst continuing to be cost effective. Information and Communication Technology (ICT) clearly has a key role here for those with access to such provision. The core provision of Athabasca University (2002) is a good example of how an institution can be focused on the individuals through developing the use of ICT whilst keeping costs down. It greatly helps of course that Canada has an extremely efficient and cheap telephone system. On the other hand, the mentoring model of Empire State College, New York, whilst highly effective in terms of retention (resulting not surprisingly from the fact that the curriculum is built around the student rather than the student having to fit into a predetermined curriculum) is expensive in terms of staff time.

How can we widen participation and improve retention rates? Some might say this is a circle which can never be squared. At the very beginning of the OU UK the issue of retention was a key factor and in a classic article McIntosh (1975) coined the phrase 'the revolving door' to warn of the dangers of simply admitting students to programmes which may not be tailored sufficiently closely to individual needs. Clearly an institution cannot be regarded as successful simply because it attracts students. It must enable them to succeed too. The OU UK has recently completed another major review of retention issues as retention rates have been steadily falling over the years (Retention Project report, 2001). In 1998 some 38 per cent of new students in the undergraduate programme did not submit their first summative assignment. This, together with a number of other points at which the student is likely to drop out, is now the subject of developmental work to change OU systems and approaches. One direct result of this is the encouragement of tutors through a new tutor contract, to make proactive contact with all students to encourage them to submit this first assignment. The evidence is that if students do submit their first assignment the vast majority carry on to pass the course. Retention is a complex, multi-variate issue which impacts on the type of courses, their length, level, cost and relevance and also on learner support. It is argued here that a greater emphasis on more focused learner support could have the most lasting impact on retention rates if approached in a holistic manner and integrated fully into the learning process. The issue of retention should not be underestimated and learner support has a key role. Clearly, some institutions, and Athabasca in Canada is a good example here, are seen as part of a national provision and the movement of students from one institution to another is natural and not of great concern. But where an institution such as the OU UK loses over 50 per cent of those who begin its courses, then there is real cause for concern. Any business person would confirm that to lose such a large percentage of first time customers would be a strong indicator that something was radically wrong.

The Open University has always prided itself on its student service and indeed in the last few years of the external quality assurance subject review process, has scored very high grades for its student support and guidance provision. However, with continuing high drop-out rates there is no room for complacency. Unfortunately, the resourcing of regional support services has been subject to steady and systematic reduction over the past few years and it may be that the impact of this is just beginning to show. There is clear evidence that tutors appointed to the new contract mentioned above will be requiring increased opportunities for the referral of students with study skills issues to the regional support service.

Even in such a large and relatively successful institution as the OU UK there is much rethinking and action needed if the issue of retention is to be addressed successfully.

Clearly some of the changes will require changes to the curriculum and to the demands made on students by a complex and heavy assessment system, but others are directly the concern of learner support. Two examples may help to illustrate how learner support systems might help with retention. As students are increasingly able to register on-line and by telephone, it is more and more possible for them to bypass the institutional guidance services. The on-line *Learner's Guide* provides some on-line support with referral points but there is still the great challenge of ensuring students enrol on the best course for them. A much smaller institution, California State University at Monterey Bay, has a system where all enrolment is on-line but no student can embark on a programme of study until it has been 'signed off' by an adviser or faculty member. A big question faces those institutions priding themselves on openness. Are they willing to use resource and to compromise openness by introducing such approaches to ensuring students are on the right track? Another example where learner support should help retention is in the development of personal development portfolios. Much work has been done in the United States on the development of such electronic portfolios which help the student and the institution monitor progression, and there is some evidence that such systems are beginning to influence the direction of the curriculum as students increasingly demand outcomes-based evidence of their capabilities.

Designing learner support systems

What is increasingly clear is that learner support needs to be designed into distance learning programmes at the initial planning phase and support should be 'fit for purpose'. It cannot be unlimited, a 'Rolls-Royce' model because, after all, someone (normally the learner) has to pay for it. So learner support systems have to relate to different cultures, different economic systems, different learners (either individuals or in groups) and different programmes of study.

A number of key questions arise then. Should learner support be available to all students or just those who may need it? Should some kinds of learner support, e.g. vocational guidance or other specialist support, be paid for additionally by those benefiting from it. Should student support be differentiated such that it is fit for purpose for different programmes (e.g. undergraduates, access courses, postgraduate). The dilemma for large institutions with a wide range of programmes is that as attempts are made to differentiate learner support according to the needs of students and programmes, the increased flexibility is provided only at the cost of increased complexity. This is a major unresolved issue in learner support.

There are arguments for different kinds and levels of support for different programmes of study, e.g. the OU Open Access programme where all learner support is provided for all students by a tutor on the telephone. Here students do not have any face-to-face tuition and preliminary surveys suggest they do not want it, especially if it means significant travel. Instead they are able to telephone the tutor whenever they wish (within reason) and the tutor is proactive in telephoning the student at the beginning of the course and at fixed points during the study period. The impact of information and communications technology on student support is addressed later.

Can learners influence the curriculum?

The current approach of most distance education institutions is to devise the curriculum (i.e. what should be taught), which still too often relates to the interests of academic staff, and then to devise the assessment strategy (how does the institution know what the student has learnt?). Finally, the support system (how can we best support the student in their learning?) is put in place.

How can the learner or potential learner affect the curriculum? The economic argument here is that if students, potential students or other stakeholders can make clear (or if we can develop more sophisticated research tools to predict) what it is they wish to learn, then systems would become more cost effective through the alignment of demand with supply thus enhancing both recruitment and retention. The mentoring approach of Empire State College, New York, is a prime example here. Rather than fit the student to a pre-determined curriculum, the curriculum is built up around the students' real needs and Moore (1980) comments 'adults who work at their real needs are highly motivated, do not drop out and rarely fail'. The Empire State model seems inherently expensive as it is predicated on the development of individual curricula, but on the other hand retention rates are high.

It is a current fashion to decry notions of a producer-led curriculum in education.

However, if the curriculum is not producer-led how should it be constructed? This chapter is not about curriculum development as such although it is impossible to separate out the curriculum from the ways in which students are supported in their learning. The market is playing an increasing role in the determination of the curriculum. No longer is it possible, certainly in commercially aware distance teaching organisations, for the curriculum to be determined simply by the experience, skills and knowledge of those employed to produce learning materials. Courses have to attract students, either because of their intrinsic interest, because of their value in increasing employability, or their essentiality in terms of professional updating or indeed a mixture of all three. Increasingly governments expect education to play a role in contributing directly and explicitly to their economic, social and cultural agendas.

The value of learner support in marketing

One of the major principles of marketing is that of feedback from the customer to the producer. Those working in learner support have a great opportunity to help here by providing systematic feedback both from current and potential learners. Unfortunately many institutions do not have the systems in place to ensure this valuable data is collected in a usable way.

Learner support systems, if designed carefully, ought to be able to provide for more market intelligence than they do and such feedback should be taken seriously by those designing the curriculum. This in turn should demonstrate the economic value of learner support by increasing registrations and there are signs that this is beginning to happen in the OU UK.

Learner Advisers now collect requests for courses which the institution does not provide and new systems are being developed to collect this systematically. There is an enormous and relatively untapped information base resulting from enquiries from the general public about courses which an institution might not currently offer.

In terms of the quality of the teaching, academic tutors also provide feedback to course teams about the content of the courses and the assessment policy and practice indicating, for example, which sections are exciting and stimulating, which are too difficult for the learners and which are dull and convoluted. The new tutor contract builds in the requirement of all tutors to provide such feedback.

Students are increasingly asked for their views on the quality of tuition provide by tutors. For example in the Open University in the East of England, all students are given a feedback card to comment on their tutorials and the work of their academic tutor and throughout the University tutors are encouraged to use the toolkit entitled *How do I know I am doing a good job?*

Changing learner expectations and customer service

Another aspect of change is the change in learner expectations. Student behaviour has altered over recent years and although many dislike the notion of students as customers, certain aspects of learner support need to be dealt with in a very business-like and professional manner. The contrasts shown in Table 9.1, modified from an internal Open University UK report, illustrate some of the changes which are taking place.

To put it bluntly, students' benchmark the services provided by educational institutions against the best commercial service they receive from banks or other organisations and they will look elsewhere if their needs are not met. The OU UK retention project (2001) comments that there are fewer students than ever before continuing to study with the University after their first year. The importance of the student as consumer is increasingly acknowledged by the UK government and the new quality assurance framework will include a key role for students. Margaret Hodge (2002), Minister for Lifelong Learning and Higher Education, recently announced that 'students will be put centre stage in the drive to raise standards. The views of students will be taken into account in a new national survey of what they think of their courses, their teaching and their institutions'. The OU UK has an excellent record of seeking feedback from students at a generic level. What is now needed by us and by many institutions is feedback of a nature which allows for direct and rapid action to improve services. Learner support services should be intimately involved in this process and this is a further example where these services should demonstrate their added value and contribution to improving student retention.

A final example illustrates the difficulties here. At a recent meeting for 250 enquirers to the OU UK in Cambridge there was general disbelief that they would have to wait nearly nine months to start their chosen course. 'We want to start now' was the refrain! The University is aware of this but also aware of the complexities involved in moving to a more frequent start date. Athabasca University in Canada is able to offer monthly start dates but only at the expense of not having cohorts of students and therefore losing the positive aspects of peer group support. For a large institution, acting on feedback is not necessarily a straightforward matter.

Table 9.1 Contrasts in student behaviour

Yesterday	Today
Respectful of academics	Demand good teaching
Compliant	Expect personal service
Loyal	Disloyal
Accepting (of institutional errors)	Assume their needs come first
Committed to the long haul	Impatient
Worked within the system	Will leave and go elsewhere
No IT skills	IT literate
No IT access	IT access increasing rapidly
No bench marks for quality of support	Huge expectations of quality

What does learner centredness mean?

Can learner centredness improve retention and what is the role of learner support as an advocate for such concepts? One of the arguments for a new way of thinking about student support is how systems might change if the student is the starting point. Tait (2000) argues that the whole process of devising a distance education programme should start with identifying who the students are and identifying their needs.

Assessment is a very specific aspect of learner support. What might a student-centred assessment system look like? Assessment is the way in which an institution demonstrates to itself and to quality assurance agencies, how well students are doing. It is also, crucially, a way of students themselves checking on their progress. It can be argued that the existence of continuous assessment in addition to examinations is learner centred in that it provides regular feedback and evidence of progress to the learner as well as the institution. In some institutions students are able to determine when to take their examinations. At Athabasca University students select a time, book a place in an examination centre or arrange for an invigilator in their home area.

Flexibility in assessment provision for disabled students, for students who are travelling or whose work commitments might prevent them from taking an examination at a particular time, is critical, and the OU UK has led the field in its flexibility in this area. However, there are a number of longstanding unresolved issues in relation to assessment practices. A classic example is the inability of the institution to provide early resit examinations to students who pass continuous assessment and just fail the examination. Evidence suggests that less than 20 per cent of students awarded a resit are willing to wait the full year before they can resit again, whereas at Athabasca, students can resit at a time which suits them. There may be a general principle involving size here. Are the very large institutions in danger of becoming less learner centred as their size poses really severe logistical problems in remaining learner centred?

The impact of information and communication technology (ICT) on learner support

In rethinking learner support it is clearly important to examine the impact of ICT. The OU UK's overall approach is one where course materials are produced centrally and distributed to learners who are then supported locally by academic part-time tutors and by staff in regional centres. This is an example of an 'industrial model' of distance learning. Other systems involve far more direct contact between the originator of the learning materials and the student (Steyn, 2001). In many ways the advent of ICT is helping those systems where the course producer also teaches students directly. However, in the industrial model the ability now of students to make direct contact with course producers is raising significant issues about the structure of such systems. In addition, students whose experience of collective and tutor support was limited to small and relatively local groups, can now join in national computer conferences which enable a wide range of input from many tutors, student and course producers.

ICT is also influencing the way in which tutorial provision is structured. This was discussed in detail by Bernath (2001). Essentially, a tutorial pattern which had previously involved regular fortnightly sessions in local centres, has been replaced successfully by a system which involves a residential weekend at the start and towards the end of a course, with student–student and student–tutor interaction taking place electronically between these two residential events.

There are also many issues relating to teaching and supporting students on-line which are clearly going to make significant impacts on learner support in the future. At an OU tutors' meeting in May 2002 considerable concerns were raised regarding the University's expectation of tutors to provide on-line support for students in the future.

How can we demonstrate to institutional decision makers that learner support is effective?

We are encouraged to measure everything today. Evaluation and feedback is regarded rightly as being very important. Student feedback is one thing; objective, measurable evidence is another. One of the major difficulties facing researchers into learner support is the lack of opportunity to plan experimental work with single variables and controls. Moral considerations prevent the notion of providing one kind of service to one cohort of students, and another, perhaps less expensive, service to another group for the purpose of research – and yet this is done in the medical profession. Why can we not grasp the nettle and try to acquire some really hard data about the impact of learner support? We need to demonstrate the added value of student support if we are going to convince the managers of institutions that it is worthwhile allocating resources to this aspect of distance learning.

Simpson (2000) quotes small scale research which suggests that support from 'family and friends' and from employers and from fellow students is more valued by students than support from tutors. Clearly, if the support from employers involves time off work and financial support then this would not be surprising; similarly if friends and family are supportive in terms of enabling the student to find the time and space to study, again valuing, such support would not seem to be surprising. In both cases the support is 'free' and is an added bonus for the student and the institution. But what of the support provided by the institution (and paid for by the learner)? How can we demonstrate clearly that regular access to a tutor or adviser, or face-to-face tuition helps improve individual and group retention rates?

One of the key elements of academic student support, and one to which a great deal of effort and thought has been applied over the past thirty years, is that of correspondence tuition: the commenting by the tutor on individual student scripts. This is the ultimate individual academic support in all forms of distance education. The student and the tutor interact over materials the student has produced. Learning from tutors' comments on scripts/assignments is taken almost as a *sine qua non* of academic support in distance learning. Not all institutions provide such feedback, e.g. in the China Central Radio and Television University with tutorial groups reaching 200 per tutor this is not possible. So where is the evidence that students learn effectively from this ultimate form of learner centredness? Do those institutions which simply grade assignments have higher drop-out rates? It seems that there is a whole area of core distance education provision which could benefit from further research. A research programme which examined in detail the way in which students use and learn from tutors' comments on assignments is urgently needed. Is any institution bold enough to set up a controlled experiment which could provide hard evidence of the value of this key interactive aspect of distance education systems?

Conclusion

This chapter has examined the changing role of learner support in distance education. It argues that learner support is just as important for the financial health of an institution as the production of teaching materials. It can be regarded as critical to income generation in three ways:

- widening participation in the context of recruitment and retention;
- contributing to market research;
- Being the public face of the institution by providing high quality services which may be the unique selling point of an institution in the future.

Those institutions which are successful in the future may find that it is the quality of their learner support services which provides the competitive edge as more and more learning materials become available from a wide range of providers. Institutional managers will continue to regard learner support as an optional 'add-on' at their peril.

References

Bernath, U. (2001) Challenges for study centres in an electronic age. Keynote address to the 9th Cambridge International Conference on Open and Distance Education, Cambridge, October 2001.

Hodge, M. (2002) Various announcements from the Minister for Lifelong Learning and Higher Education.

Hülsmann, T. (2000) *The Costs of Open Learning: A Handbook*. Bibliotheks-und-informationssytem der Universität Oldenburg, Germany.

McIntosh, N. (1975) Open admission – an open door or a revolving door, *Universities Quarterly*, March.

Mills, R. and Tait, A. (eds) (1996) *Supporting the Learner in Open and Distance Learning* (London: Pitman).

Moore, M. (1980) Continuing education and the assessment of learner needs, *Teaching at a Distance*, 17, pp. 26–9.

Norquay, M. (1986) Educational radio, in Mugridge, I. and Kaufman, D. (eds), *Distance Education in Canada* (London: Croom Helm), pp. 247–59.

Paul, R. (1988) If student services are so important why then are we cutting them back? Keynote address in Developing Distance Education, International Council for Distance Education Conference Proceedings, Oslo.

Retention Project (2001) Open University UK Internal Report (OU/01/1).

Rumble, G. (1994) The economics of mass distance education, in Harry, K., Keegan, D. and John, M. (eds), *Distance Education: New Perspectives* (London: Routledge).

Simpson, O. (2000) *Supporting Students in Open and Distance Education* (London: Kogan Page).

Steyn, T. (2001) Did we meet your learning needs? Exploring the experience of post-graduate learners in distance education in South Africa, in Mills, R. and Tait, A. (eds), *Supporting the Student in Open and Distance Learning*, Collected Conference Papers, from the 9th Cambridge International Conference on Open and Distance Education, Cambridge, 2001.

Tait, A. (2000) Planning student support in open and distance learning, *Open Learning*, 15 (3).

Yapp, C. (2002) The annual public lecture, Cambridge Regional College, Cambridge, UK.

10 Distance higher education and library services in Japan

Chieko Mizoue

Introduction

The terms 'distance education' and 'e-learning' have gained currency in higher education circles in Japan during the past few years. This trend can be briefly summarised as 'what they want, when they want it, and where they want it', using available network technologies. The technological diversity of distance education consists of telecourses, audio and video teleconferences, closed broadcast and cable television systems, microwave compressed and full motion video, fibre optic networks, and satellite-based and computer networks. In all, twenty-two delivery systems have been categorised (Jones, 1997). Computers and networks can make library services more readily available for distance learners. The need to provide access to higher education at a distance has been recognised as a top priority in many countries. Despite the rush by academic planners to mount distance educational programmes, the impact on university libraries has been minimal until recently (Lee, 1999). In particular, Japan's university libraries had not begun to identify the special demands and problems of this new group of learners, although Japan has a long history of correspondence courses at the level of higher education.

There are few accounts in the literature that systematically describe the delivery of library services to distance learning programmes in Japan. In this chapter, as a modest contribution to the subject, I would like to attempt an examination of the practices and problems of implementing a library delivery system to distance learners by using the past survey data in Japan, and to provide some recommendations for future action to libraries that support distance learners.

First, I will briefly examine distance higher education in Japan, and the relationship between students, university libraries, and public libraries. I will then suggest that university libraries should forge links with public libraries to enable more effective distance education.

Reform of higher education in Japan

Japan's higher education system has been changing with the advances in the telecommunications field. This change has occurred due to the following three circumstances:

1   The knowledge and skills that people learn at college quickly become obsolete because of advances in the telecommunications field;
2   Japan's excessive emphasis on individual educational background, with the labour practices of lifetime employment and once-a-year recruitment of new university graduates, has had serious adverse effects on the provision of lifelong education. The number of adult students is still very small, although labour practices and the recruitment system are changing and the number of adult students is gradually increasing; and
3   Since declining birthrates have led to a decrease in the number of 18-year-olds, more attention is now being paid to older learners, and systems are being developed, including distance education, that would suit a variety of learners at different stages of life.

It is therefore necessary for Japanese universities and colleges to create a culture of lifelong learning. This entails creating a society in which people can freely take advantage of learning opportunities at any stage of life, one in which their learning achievements will be adequately evaluated.

One reform is to make practical use of open-distance education. Much of the research on the technology needed to carry out open-distance education has been conducted in Japan, and has focused on the so-called 'hard facets' of the issue. These results showed that distance higher education could be made practical by the use of communications satellites, teleconferencing and the Internet.

On the other hand, less attention has been paid to supporting distance learners. It seems to me that the quality of educational services, the so-called 'soft facets', has received scant attention. One example is represented by library services for distance learners.

In 2000, the University of Library and Information Science in Japan started a distance learning class via a teleconferencing system between the Tsukuba main campus and its Tokyo satellite campus. We offer graduate classes using this system.

The number of graduate students who study only at the Tokyo satellite office is very limited, and they are not provided with any special library services, only those offered to on-campus students.

Therefore, all students come to the university library to access services, although some services, for example, on-line public access catalogue (OPAC) may be accessed via home computers. OPAC is a computer-based and supported library catalogue (bibliographic database) designed to be accessed via terminals so that library users may directly and effectively search to retrieve bibliographic records without the

Table 10.1 Enrolment in the graduate schools of ULIS in 2001

	Master's programme	Doctoral programme
Main campus only	72	45
Main campus and satellite office	34	0
Satellite office only	7	0
Total	**113**	**45**

assistance of a human intermediary such as a specially trained member of the library staff (Young, 1983, p. 157). Book borrowing and inter-library loan services, however, are only available to students who come in person to the library. The library services provided by ULIS are typical; they are not rare.

While distance learners may obtain some necessary information through the Internet and computer networks, study at universities and colleges requires a student to fully utilise university library services. Some library services may be inaccessible to the distance learner.

A brief history of distance higher education in Japan

Before World War II, some Japanese universities published lecture notes intended for adult learners who were not regular students. These lecture notes were reportedly very popular and many adult learners utilised them, even though universities did not provide any educational services or guidance for them.

The School Education Law was enacted in 1947. This law established official university correspondence courses. Subsequently, the Ministry of Education carried out drastic reform of the higher education system. In 1950, a few universities, including Keio University and Bukkyo University, formally established correspondence courses. Japan's official history of distance higher education, therefore, goes back more than fifty years.

Currently there are ten junior colleges, twenty universities, and six graduate schools offering distance higher education. Approximately 240,000 students are categorised as regular students. In addition, there are several categories of non-degree students. For example, at the University of the Air, there are one-year non-degree students, one-semester non-degree students, research students and special audit students.

The University of the Air is the largest distance higher educational institution in Japan. Learning materials are offered only through broadcast and printed materials. Student enrolment in broadcast lectures began at this university in 1985, and currently about 87,000 students are enrolled. Approximately 60 per cent of them study degree courses. It modelled itself upon the Open University UK. In 1967, the Social Education Committee (established by Japan's Ministry of Education) researched the use of television and FM radio for specialised educational broadcasts, and reported its findings in 1969. At that time, many television stations had begun to operate in the UHF band. The Japanese government wanted to use this new television wave as an educational tool, since the idea of 'life-long education', a concept that UNESCO advocated, had become popular.

The Ministry of Education and the Ministry of Posts and Telecommunication together officially established the University of the Air in 1983. The University of the Air requires an enormously complex technological system, since its lectures are delivered entirely via broadcast. More recently, however, communications technologies like teleconferencing systems and computer networks have enabled universities and colleges to deliver distance education without such huge investments in technology. In 1998, the Ministry of Education decreed that not only correspondence course students but also regular students could obtain college credit through distance learning. The maximum permissible number of credits earned through distance education for a regular student attending a four-year university course is currently sixty credits, half the amount needed to graduate from university.

Subsequently, the Ministry permitted Master course distance programmes at four universities in 1998. By the year 2000, six graduate schools were offering such programmes. The University of the Air offering Master course began programmes in 2002.

That said, distance learning degree courses offered in Japan are limited compared with other countries. However, there are many distance programmes in the fields of private preparatory schools and business and vocational schools. This limited number of degree courses shows how strongly the Ministry of Education controls the administration of colleges and universities. It may have until recently still tended toward sustaining traditional learning at higher education; it has now just begun to change its policies of control.

Distance learning courses and library services

Kate Stephens and Lorna Unwin of the University of Sheffield, in the United Kingdom, have classified distance courses into the following typology (Stephens and Unwin, 1997):

> *Type A*: The self-contained course. Students study from packaged materials (usually text-based but could include multimedia) and are not expected to read or to consult sources beyond the supplied material.

> *Type B*: The expandable package. Students study largely from packaged materials but wider reading (and hence the use of libraries) is recommended for certain sections of the course, notably a final dissertation or project.

The Type A course providers justify self-containment on the grounds of equality or on the grounds that students have to study the boundaries by choosing the necessary sources. Therefore some students may not have access to libraries. Type B courses, which are common in Japan and other countries, are consistent in that their providers recognise the problems of equality, and they believe that students should develop their knowledge and skills by themselves. Therefore, students must have access to libraries. Above all, the graduate students in distance courses cannot write a dissertation or final project without using libraries.

That is to say, universities with distance learning courses have the responsibility to provide library services for their own distance learners. What kinds of library service should be provided for them?

Traditional students using a library do the following:

- Search for materials using indexes and bibliographic data
- Search using catalogues

- Consult the reference section when not sure how to proceed
- Borrow materials, sometimes using inter-library loan services
- Photocopy library materials
- Search for materials when finding information and ideas related to their specific interests

In the past, students could not utilise these services without physically going to a library. Recently, some of these services are available through the Internet and can be accessed from home. For example, some students can borrow or arrange for photocopying services by mail, but in many cases in Japan, the students must come to the library in person for such services. If the materials are not digitised, it is necessary to come to the library.

Based on this traditional way of using the library, I would like to examine library services for distance learners in Japan. Although distance courses in Japan have a long history, there is little research concerning the relationship between correspondence courses and library services. People in higher education, in general, have regarded the primary role of university libraries as one for research, not for education. Since this thinking is still prevalent, faculty and staff do not take into consideration library services for distance course students, who frequently do not visit university campuses.

Public libraries, too, have been uninterested in the specialised studies of adult learners who are learning through distance courses. Rather, public libraries have catered to the non-academic library user.

But at Chuo University, a large, private university, the university selects one institution from each prefecture, for example a public library, private university library, or professional college, and donates several hundred books that are deemed essential for correspondence study. This collection is known as *tsukyo bunko,* or a collection for correspondence study (Matsumoto, 1981, pp. 686–7).

Bukkyo University, another private university, has a borrow-by-mail service, but few students take advantage of this service because either the mail charge is expensive and/or the materials may not arrive promptly. However, most Japanese universities require correspondence students to come to the library directly to access library services. Due to this inconvenience, many distance education students use the other libraries when they need materials. One study showed that 'using public libraries' and 'buying necessary books by oneself' are the highest priorities when students need to write a report. In 1978, when the students of Bukkyo University needed to write a report, 38.3 per cent of correspondence students went to public libraries, and 5.2 per cent went to other libraries (Marsumuro and Kawasaki, 1982, pp. 33–51). In the same year, at Keio University 64.5 per cent of correspondence students used public libraries; the average rate of use of public libraries in Japan at that time was 4.7 per cent (Fujibe, 1979, pp. 183–211). However, public libraries do not really meet the demands of university students. Most public libraries do not possess a collection of specialised books in academic fields. Matsui reported that 198 titles (more than 40 per cent) of reference books required for the teacher certificate distance course programme were not in the three public libraries of one city (Matsui, 1990, p. 210). These results show us that neither university libraries nor public libraries fulfil the role of providing library services for distance learners.

The University of the Air and library services

The University of the Air's academic programme consists of classes broadcast over television and radio, printed course materials, guidance by mail, and classroom instruction and examination for credit at study centres. While the other distance courses are provided by the traditional universities, all courses by the University of the Air are provided via distance learning. Broadcast classes are provided from 6 am until 12 midnight every day. Programme scheduling is arranged flexibly to allow students to tune in at their convenience.

Library services of the University of the Air were initially different than those of other distance courses. The original target area, which included only the greater metropolitan Kanto region, had six Study Centres in 1985 at the onset of the academic year. The Study Centres began to offer face-to-face instruction and credit certificate examinations. At the same time, they were planning to offer academic counselling and guidance, opportunities to listen to or view the broadcast programmes and library services. The University Library, headquartered in the city of Chiba, is a comprehensive library. Smaller libraries attached to the Study Centres are utilised by students; students can access the books and journals that are in the University Library in Chiba through the Study Centre library.

In 1985, each Study Centre library had approximately 6,000 books and 50 different periodicals (Kondo, 1985, pp. 202–4). In 2001, there were 343,249 books at all Study Centres and 71 periodicals at the six main Study Centres, and 596,252 books and 1,376 periodicals at all libraries of the university (University of the Air, 2001, p. 2).

The original target area has seen enormous expansion with the help of the Communication Satellite System (CS) launched in 1998. Although not every Study Centre is located in a national university, students can access libraries attached to national universities in which Study Centres are located. In addition to this, some students can access libraries where the University of the Air makes an agreement with national/private universities for their study.

It is clear that there are not enough books and magazines for students in their specialised fields. However, students can access other university libraries. At the very beginning, staff of the University of the Air hoped that public libraries would cooperate, since students in other correspondence courses often used public libraries. However, no special collections for University of the Air students have been established at any public library, even though some public libraries make available all printed material for television and radio programmes of the university. The relationship between the university and public libraries needs to be strengthened.

Copyright issues

Instructors and providers of distance learning courses endeavour to deliver course materials at the convenience of the students while utilising technological advances to the fullest extent possible. However, permitting activities in the traditional classroom – face-to-face teaching – is problematic for different levels of students in all types of distance learning.

Japan's Copyright Law does not recognise the concept of 'fair use' – the right of someone other than the copyright owner to reproduce, distribute, adapt, perform or display a work. In the United States, teaching is listed directly in the text of the Section of 'fair use'. Additionally, the American Copyright Act provides important exemptions for non-profit educational institutions.

Japan's Copyright Law also provides exemptions for educational institutions. It is defined in Chapter II (Rights of Authors), Section 3 (Contents of the Rights), Subsection 5 (Limitation on Copyright), Article 35 (reproduction in schools and other educational institutions). It says:

> Article 35: A person who is in charge of teaching in a school or other educational institutions established not for profit-making may reproduce a work already made public if and to the extent deemed necessary for the purpose of use in the course of teaching, provided that such reproduction does not unreasonably prejudice the interests of the copyright owner in the light of the nature and the purpose of the work as well as the number of copies and the form of reproduction.

This is called 'classroom exemption'. It is permissible for teachers in formal or non-formal educational institutions for non-profit making purpose to reproduce a work to use it in the course of teaching, provided that such reproduction does not unreasonably prejudice the interests of the copyright holders (Copyright Research and Information Center, 2001). However, what is referred to as 'classroom exemption' is very restricted. School activities outside the 'classroom' cannot be met legally. Some people therefore simply ignore the law.

Moreover, no mention is made of distance and on-line courses in the Copyright Law in Japan. On the other hand, in the United States, if an on-line course contains all of the materials a student needs for the course, and if the copyright for some of those materials is not owned by the instructors, it is unlikely that the Copyright Act, USC Section 110 (2), or even fair use can be met (Gasaway, 1998). Section 110 (2) covers distance learning, but it is very restrictive. Since the Act was passed in 1976, the only type of distance learning involves television technology.

Finally, the use of audio-visual materials is very restricted in distance and on-line courses, since their use requires that permission be sought and royalties be paid when the copyright holder requests payment. Moreover, copyrights of video tapes are very complicated; no single organisation exists to manage these copyrights in Japan. Actually, it is impossible for instructors and course staff to manage these copyrights by themselves. This means that we cannot use them for distance learning.

In general, Japan's Copyright Law has tended to strengthen the rights of the copyright holder as technology has developed; it has not recognised the unique position and importance of education and distance learning by providing exemptions to the exclusive rights of the copyright holder. This may lead one to conclude that library services for distance learners in Japan lag far behind those in other countries.

Teaching and learning styles in distance education have dramatically changed in the past two decades. The basic conception of current Copyright Law in Japan was created in a period when face-to-face teaching was the norm. However, teaching and learning may change in the future. We should redefine the meaning of face-to-face teaching in the era of on-line learning, and the balance between copyright holders and distance learners should be reviewed in favour of facilitating distance learning.

Facilitating library services to distance learners

Currently, not only distance education institutions, but also traditional universities and colleges offer distance education services to a growing number of students. Given that university libraries are traditionally set up for on-campus use, libraries are necessarily faced with the challenge of restructuring and re-orienting their services to accommodate off-campus users as well.

Most university libraries, for instance, should extend their hours and the goals of library services, not only as a social service but also as an educational service for adult distance learners. If many universities providing distance education courses make their library services widely available to their communities, distance learners will have access to library services anywhere. This means reciprocal utilisation in the field of library services.

Universities should also form close relationships with public libraries. Public libraries should give priority to the needs of distance learners to the fullest extent possible. While it is impossible for each public library, from a physical or financial point of view, to build a collection in all fields of distance education courses, public libraries could have complementary roles. For example, one public library could maintain a collection of books on economics, while another concentrated on titles in political science. This co-ordination of effort would also save money that would be wasted if libraries in the same area were purchasing the same books. Also it helps distinguish the public libraries by virtue of their specialisation.

As educational organisations become more cost-conscious, the increasing number of cooperative ventures with other libraries will be driven by political and financial concerns. Libraries of all kinds will be making agreements among themselves to underwrite the high cost of technological services.

In Japan, we need to shift the discussion away from the purely technological problems of distance education toward educational services for students, including the relationship between universities and other libraries. We should aim to provide hybrid library services, electronic and traditional services, not only to on-campus students but also to off-campus students.

References

Copyright Research And Information Center (2001) *Copyright Law of Japan*, http//www.cric.or.jp. This is translated by Oyama Yukifusa *et al.*, but is not an official translation by Agency for Cultural Affairs, Japan. *Copyright System in Japan*, http//www.cric.or.jp.

Fujibe, A. (1979) Public libraries and correspondence course students (Japanese), *Library and Information Science*, 17, pp. 183–211.

Gasaway, L. (1998) Distance learning and copyright, *The Journal of Library Services for Distance Education*, 1 (2), http://www.westga.edu/library/jlsde/.

Jones, M. (1997) High five for the next five: libraries and distance education, *The Journal of Library Services for Distance Education*, 1 (1), http://www.westga.edu/library/jlsde/.

Kondo, K. (1985) The university library and guidance at the University of the Air (Japanese), *Toshokan-Zashi*, 79 (4), pp. 202–4.

Lee, A. (1999) Delivering library services at a distance: a case study at the University of Washington, *The Journal of Library Services for Distance Education*, 2 (1), http://www.westga.edu/library/jlsde/.

Marsumuro, T. and Kawasaki, H. (1982) Distance learners and library (Japanese), *Toshokan-Kai*, 34 (1), pp. 33–51.

Matsui, I. (1990) Students of correspondence courses (Japanese), *Toshokan-Kai*, 42 (3), pp. 206–14.

Matsumoto, T. (1981) 'Tsukyo-Bunko' at the correspondence course of Chuo University (Japanese), *Toshokan-Zashi*, 75 (11), pp. 686–7.

Minai, H. (2000) Issues of library services and distance learning in Japan (Japanese), in AudioVisual Education Association (ed.), *Research Report of Lifelong Learning with New Technology* (Tokyo: Audio-Visual Education Association).

Mori, T. (1987) Students and library services in the University of the Air (Japanese), *Gendai-No-Toshokan*, 25 (1), pp. 50–6.

Stephens, K. and Unwin, L. (1997) The heart of matter: libraries, distance education and independent thinking, *The Journal of Library Services for Distance Education*, 1 (1), http://www.westga.edu/library/jlsde/.

University of the Air (2001) *Outline of University of the Air 2001*, p. 2.

Young, H. (ed.) (1983) *The ALA Glossary of Library and Information Science* (Chicago, IL: American Library Association).

11 Changing entrenched learner support systems

Vision and reality

Evelyn Pulane Nonyongo

Introduction

Integrated and well-functioning learner support services are one of the central distinguishing factors between correspondence education and distance education or open and distance learning (ODL), the preferred term in recent years. Learner support is but a sub-sector of the total ODL system and change in this sub-sector is informed by the nature and philosophy of the total ODL system of the country and the institutions concerned. Changing existing learner support systems that have been 'entrenched' over a number of years is not easy. International distance education experience has thus tended to favour establishment of completely new ODL institutions with quality integrated learner support systems rather than attempting to change existing systems and institutions. In the United Kingdom, for example, a new institution, the Open University, was established by Royal Charter in 1969 even though some form of correspondence education had been in existence in the UK for a number of years. The University of London external degree programme, though mainly an examinations service, provided opportunities for adults to register for degree courses, study largely on their own or with some support from private commercial colleges and then write examinations. This service was also available to international students and the writer is a product of the University of London external degree programme. Similar examples of the establishment of new provincial or national institutions can be found in Canada, with Athabasca University and the Open Learning Institute, and in Pakistan with the Allama Iqbal Open University (Koul and Jenkins, 1990). In Africa, Tanzania and Zimbabwe have followed the same route and new institutions, the Open University of Tanzania and the Zimbabwe Open University have been established. Nigeria is also investigating the possibility of establishing an Open University and a delegation has recently visited South Africa for this purpose. The UK experience of establishing completely new ODL institutions and its Open University model have, thus, spread to other countries. Replication of these types of institutions in other countries indicates recognition of the success of this route of operation and model of institution.

Two southern African countries, Botswana and South Africa, have, in contrast, taken a different route in addressing the issue of access to secondary and higher education through ODL. They have decided to change existing institutions and create from this base new institutions with improved and well functioning learner support services that encapsulate the vision of distance education spelt out in their national policies. The route chosen by these countries is not easy and according to Perry the reasons for this are related to the fact that:

> the inertia inherent in established educational systems is normally too strong to permit high speed change. Inertia stems both from the sheer complexity of educational systems and from networks of vested interests concerned with maintaining them.
>
> (cited in Koul and Jenkins, 1990)

In view of the potential difficulties of attempting major and high speed change, sharing the experience of two institutions in two southern African countries that are grappling with change in contexts different from the above international experience should be useful to ODL practitioners and other countries intending to transform their systems. The two institutions chosen for this analysis are different in a number of ways. One is a university and the other a secondary education college. The shape, size, focus, variety and levels of courses and/or programmes offered and complexity of operations of the two are vastly different. The number of years in operation also differs greatly with one of the institutions having over fifty years experience as a dedicated distance education institution and the other only about half of that time. The two were chosen for these reasons. First, they represent attempts to change distance education learner support systems in southern Africa at two different, but crucial, levels of educational provision: higher and secondary education levels. The routes followed by these countries in transforming their systems are similar, though there are contrasting differences. Both countries have decided to build on their history of distance education and to establish new institutions from existing ones, that is 'born from an existing operation' as described in the Botswana documents (BOCODOL, February 1998, p. 3).

The two institutions, are, however, at different stages of implementing the new policy. One is relatively far in implementing its strategies for a transformed and new institution. The other is grappling with internal change prior to the new government directive of merging three current national ODL institutions to create a new one.

This chapter analyses the two institutions' progress in changing their original learner support systems including the success, difficulties, the extent to which the 'inertia' mentioned above has affected the implementation of change, and some of the lessons emerging from their experience.

Brief description and comparison of the two southern African examples

A brief description of distance education in both countries is necessary to understand the reasons for the envisaged changes in learner support. The description will also include the learner support systems in operation prior to change in the two institutions that are the subject of this chapter, namely the Botswana College of Open and Distance Learning (BOCODOL) and the University of South Africa (UNISA).

Botswana

Prior to 1960 Botswana was mainly a consumer of distance education programmes provided by other countries: South Africa, Zimbabwe and Britain. Botswana played a limited role as a provider of distance education in 1960 with the Salisbury Experiment. This was a collaborative teacher training programme through which Botswana teachers enrolled with the Salisbury Correspondence College in Zimbabwe, did the practical part of the course at the Lobatse Teacher Training College in Botswana and on completion of their course were awarded the Elementary Teachers' Certificate by the Ministry of Education in Mafeking in South Africa (Mphinyane and Selepeng-Tau, 1998). Full-scale involvement as provider of distance education began with the Franscistown Project (1968–73) which upgraded 700 untrained teachers and is said to have achieved a success rate of 88 per cent. The success of this project led to the establishment of the Botswana Extension College in 1973, and in 1978 this college became a unit of the newly established Department of Non-Formal Education (DNFE) in the Ministry of Education. From 1979 the University of Botswana also became involved in the provision of distance education (Mphinyane and Selepeng-Tau, 1998).

Botswana undertook a major review of education in 1993. The resultant Report of the National Commission on Education expressed concern at the absence of policy on out-of-school education and recommended:

- that a clear policy be developed for 'a responsive and relevant out-of-school education system', and
- the establishment of a Distance Education College to exploit the potential of distance education as a key component of such a system.

(BOCODOL, 1998, p. 2)

The Establishment of the Distance Education College to cater for out-of-school young people and adults was in 1994 endorsed in the Revised National Policy on Education, Government White Paper No. 2. This policy document also made provision for the University of Botswana Centre for Continuing Education as the second distance education provider which would offer 'an increasingly wide range of tertiary-level programmes at a distance' (BOCODOL, 1998, p. 3).

The new college mentioned above and which has since been launched and named Botswana College of Distance and Open Learning (BOCODOL) is described in its project proposal as:

a new initiative, distinctive in status, purpose and organisation. Though born of an existing operation, the College will be transformed from a centralised traditional distance education, to an institution providing learning open to all. It will have a small but strong central management and production unit and a decentralised delivery system with a regional focus to take learning to the people.

BOCODOL's original learner support system

The learner support services that BOCODOL inherited from the DNFE consisted of these six elements: tutor marking, tutorials at study centres, teaching at weekend courses, learner advice, radio teaching and district visits (Molefi and Mphinyane, 1998). Secondary schools were the main venues of tutorials, and part-time tutors were recruited from secondary school teachers. The centres operated three or four times a week between 17:30 and 20:00 in the evenings. Tutors at these study centres provided face-to-face tutorials which were said to 'entail tutors being approached by students, requesting them to explain areas of difficulty in the workbook being studied' (Molefi and Mphinyane, 1998). Tutors also marked assignments and were expected to give guidance on subject content when marking. Additional face-to-face support was provided through weekend courses that were presented by DNFE full-time staff at the different centres. District visits, on the other hand, were undertaken by Gaborone headquarters' staff to provide further support to tutors, learners and DNFE district staff. Learner advice was another element of support that was provided by different levels of staff and utilised media like telephone, radio, print and face-to-face. Radio and audio cassettes were also used for content teaching and counselling purposes.

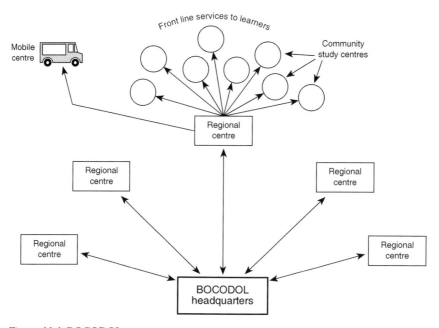

Figure 11.1 BOCODOL structure

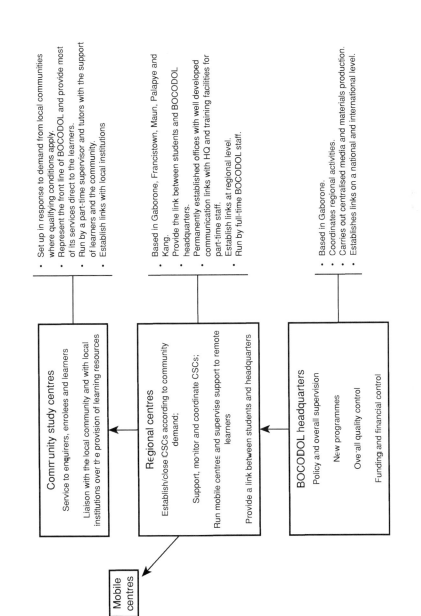

Community study centres

Service to enquirers, enrolees and learners

Liaison with the local community and with local institutions over the provision of learning resources

- Set up in response to demand from local communities where qualifying conditions apply.
- Represent the front line of BOCODOL and provide most of its services direct to the learners.
- Run by a part-time supervisor and tutors with the support of learners and the community.
- Establish links with local institutions

Regional centres

Establish/close CSCs according to community demand;

Support, monitor and coordinate CSCs;

Run mobile centres and supervise support to remote learners

Provide a link between students and headquarters

- Based in Gaborone, Francistown, Maun, Palapye and Kang.
- Provide the link between students and BOCODOL headquarters.
- Permanently established offices with well developed communication links with HQ and training facilities for part-time staff.
- Establish links at regional level.
- Run by full-time BOCODOL staff.

BOCODOL headquarters

Policy and overall supervision

New programmes

Overall quality control

Funding and financial control

- Based in Gaborone.
- Coordinates regional activities.
- Carries out centralised media and materials production.
- Establishes links on a national and international level.

Mobile centres

Figure 11.2 The new model for learner support

Some of the concerns raised about the BOCODOL distance education and learner support services include the centralised nature of the provision (BOCODOL, 1998, p. 3), the quality of services provided in the various elements of learner support (for example in tutoring, counselling and administration), and management (Molefi and Mphinyane, 1998; Nonyongo, 1999). BOCODOL has begun to address these weaknesses as the later sections of this chapter will demonstrate.

South Africa

South Africa has thirty-six public higher education institutions consisting of twenty-one universities and fifteen technikons (tertiary level institutions with a vocational bias). Three of these, representing two universities and one technikon, are distance education institutions. One of the three, the University of South Africa (UNISA), has been a dedicated distance education institution since 1946 and is thus the 'first public university in the world to teach exclusively by means of distance education' (UNISA, 2001, p. 2). The second, Technikon SA (TSA) was established in 1980 to cater for tertiary level technical and vocational education. The Vista University Distance Education Centre (VUDEC), is part of Vista University which was established in 1981 on the recommendations of the commission appointed to 'investigate the university needs and requirements of urban Africans in Republic of South Africa' (SAIDE, 1994). In 1996 these three ODL institutions collectively enrolled 225,000 students (NCHE, 1996, p. 120).

The weaknesses of South African distance education are well documented (SAIDE, 1995). The 1996 Report of the National Commission on Higher Education (NCHE) also recognised that the 'extent of the distance/correspondence education infrastructure is impressive' but that there were 'serious concerns about the efficacy, appropriateness and cost-effectiveness of current distance education provision' (NCHE, 1996). The commission summarised the weaknesses in the current provision of distance education as consisting of :

- low success in terms of throughput and completion rates;
- correspondence nature of programmes offered in comparison with well-functioning distance education;
- inadequate learner support which is exacerbated by the lack of a co-ordinated regional network of learning centres;
- limited enrolments in many courses which negate the potential economies of scale;
- current subsidy arrangements not encouraging the development of learner-centred educational models.

The central recommendations made by the NCHE were adopted in subsequent policy development documents like the Education White Paper 3: A Programme for the Transformation of Higher Education (1997) and the Higher Education Act. In all these documents the transformation of distance education is located within the country's broader process of political, social and economic transition, overcoming social-structural inequalities, contributing to reconstruction and development, and positioning South Africa to engage effectively with globalisation. Recent documents have moved the policy development process to the implementation stage. The Council on Higher Education's Size and Shape of Higher Education Task Team Report, *Towards a New Higher Education Landscape: Meeting the Equity and Social Development Imperatives of South Africa in the 21st century, June 2000*, presented proposals to the Minister of Education on the restructuring of the higher education system. The *National Plan for Higher Education, February 2001*, was then the Minister's response to the advice from the Council on Higher Education.

UNISA's original learner support system

UNISA policy documents mention four categories of learner support strategies provided: print-based, contact, technology enhanced and environmental support strategies (UNISA, 1997). These are further explained as follows:

- Print-based strategies include strategies built into printed materials and separate support materials additional to course content, for example generic study skills, separate course-related printed materials on learning skills, and separate access courses including accredited courses.
- Contact strategies which are aimed exclusively at establishing contact between teacher and learner, and include correspondence-based contact strategies (like comment on individual assignments, personal letters and faxes) and face-to-face contact strategies.
- Technologically enhanced strategies which include a range of multi-media support strategies aimed at direct contact strategies such as the Internet, Student-on-line, computer-based study programmes, video and audio conferencing and cassettes, etc.
- Environmental support strategies which consist of the provision of certain facilities, e.g. library, study space for individual and peer group study, and generally facilities that enhance the development of a learning environment.

The major changes that are described below are in the categories of contact and environmental support. However, this does not mean that changes have not occurred in the other two categories. In the print-based strategies, for example, the materials development process was changed and the quality of the products greatly improved by the introduction of the team approach and the development of more interactive and learner-centred materials. In ICT a new directorate has been set up and plans are afoot to improve UNISA's utilisation of ICT.

Transforming learner support in both institutions

Transformation is taking different formats in these two institutions. BOCODOL began its mandate of forming a new institution in 1998 and has for the past three years been implementing this mandate. UNISA has on the other hand been responding to criticisms about its distance education and not necessarily establishing a new institution. In terms of the Minister of Education's plan for transforming the higher education ODL system through a merger of the current three public distance education institutions, the merger should have taken place by April 2002, but legal challenges to the merger at first by Vista and lately by UNISA, have delayed the process.

BOCODOL's new learner support system

As a new institution 'born of an existing operation', BOCODOL began the process with strategic planning which culminated in the July 1998 BOCODOL Strategic Plan. Implementation of the learner support transformation is in process and has gone through various stages. The first was a review and assessment of the learner support system undertaken in June 1999 (Nonyongo, 1999; Tait, 1999). The review confirmed and fleshed out in some detail the weaknesses mentioned above about the existing learner support system, and prioritised the recommendations made into those that can be carried out quickly and relatively cheaply and those that are relatively easy to carry out but have heavy demand on resources. The review, *inter alia*, noted some of the difficulties of building a new system from an existing operation and prolonging the marriage between the two. For example, the review noted that the 'negative attitude about distance education in Botswana partly emanated from some of the weaknesses that BOCODOL is inheriting' from the DNFE system, and that interim arrangement of sharing staff at regional offices between DNFE and BOCODOL activities were creating problems related to accountability, communication and prioritisation of one programme's activities over the other.

The second stage in the process of changing the learner support system began with a Retreat held in March 2000 aimed at enabling BOCODOL to make significant improvements in the services provided to learners and developing a new model for learner support. The Retreat participants came from the relevant stakeholders in learner support including learners, tutors and representatives from the DNFE. The Retreat thus ensured a common understanding and all stakeholders' ownership and commitment to the plan. The new plan radically changed the learner support system. It changed the centre of service provision to learners from the DNFE District Offices to community study centres and thus gave community study centres greater power and provided for greater community involvement at that level (see Figure 11.1). Figure 11.2 shows the functions of each of the three tiers of the new model: Headquarters, Regional Centres and Community Study Centres. Criteria for developing community study centres and for the grouping of villages that will be serviced by a study centre were also developed at the Retreat. The plan also included provision for piloting a new learner support system in two regions, and criteria and methods of evaluating these pilots.

The third stage involved the development of an operational plan for the imple-mentation of the new learner support model in two pilot regions: Gaborone and

Kang. BOCODOL's Gaborone region covers the south central part of Botswana while Kang includes Kgalagadi and the western parts. Some of the outcomes of this phase were:

- an operational schedule for the first year of the pilot covering tasks, responsible people, deadlines and required resources;
- tutorial support schedule for face-to-face and correspondence tutoring;
- staff development and training mechanisms;
- mechanisms and processes for monitoring and evaluation of the pilot.

BOCODOL's plan is to operate from a total of five regions. The other three regions are Central, North and North West Botswana.

The pilot was launched on 23 April 2001and the operational plans developed in stage three above are being implemented and monitored and evaluated regularly. BOCODOL seems to be on course to being the new institution consisting of a 'decentralised delivery system with a regional focus to take learning to the people' as envisaged in the 1994 Revised National Policy on Education, Government White Paper No. 2.

However, even in an institution as committed to speedy and radical change of the learner support system as BOCODOL, old traditions take time to die and the parapets of resistance often rise in various ways and thwart progress. The latest monitoring and evaluation report (Roman, August 2001) highlighted the difficulties of changing the following entrenched traditions :

- Teaching and learning with regard to expectations, roles, responsibilities and practices of both tutors and students. On the one hand, tutors are said to be 'still entrenched in the DNFE culture when they were not required to do much' in that they still continue to use the lecture method, and some use face-to-face tutorial sessions to do other work like marking written assignments instead of attending to learners' needs and problems. On the other hand, learners expect to be taught and tend to be passive in the teaching/learning situation. These problems are, of course, prevalent in most distance education systems, but the main reason for BOCODOL's concern is to ensure that they are reduced rather than perpetuated.
- Institutional practices and recognition that change cannot be achieved cheaply. Demands for staff to introduce radical change in approaches and workloads (for example, development of lesson plans for tutorials, encouraging active participation, giving more support to learners experiencing problems) need to be matched with comparative remuneration. BOCODOL introduced a new tutor payment system with the pilot and increased tutor fees by 100 per cent (from 15 to 30 Pula) above those previously paid by DNFE. Though demands for extra pay are, from the staff's point of view, never adequately addressed, it is important that in reviewing fees institutions take into consideration that part-time tutors fees include none of the benefits enjoyed by full-time staff and should, therefore, regularly review fees in

line with similar institutions' practices, in consultation with the staff concerned, with the reasons for the amount provided. Reducing the total number of tutorial hours when fee increases are introduced does not solve the problem, because it, in effect, reduces the support given to students. BOCODOL is aware of tutor dissatisfaction and has undertaken to review tutor fees and other elements of the learner support system as they move towards institutionalisation of the new system.

- Inter-departmental/divisional problems which in essence relate to perception of status similar to the academic and non-academic divide in higher education. An example in BOCODOL's case is the Course Development Department's outlined perception of their department's tasks as BOCODOL's core business and 'unwillingness to scrutinise the effects of the quality and efficiency of their work on other departments' (Roman, April 2001). Such perceptions negate attempts to integrate sub-systems and processes, and devalue the important role played by learner support staff in the whole ODL system. To address this problem and build consensus on the way forward, BOCODOL has introduced a Project Monitoring and Evaluation Committee which meets fortnightly and consists of heads of Divisions and the Directorate.

But what is important is that the BOCODOL's monitoring and evaluation strategy is identifying, on an on-going basis, these areas of resistance, raising the issues with stakeholders and coming up with recommendations on how to address them. There is also recognition in these monitoring reports that entrenched traditions need a longer time to address than originally envisaged and that BOCODOL, for example, needs to be pragmatic by regarding the paradigm shift 'as a long-term goal and in the short-term to reform the training' (Roman, August, 2001, p. 11). Equally important is that BOCODOL is taking the recommendations seriously, reflecting on them and introducing appropriate action. Above all, BOCODOL's management has taken a strong leadership role in regularly articulating the agreed vision, ensuring that implementation is on course and that the monitoring and evaluation recommendations are being addressed.

Recent changes to the UNISA learner support system

With regard to UNISA, the period from 1994 to date has seen the introduction of a number of changes within the learner support system and the institution generally (for example, the introduction of the team approach in materials development and general improvement of the quality of the learning packages, etc).

The learner support changes began in 1994 with a joint SACHED Trust and UNISA pilot project of decentralised learner support in two of the SACHED learning centres in Johannesburg and Pretoria. In 1995 this became a UNISA owned and driven programme when the Department of Student Support (DSS) was established with the mandate to facilitate:

- The establishment of a receiving structure from which various student support processes could be generated. This structure would be in the form of provincial UNISA centres which could be organically linked to a network of community-based study centres.
- Establishment of an integrated student support system which includes a face-to-face tutorial system.
- The formation of a well-functioning student representative council which could enhance student participation and involvement in all the key decision-making bodies of UNISA.
- The development of a Financial Aid Bureau which would open access and ensure sustenance for the financially disadvantaged, but academically deserving, students of UNISA (UNISA Council, 1994, p. 34).

Since 1995 the DSS has achieved considerable success in the establishment and further development of the so-called receiving structure through which face-to-face tutorial services are provided in six major cities of South Africa. Three of these centres are located at the UNISA regional centres in Cape Town, Durban and Pietersburg. The rest are mainly DSS operations and are located in Pretoria, Johannesburg (sharing space with a branch of the UNISA Library Department) and Umtata. Through these learning centres, DSS has developed a solid foundation for future establishment of a wider network of learning centres. Among the operational processes and procedures in place in these centres are:

- Local tutor recruitment, training, payment, monitoring systems.
- Collaborative development of year plans in conjunction with forty-two academic tutor coordinators nominated by thirty-nine participating academic departments.
- Collaborative development of tutors' and students' manuals and training packages. Several of these packages are already available.

In addition, some of these centres began piloting, with limited success, the establishment of community-based learning centres. But today, due mainly to finance and staffing problems, none of these community-based learning centres are operational.

The DSS has also played an important role in the establishment of a national Student Representative Council (SRC) at UNISA. The SRC has become a recognised UNISA activity whose members are represented in all the central UNISA decision-making bodies like Council, Senate, the Institutional Forum, etc. The SRC is funded from a central levy included in the registration fees. One of the reasons for the successful recognition and integration of the SRC in the UNISA system is that the SRC is a strong collective force within UNISA, consisting mainly of youth who are full-time students (that is, not employed). They actively participate in the activities of – and are supported in various initiatives to transform universities – by other universities' SRC and political students' organisations like the Congress of South African Students and Pan African Students Organisation. This strong national force has used various means, for example campaigns, sit-ins and marches, to get recognition and integration in most universities' systems including the UNISA system. But some of the major weaknesses of the UNISA SRC is that it is not fully representative of UNISA students. Its membership continues to consist of full-time students and thus it mainly tends to prioritise the needs and views of full-time students. There are also no clear accountability mechanisms between the SRC and part-time students who are the majority of UNISA students and are thus the main source of SRC funding because the SRC levy is paid by all UNISA students.

The Financial Aid Bureau (now called the National Students Financial Aid Scheme, NSFAS) operates as part of the national government scheme to assist disadvantaged students financially. Since the inception of FAB/NSFAS in the DSS, it has between 1995 and 2000 successfully distributed a total of R61.3 million to needy students. In 2001 alone a total of R26.5 million was received and distributed. Annually the department has accounted to the relevant government structure on how the money was used within the stipulated guidelines. The success of this operation emanates mainly from the fact that it is a government-funded operation with clear national operational guidelines, procedures and accountability structures and, importantly, that the DSS has developed the capacity to implement the scheme within a short period of time. In recognition of this capacity UNISA has begun discussions with the DSS for all other UNISA student bursary or sponsorship arrangements to be managed from the DSS scheme.

From the above, it is clear that the UNISA DSS has had substantial success in implementing the above aspects of its mandate and that it has contributed greatly to changing the UNISA learner support system. However, with regard to integration of the face-to-face tutorial sub-system within the total UNISA system, it is here where the difficulties of changing entrenched systems have surfaced, and resistance is great. A critical evaluation of learner support at UNISA by an internal team set up by management in 2000 (Ngengebule *et al.*, 2000), highlighted that learner support is still not integrated in the system. Some of the 'fortifications' and 'trenches' used to thwart the successful integration of learner support were said to include:

- Continuing to conceptualise and implement the face-to-face tutorial pro-gramme as an add-on system. This has made the DSS participants, that is, tutors, learners and staff, feel not recognised and appreciated and they metaphorically describe their situation as that of an 'elephant and an ant' (Moore, 2000). The DSS has minimal influence on the development of learning materials and the teaching of academic departments (Mackintosh, 2000), even though DSS tutors interface regularly with learners and could make valuable inputs on the problems tutors and learners face on the ground. Similar face-to-face support provided by academic departments, viz. discussion classes, are kept separate from the learning centres' tutorial programme.
- Continuing to locate the DSS in the administration section of the university and thus minimising the chances of academic recognition and integration.

- Maintaining a separate financing arrangement for DSS face-to-face tutorials. UNISA covers the infra-structural costs of running the DSS, like full-time staff salaries and benefits, premises, equipment, but not the face-to-face tutorial costs like payment of tutors and tutor development activities. Students joining the face-to-face tutorial programme pay a separate registration fee for this service. Most of the students who require high levels of support are typically the ones who do not have the economic means to finance this additional cost, and the drastic (62 per cent) drop in face-to-face tutorial enrolments in 1998 (see Table 11.1) was because of a substantial increase in tutorial fees from a flat fee of R65 per year irrespective of the number of courses to R60 administration fee plus R160 per course. With the introduction of even more reduced face-to-face tutorial fees of R100.00 per semester irrespective of the number of course registrations in 2002, the DSS is predicting that the annual registration figures will match the 1996–7 numbers. The first semester registration numbers are 6,770 students as at 2 May 2002, (UNISA/DSS weekly enrolment figures). This is, according to the DSS, a clear indication that disadvantaged learners are excluded from the face-to-face tutorial sessions by the fees charged for this service.

Attachment to UNISA's tradition of correspondence education, the assumed threat to jobs at headquarters, the potential relocation to far away regional centres and the assumed lower status of learner support positions, are some of the factors contributing to resistance to integration of learner support. In addition, the absence of a co-ordinated direction from management also play a role. This manifests itself in the absence of a common vision of a transformed learner support system at top management levels. From the government's side, delays in changing the funding formula to include learner support needs in ODL also contribute greatly to the problem, because, indeed, learner support costs are substantial and to establish and maintain a countrywide network of effectively operating learning centres cannot be implemented by institutions single-handedly without substantial assistance from government and other donors.

In this instance the strong forces for radical change seem to have been absent. Some of the reasons for this are related to priorities of potential agents of change. The current trend within forces like the SRC, UNISA Council and trade unions is to prioritise issues of governance and employment equity above transformation of

Table 11.1 Tutorial programme head count enrolment 1995–2001

Year	Number	% Increase/decrease
1995	4,813	
1996	11,447	+ 13.8
1997	11,922	+ 4
1998	4,475	− 62
1999	5,467	+ 22
2000	5,278	− 3
2001	6,032	+ 14

learner support. The influence of the other two external forces, SACHED and SAIDE, seems also to have waned greatly. The incorporation of the SACHED learner support programme into UNISA contributed to the democratic ethos of DSS activities, but removed SACHED's lobbying capacity as an external force. SAIDE's priorities seem to be somewhere else as well.

One of the recommendations made in the learner support critical review mentioned above is that UNISA, as part of its ICT development strategy, should pilot using ICT to integrate, strengthen and effectively co-ordinate learner support in the learning centres and the emerging multi-purpose Community Centres that are part of the government's education and ICT transformation strategy.

But, despite these weaknesses, it is clear that in comparison to the period prior to the SAIDE report, these changes have seen major improvements in the UNISA ODL system. However, when one compares BOCODOL and UNISA, it is also clear that the latter is trying to change its system piecemeal, and in some instances without the strong leadership and co-ordinated approach adopted by the former.

Merger as impetus for learner support change

The new policy implementation initiative recommended by the Department of Education through merging the three ODL institutions mentioned above had the potential to provide the required impetus to effect radical change similar to that effected in BOCODOL. The new National Plan for Higher Education (DoE February 2001, p. 62) recommends, *inter alia*, that:

> a single predominantly dedicated distance education institution that provides innovative and quality programmes, especially at the undergraduate level, is required for the country. The opportunities that the present distance education institutions have created for students in Africa and other parts of the world must be maintained and respected.

The single institution would be established through 'merging UNISA, TSA and incorporating the distance education centre of Vista University into the merged institution.' Among the advantages mentioned are that such a single dedicated distance education institution will:

- develop a clear focus and strategy for the role of distance education in contributing to national and regional goals;
- develop a national network of centres of innovation, which would enable the development of courses and learning materials for use nationally, thus enhancing quality within the higher education system;
- develop a national network of learning centres, which would facilitate access and co-ordinate learner support systems;
- enhance access and contribute to human resources development within the SADC region in particular and the continent as a whole;

- enable economies of scale and scope, in particular ensuring that advantage is taken of the rapid changes in information and communications technology, which are expensive and where the additional investment is unlikely to be within the capacity of any one institution.

This new South African initiative is very similar to that found in Botswana with BOCODOL. It is creating a new institution from existing operations and aiming to transform the learner support system through the development of a national network of learning centres which would facilitate access. It is also incorporating an external force to assist the transformation, in the form of a Working Group appointed by the Ministry and tasked to 'facilitate the merger including the development of an implementation plan'.

The South African initiative is, however, of greater magnitude and complexity. It is merging three tertiary institutions that have a total year-2000 head count enrolment of 180,000 (UNISA: 110,000, TSA: 60,000 and VUDEC: 10,000) and whose areas of operation and specialisation differ. One institution is a dedicated distance education technikon and two universities, one a dedicated distance education institution and the other a part of a dual mode operation. While these differences might be beneficial in terms of facilitating integration of education and training (for example through sharing the Technikon's vocational education experience and the two universities' strong academic experience), existing genuine concerns and prejudices about status and quality of technikon and university qualifications, and staff's academic status, will be some of the thorny issues that need to be addressed. This merger will also bring together three institutions with different entrenched traditions, cultures, organisational structures, etc. and will therefore be even more difficult to effect than was the case with BOCODOL and its predecessor the DNFE. In addition, resistance to strong government intervention in higher education and issues of institutional autonomy and academic freedom are likely to feature more strongly in the South African situation, and have already done so, than they have done in BOCODOL, which operates at secondary education level, and in a country where government intervention is often passively accepted.

But be that as it may, the attempts in BOCODOL and UNISA to transform learner support provide some lessons worth noting in any attempt to transform existing operations.

Lessons from both countries' experience

Below are five of the central lessons emerging from the two countries' experience.

Shared vision

There must be a shared vision among all stakeholders. The vision encapsulated in the policy frameworks should become, in practice, part of the institution and should drive the institution's implementation strategy. Recognition of institutional weaknesses, and preparedness to address them, are part of this process. This does not exclude challenging emerging policies and suggesting alternatives. At both national and institutional levels, mechanisms used to arrive at a shared vision include wider stakeholder consultation, followed by revision and eventual finalisation of policies. The road to finalisation might be long and bumpy but once reached the institutions concerned need to own the vision and run with the process of implementation. BOCODOL seems to be doing fairly well. UNISA and its merger partners are at the beginning stages of developing a merger implementation plan and the road ahead is still unclear. The UNISA and other universities' challenge to the Ministry's merger plans can be interpreted as attempts to arrive at a mutually agreed vision of the process and nature of the envisaged new institution. Certainly, unilateral Ministerial decision of some of the aspects, for example the name, Open Learning University of South Africa, for the new institution, will continue to meet with opposition from most quarters including UNISA alumni and other partners, and indicates the kind of bumpy road that lies ahead. But an even more difficult issue is the nature of the merging partners: are they equal and can they be equal when in their current status they are not deemed equal? The UNISA situation thus presents difficulties of arriving at a shared vision which was not the case in BOCODOL.

Strong leadership

At whatever stage institutions are in the development and implementation cycle, strong leadership is crucial. Change is difficult and creates fear and resistance mechanisms. By taking a strong leadership role, management can help to clarify the vision, direct the process of change and assuage fears while ensuring that barriers to change are nipped in the bud. Regular communication about the new direction, and addressing some of the emergent issues including staff training and development needs, should be part of this process. Success can be achieved if management is united, committed to change, driving the process collectively and delegating but not relegating responsibility. The kind of leadership required is one that can 'encompass a number of management and governance styles; a sense of purpose and direction that will provide meaning for and the integration of the various activities and functions throughout the institution' (Paul, 1990, p. 67). BOCODOL's new leadership seems to be on track with regard to this aspect. UNISA has had problems, but hopefully the new, larger management team established last year which has addressed the racial equity problems, though still weak on gender equity, will bond into a strong team that will steer the ship towards a shared vision and eventual best destination in the interest of the country.

Acceptance of external assistance and criticism

Criticism both positive and negative helps to improve provision. By forcing institutions to view their strengths and weaknesses through the eyes of another person/people, criticism encourages institutions to effect change. In South Africa the role played by NGOs like SACHED and SAIDE in highlighting the weaknesses of the UNISA learner support system was crucial and has helped UNISA to introduce some of the changes mentioned here. Both the Botswana and South African governments have also played a major part in this in recognising the weaknesses of their system and suggesting change. From the concerned institution's side, recognising weaknesses, seeking and accepting assistance is also very important.

Monitoring and evaluation

The BOCODOL experience highlights the importance of on-going monitoring and evaluation (both internal and external) in identifying strengths, weaknesses, problems, etc. early enough and seeking ways of addressing anything that might affect implementation adversely. The role of management in driving the process of implementing the recommendations emanating from the monitoring and evaluation strategies cannot be over-emphasised. At university level, where research is one of three main functions, reflexive research on institutional operations and practices should play a central role in assisting institutions to reflect on their provision and introduce the required improvements.

Adequate resources

Learner support activities are not cheap and subsume substantial amounts of institutional budgets since recurring costs are subject to yearly increase due to inflation and other factors. They are, however, essential components of the ODL system and generally assist in breaking the isolation of learners and reducing the high drop-out rate associated with this system of education. The difficulties of setting up an adequate system in countries with a large rural population with limited infrastructure and not enough educators with the relevant qualifications in these areas should not be underestimated. But, with greater commitment to expanding services to most learners and to cooperating with other structures operating in areas where registered learners reside, institutions can greatly improve access to these services. It is important that governments recognise the difficulties faced by ODL institutions in providing access to learner support services generally, and especially in remote areas, and assist institutions by allocating resources for learner activities to ensure meaningful transformation of learner support. Institutions on the other hand, should also be fair in their allocation of resources and not short change learner support activities.

Conclusion

The route taken by both countries, that is one of changing existing operations, seems to have been the best in their circumstances. In South Africa, creating a completely new institution would have proliferated institutions, while closing existing ones to create a new one would have caused immense disruption and potential turmoil because despite their weaknesses these three existing institutions attract large numbers of students and have good reputations and infrastructure. Only time will tell whether the envisaged merger will take place and result in an institution described in the current policy documents. The current struggles and delays suggest that a long time will elapse before resolution of the issues is achieved. Perhaps, in South Africa, 'inertia' from the 'networks of vested interest', is beginning to set in and entrench the *status quo*. One thing that points to the contrary is that despite the legal challenges to the aspects of the merger, the three institutions are still actively involved in the merger working groups and inter- and intra-institutional task teams. These groups are representative of most of the relevant stakeholders in these institutions and are likely to debate the issues around learner support holistically and achieve some results. In contrast, BOCODOL is well on the way to the envisaged new institution. For this country, the type of route taken towards change seems certainly to have been seen as the best by the stakeholders concerned. It was important that the existing DNFE infrastructure was used to facilitate transition and ensure minimal disruption for students already in the system. In comparison with the UNISA situation, it is also crucial to recognise the major differences in terms of size, level, complexity and number and nature of institutions involved in the envisaged change.

References

BOCODOL (1998) *Project Proposal for Botswana College of Distance and Open Learning*, prepared by the Project Memorandum Sub-Committee for Submission to the Planning Committee, unpublished (Gaborone: BOCODOL).

CHE (2000) Council on Higher Education. Size and shape of Higher Education Task Team Report in, *Towards a New Higher Education Landscape: Meeting the Equity and Social Development Imperatives of South Africa in the 21st Century* (Pretoria: CHE).

DoE (2001) *National Plan for Higher Education*, Ministry of Education. February 2001 (Pretoria: DoE).

Koul, B. N. and Jenkins, J. (eds) (1990) *Distance Education: A Spectrum of Case Studies* (London: Kogan Page).

Mackintosh, W. (2000) *Perspectives on Student Learning and the UNISA Distance Education Delivery System*, unpublished (Pretoria: UNISA Press).

Molefi, F. and Mphinyane, O. (1998) The distance education division of the Department of Non-Formal Education, in Nonyongo, E. P. and Ngengebule, A. T. (eds), *Learner Support Services: Case Studies of DEASA Member Institutions* (Pretoria: UNISA Press).

Moore, C. (2000) *Report on Tutor/academic Workshops – Input into the DSS Workshop for 2000* (Pretoria: UNISA Press).

Mphinyane, O. and Selepeng-Tau, O. S. (1998) Overview of distance education development and programmes in Botswana, in Nonyongo, E. P. and Ngengebule, A. T. (eds), *Learner Support Services: Case Studies of DEASA Member Institutions* (Pretoria: UNISA Press).

NCHE (1996) *National Commission on Higher Education Report: A Framework for Transformation* (South Africa: The Research and Management Agency).

Ngengebule, A. T. and Nonyongo, E. P., Smit, L., Van Schoor, W. A. and Mackintosh, W. G. (2000) *A Critical Evaluation of Learner Support at UNISA: Commemoration of the Y2K As the Year of Learner Support at UNISA* (Pretoria: UNISA Press).

Nonyongo, E. P. (1999) *Review and Assessment of the BOCODOL Learner Support System*, unpublished (Gaborone: BOCODOL).

Nonyongo, E. P. and Ngengebule, A. T. (eds) (1998) *Learner Support Services: Case Studies of DEASA Member Institutions* (Pretoria: UNISA Press).

Onions, C. T. (ed.) (1973) *The Shorter Oxford English Dictionary on Historical Principles* (Oxford: Clarendon Press).

Roman, M. (2001) *Draft Learner Support Consultancy Report, Part 7, 30 July to 10 August 2001*, unpublished (Gaborone: BOCODOL).

South African Institute of Distance Education (SAIDE) (1995) *Open Learning and Distance Education in South Africa: Report of an International Commission, January– April, 1994* (Manzini: Macmillan).

Tait, A. (1999) *BOCODOL–BATH Partnership Project: Learner Support Consultancy Report*, Centre for Continuing and Distance Education, University of Bath.

UNISA (1994) *The UNISA Learning System: A Working Document*, unpublished (Pretoria: UNISA Press).

12 Lost and found

Open learning outside the doors of academe

Jennifer O'Rourke

As contemporary open and distance learning (ODL) enters its fourth decade and approaches organisational middle age, enthusiasm seems to be waning among some pioneering institutions for its original goal of extending educational opportunity to those who had been left out. The mantra, coined by the OU UK, to be 'open as to people, places, methods and ideas' now appears less often in open learning publications than references to customers, markets and cost-recovery. Many academic institutions that have recently adopted ODL see it as a means of capturing a niche market for its academic specialties, preferably by serving profitable, fully employed learners through advanced information technologies. As one critic puts it, 'the implication is that choosing a particular university, following a particular regimen, will turn the student into a specifiable and identifiable product' (Franklin, 1990). When ODL seems poised to be in the vanguard of what Tait (2000) terms 'the marketisation of education', it leaves the nagging question about the re-marginalisation of learners that are no longer sufficiently rewarding for institutions to serve. Fortunately, there are some new models offering flexible, responsive distance learning emerging from innovative organisations that are not part of the competitive academic ethos.

The broad questions about the apparent right turn in ODL are presented here as a backdrop to the main theme of this chapter: an exploration of what has been achieved recently by non-academic organisations that have offered original and creative ODL programmes to learners in challenging situations. We will also consider some questions prompted by these examples, and whether their lessons about 'good practice' (Calder, 2000) can be applied elsewhere.

Those with a longer view of organisational history often refer to the phenomenon of small, innovative organisations that have the right idea at the right time, flourish, expand, and then become institutionalised and inflexible, only to be displaced by another small, innovative organisation that has a good idea, and so on. Is it possible that in the field of open and distance learning, a new kind of organisation might be better able than established providers to respond to the need for genuinely accessible learning? Perhaps this new kind of provider is already here, and is quietly operating in areas that are considered unrewarding for the established academic ODL institutions.

Following are three examples of responsive, individualised open learning offered by organisations that have not joined the stampede for customers. These are courses offered by non-profit agencies or non-government organisations (NGOs) for whom market share is not an issue. My experience with them was as course author, researcher, or tutor. They have been chosen as illustrations because of the strong learner focus in their design, learner support and administration, all of which contributed to the quality of the learning process. They raise questions about whether it might be easier to maintain a learner focus outside the competitive academic context, and about how learning is affected by the organisational and operational goals of the provider. There is no claim that these examples are either unique or representative; just the observation that they can provide models for serving learners in a flexible, responsive way.

Near the end of this chapter, we will come back to the larger questions, and consider whether lessons from these situations might be more widely applicable to other ODL programmes. Along the way, we will reflect on how the values and ethos of the provider shape the learning experience.

Common features: otherness, altruism and situated learning

At first glance, it seems that there would be few commonalities among the following distance learning situations: a course in effective writing for staff in a UN agency, a course in writing project proposals for professionals with a common interest in environmental issues, and a basic literacy programme for adults. But even though the learner populations were quite different, all learners shared some characteristics of 'otherness' as Tait (1999) terms it, by virtue of being outside the dominant western countries, cultures or economies. Moreover, the providers were all agencies operating in the social and environmental field: they shared what might be called 'a culture of altruism' and feature what Tait (1999) describes as 'non commoditised relations, which are not subject to the imperatives of profitability and the associated instrumental rationalities of managerialism'. These factors and the importance of situated learning (outlined below) may be the reasons why similar themes emerged about learner support, despite differences in course content and delivery methods.

All three courses were designed for what is now termed situated learning. The concept of situated knowledge expands Schön's (1987) idea of reflective practice by recognising the importance of using everyday experience and personal interaction to take reflection to the next stage: insight. Insight, in turn, leads the way to practical applications of new learning. In an article on professional development for teachers, Leach (1999) explains how situated knowledge links learning with everyday practice.

Situated knowledge becomes the crucial component which drives reflection and in turn the process of learning. This perspective challenges traditional dichotomies between theory and practice, institutional (or school) learning and everyday learning, between thinking and doing, mind and body. As an account of learning it presents a view of cognition as ongoing, unfolding and experiential, which has important insights not only for curriculum development but also for learner support in teacher education.

This view of learning as a holistic continuum makes sense not just for teacher education, but for many situations in which learning is an essential thread in accomplishing everyday tasks. In this context, learners are not expected to make all the connections between theory and practice on their own: instead, support 'must be centrally grounded in social practice, recognising that knowledge is constantly created and transformed at the intersection of the dialogue between people, their collective knowledge and experience, in particular settings and context' (Leach, 1999).

In all three learning situations, personal mentoring or tutoring helped learners to make the links among three elements: their own experience, course content that presented principles of good practice, and the application of these principles to their everyday work and life. In addition, the course design and programme administration focused on the needs of the learner, rather than the needs of the provider.

An overview of the programmes

Before exploring how individual and organisational support was conceptualised and how it evolved in each situation, here is some background about each programme and its provider.

Effective Writing for UNHCR is a customised course developed in response to an identified need for clearer written communication among staff within that organisation. UNHCR, the United Nations High Commission for Refugees, is the United Nations agency that provides immediate and longer term support for refugees displaced from their homes by conflict or natural disasters. Most of the approximately 5,000 international staff work away from their own countries in the field, either on site where refugees are gathered, or in nearby regional offices. For many staff, English is an additional acquired language.

The Commonwealth of Learning provided the open and distance learning framework for development and delivery of the course. The course author, Maree Bentley, consulted widely with UNHCR staff and conducted an extensive review of written communication at UNHCR throughout the course preparation stages. *Effective Writing* presents the principles and practice of good writing in the context of the UNHCR organisation, and incorporates many examples from typical situations that staff encounter. As a result, the course enables participants to see good communication practice in terms of their own daily reality, and invites them to apply the principles of good writing to their own work.

The course is structured as a print package with integral tutorial support provided by email. The print package consists of three modules, but learners complete only two. A common first module covers the basic principles of effective writing. The next modules focus on different types of writing that are typical of different roles within the organisation; either daily written communication, such as memos, faxes, emails and letters, or more extensive and formal reports that are required regularly at UNHCR. The learners and course administrators identify the second module that best meets their needs.

The course is designed to require about forty hours of study time. Learners have six months to complete it, and set their own individual schedule for completion of each of two modules, so they can accommodate their studies within their other commitments, such as year-end reporting or special missions to other locations. Assignments for each module are based on the learner's own work-related writing: they enable the writer to analyse and reflect on the work and obtain detailed feedback and suggestions from their tutor. Each learner is assigned to a specific tutor. Tutors work with up to fifteen participants at once, maintain regular email contact with each learner, answer questions from learners about the module activities and assignments, and provide assessment for each assignment.

Writing Project Proposals was developed for LEAD International, an organisation that promotes greater awareness of environmental issues among present and future decision makers. The centrepiece of LEAD's work is a two-year training programme provided to about 200 mid-career professionals working in business, government, academia, NGOs and media in thirteen regions worldwide. Although participants complete their training programmes in English, the majority are not native English users. Many graduates of the programme continue their affiliation with LEAD by serving as resource people for LEAD programmes, participating in continuing professional development, and by maintaining contact with others from their cohort. (LEAD uses the term 'the LEAD family' to encompass LEAD Associates, [current participants in the two-year programme], LEAD Fellows, [programme graduates] and staff of the LEAD organisation in its central and regional offices.)

LEAD identified a need among LEAD Fellows and Associates for enhanced skills in writing proposals, so they could obtain funding to implement specific environmental projects. LEAD felt this need could be best addressed by a distance programme, and the Commonwealth of Learning provided the distance education expertise for the development of the course. The course consists of a print package and email tutorial support. (Recently, a CD-ROM was developed based on the print package). Participants were expected to have the basic project concept in place before they began the course, so they could proceed with the proposal writing stages during the course. The *Writing Project Proposals* materials present the principles of proposal writing and real-life examples, and are designed to enable participants to work systematically on their own project proposals. Mentors responded to individual questions, provided regular feedback on participants' work, and guided an email conference among those in the mentor's group.

The pilot session was originally structured as a paced ten-week course: the rationale for pacing was to enable participants to discuss each week's topic in a computer conference. However, it soon became evident that maintaining the pacing was not feasible, because participants' workloads and differences in preparedness for proposal writing meant that they could not complete each stage according to the same schedule. As well, their main focus was on completing the research and consultation steps needed for their own proposal, and they had little or no time left for participation in an electronic discussion. The programme schedule was extended to allow participants greater flexibility in completing each stage. Most of the interaction was between participants and their mentors, rather than among participants; participants tended to focus on completing their own proposal while juggling demanding jobs and life commitments.

Both the UNHCR and LEAD programmes are provided to professionals who, for the most part, have already achieved a significant level of education. In that sense, they cannot be regarded as excluded from educational opportunity. But in other senses, they are not typical of mainstream learners served by academic institutions, and they share characteristics of those who are most likely to be marginalised by more conventional ODL (Tait, 1999).

Almost all the UNHCR staff and most LEAD participants were working and living outside the wealthier countries of Europe and North America. In UNHCR, many staff are working in very isolated and difficult conditions, and all, directly or indirectly, serve as advocates for refugees, a segment of the world population that is often excluded from the most basic life opportunities. The commitment of LEAD participants to environmental issues often sets them apart, especially where influential segments of society support political, social and economic goals that conflict with environmental sustainability. In addition to working for causes that are outside the mainstream, both UNHCR and LEAD learners face language and cultural divides, as they work in fields where the dominant language is English.

The third example is different in many respects from the first two, in terms of content, learner profile and technologies. But the AlphaRoute literacy project shares a significant common feature – a learner-focused course. Funded by provincial and federal government agencies in Canada, and implemented by AlphaPlus, a non-profit organisation, the AlphaRoute project has developed and piloted a series of web-based literacy programmes. Participants in a 1999 pilot programme worked with the web-based materials over a ten-week period, at six different literacy centres in Canada. Designed for people with skill levels ranging from minimal literacy to early secondary school level, and for both English and French speakers, the programme covered basic language content (vocabulary, grammar and usage) and incorporated this content into everyday life issues, such as health, employment and recreation. Visuals, graphics, animation and sound were used to guide learners who had limited reading skills. Although the programme was structured so that learners had to complete some self-assessment activities in sequence, they were also able to explore the whole site and try out different areas. On-site co-ordinators provided help to ensure that learners could get into the site; more advanced technical support was available by phone and on-line. All AlphaRoute learners worked with a mentor, who was available by email and by phone, and who provided individualised feedback on their assignments. A 'café' area in the site enabled learners to meet each other at a distance, and engage in group discussions on significant topics, such as euthanasia. Several learners formed an on-line writers' group to share their own personal writing, including their poetry, with each other.

These AlphaRoute learners were young adults who had English or French as a first language. Some were living in very marginal circumstances, and all of them, to varying degrees, were restricted in work and life opportunities because of their limited literacy skills. Interestingly, learners said that one appeal of the course was that they would be able to tell their friends that they were working on computers: for people who often felt like outsiders, it was a chance to operate in what is considered the mainstream.

Common themes in learner support

Learner support is usually set into two broad areas: administrative services and support for learning. Since these situations involved no fees or formal academic accreditation, there were fewer administrative tasks than in an academic context. The UNHCR's staff development department recruited and selected learners for the *Effective Writing* course; COL administered the record-keeping tasks during course delivery and co-ordinated input from tutors. LEAD recruited participants from among LEAD Fellows and Associates; programme delivery was coordinated by a tutor who worked closely with LEAD's training programme director. Most AlphaRoute learners were already affiliated with one of the pilot sites, and were recruited by the site co-ordinators, who also handled basic administrative tasks. In all three cases, the first point of contact for the learners was an organisation with which they already had a meaningful connection. As well, in each situation, even though the course administration was primarily handled by one or two people, there was a 'continuity of concern' for the learner that was characterised by prompt attention to questions from learners, tutors, and in the case of AlphaRoute, local site co-ordinators. However, the main focus of this discussion of learner support is on that provided by tutors. (In two of the courses, tutors were termed mentors.)

Support for learning is categorised by Lebel (1989) into four areas: cognitive, metacognitive, affective and motivational. In these situations, cognitive support involved all those activities that helped learners to enhance their knowledge and skills; identifying the strengths and weaknesses of their work; pointing out additional resources that might be helpful, and so on. Metacognitive support helped learners develop more effective approaches to learning, and recognise the significance of what has been learned and how it can be applied in different contexts. Affective support acknowledged that the learners had to contend with some very challenging situations, both in their work and everyday lives. Tutors/mentors provided motivational support by keeping in touch through email, letting learners know that they cared about their progress, and maintaining what a colleague calls 'the ongoing hum of awareness'.

All the courses described above were challenging experiences for the participants. In two situations, they were working in an unfamiliar language; in the third, they had limited skills in managing their own learning and were working with unfamiliar technology. When work and/or life situations took priority for weeks at a time, and learning was interrupted, regular contact from a mentor or tutor helped to sustain a sense of continuity.

Support was an essential factor in helping learners to individualise the learning process and apply it in their own context; in other words, to engage in situated learning. The UNHCR and LEAD participants had to apply the resource materials to their own work situation and infuse them with their own experience: they could not treat the course as an academic exercise. The AlphaRoute learners had to determine the level and resources that were right for them, and apply what they were learning to situations that were relevant to them. Tutors/mentors had to reach into their learners' worlds, to learn about their participants' goals and contexts in order to respond appropriately to their work.

The following samples of learner comments show how they experienced each kind of support:

> Cognitive: 'She [the mentor] was there to help me so I've learned where a comma should be, or a question mark, or just grammar and stuff like that.' (AlphaRoute)

> Metacognitive: 'Your explanations and comments were very clear to me. The idea to work in smaller sections and simple language is not only to be clear, but the need to express a message in a language you are not proficient in. This situation forces you to find the short way to communicate effectively.' (Effective Writing)

> Affective: 'She [the mentor] helped me feel more confident about my vocabulary, the way I speak, in every aspect of learning. She's helped me keep my frustration level down. She was like the centre of this whole thing, I think.' (AlphaRoute)

> 'The course has especially helped me to overcome my initial writer's block, to analyze and organize writing tasks, and to overcome my insecurity.' (Effective Writing)

> 'Thanks a lot, again, for not forgetting me.' (A LEAD participant, after her project plan was derailed by political upheaval in her country.)

> Motivational: 'Thank you very much for your support and guidance during the course period, without which I would not have been able to complete my assignments. There were times weeks would pass without doing my assignments due to exigencies of duty and your emails always put me back on the track. You never know how much I appreciated those emails.' (Effective Writing)

Assessment, learner response, and indicators of success

Early indications are that each of these courses has achieved success, and that the majority of participants accomplished the goals they set for themselves. Learners also noted that they feel more confident in applying what they have learned in their work and/or to future learning tasks. In the two courses which involved more formal assessment processes, most learners were successful.

In the evaluation of the LEAD pilot, the majority felt that the course helped them achieve their goals. Half of those respondents rated the course experience at 4/5 or 5/5, commenting that it helped 'by virtue of both the pressure and the learning factors', and 'the structure helped me greatly in focusing my thought with regard to the direction and issues I needed to consider in my proposal.' Most respondents (80 per cent) stated that the mentor helped them achieve their goals to a great extent (ranking this support at 4/5 or 5/5), and the rest rated mentor support as important to them. Few participants received support from their employers or work colleagues: in fact, many participants reported dealing with an additional workload while engaged in the course. Also, very few had support from other participants in the course, due to logistical problems, language difficulties and disparities of goals. Most participants said that they would prefer to be able to work on the course primarily on their own, with regular feedback from a mentor and contact from other participants. None believed the course would be valuable if they worked alone on the course materials without a mentor (Chiarelli, 2001).

The evaluation notes, 'Mentor–learner interaction was a highlight for many of the participants, who valued feedback from experienced proposal writers.' The mentors reviewed each participant's work carefully and provided detailed feedback, which involved a significant time investment. This time investment represented a cost for the course provider, but many participants said that they would be willing to pay for the course. The pilot was offered to participants on a no-charge basis. Interaction was by email, rather than the web, and access to email was sometimes a problem for some learners. One section of the course, on identifying funders, recommended using the web, but this was not always feasible for everyone: some had infrequent access, or it was very slow and frustrating. One learner suggested that good Internet access and free time were essential to work on the module effectively.

Although provisions were made for group interaction, very few learners took advantage of this opportunity by contributing to discussions. Interestingly, comments on the evaluation indicated learners would have liked to have heard more from others in the course, but they felt they had little time themselves to contribute to the discussion or engage with others. This suggests that learners may be as instrumental about learner-learner interaction as they are about other aspects of distance courses, and that they will participate in interaction only if it directly meets their own goals (in this case, a viable proposal; in other situations, academic credit).

Early indicators from the first year of *Effective Writing for UNHCR* also confirm the significance of the tutoring role. So far, 78.6 per cent of the first 300 learners have completed the course successfully, a very good result for a flexible non-credit course provided for people working in demanding jobs, often under very difficult circumstances. UNHCR credits this outcome to strong personalised tutor support. Participants attribute their achievement both to the quality of the course materials and to tutor support. These are typical comments:

'The feedback from the tutor was very detailed and good. It showed that she was interested in my work and was always willing to guide me to improve my writing skills. The course guide was very useful and helped me along the way.'

'I wish to thank all involved in the design and administration of this course and most of all my tutor who was a great help all throughout the course, always full of encouragement, patience and sound advice.'

'Even though the didactic materials are very good, the experience and dedication of the tutor is what makes the course so valuable.'

'The very positive feedback and evaluation from the tutor reassured and motivated me a lot. The course manual and style guide will certainly be useful reference tools in the future.'

It is interesting that participants in *Effective Writing* valued all three elements of the course: the course materials, the tutor support and the administrative support. Several learners commented that they will continue to use the course materials as a resource, indicating that they were well suited to their situation (the course materials received an award of excellence from ODLAA in 2001). Although the learners are primarily in touch with their tutors, they also have direct contact with the course administrator when they begin and end the course, and for any strictly administrative questions, such as rescheduling or changing modules. Unseen to the participants, the tutors themselves also receive support from the course administrator and the course author. The administrator compiles learner records, maintains contact with UNHCR staff development office, and helps to resolve any difficult administrative issues. Once a month, a four-day on-line discussion session is open for tutors to exchange ideas and raise issues: the course author facilitates many of these sessions, and is present for almost all of them. As a result, tutors feel connected to each other and to the programme, even though they are working one-to-one with individual learners. Initially, these sessions were planned just for the start up phases of the course, but tutors indicated they would like to continue this regular communication, and they have become a regular feature of the programme. The issue of support for tutors usually receives very little atten-tion. The effectiveness of some of the simple strategies used for *Effective Writing* such as egalitarian administrative support and short on-line tutor discussions indicates that supporting tutors is not difficult or costly, if there is an organisational commitment to do so.

Input from the AlphaRoute research was used to inform further development. The AlphaRoute programme has been expanded to serve additional learners, and to explore distance delivery to more locations. As well, two new web-based literacy courses were developed specifically for two other learner groups: the deaf commu-nity and aboriginal adults. Each course was designed with the active participation of representatives of these learner groups, and has been customised to reflect the distinctive values and cultures of each community: all are designed to incorporate strong mentor support.

What makes the difference?

Each of these three examples provided courses with a clearly identified focus on the learners' needs and goals. Academic credit was not a factor in any of these courses, which gave the provider more flexibility in customising the course to meet learner needs, and enabled the tutor or mentor to respond directly to the goals articulated by the learner. Although learners valued and worked well with the course learning materials (two in print, one on the web) that were custom designed for the programmes, learners also felt that input from their tutor or mentor made the significant difference in helping them learn what they wanted to learn.

As one writer/author notes 'A well-marked paper ends up as a dialogue on the page – an exercise of listening and learning on both sides' (Jackson, 2001). This level of tutor engagement with the learners is in contrast to the prescribed role of 'marker' which is often assigned to graduate students at large dual mode universities, or the piecework approach to marking in single mode institutions, both governed by goals of cost-efficiency in large scale distance teaching. As well, institutional commitment to enhanced learner support may not be wholehearted when, for many distance education providers, the student who does not complete the course costs less and is more profitable than the learner who remains in a course, submitting assignments that the tutor must be paid to mark.

What are the implications of these examples?

As mentioned at the outset, this chapter is based on reflection from personal experience with three courses offered outside the academic market. These examples are by no means unique. There are a great many other providers who work outside the traditional academic ODL context. For example, the International Extension College has for many years supported organisations that offer original, customised distance learning that is appropriate to a particular context and specific groups of learners (Yates and Bradley, 2000). As well, there is no claim that these three examples address every challenge in ODL. For example, two of them followed a variation of an 'outreach' model, in which tutors and administrators were based in western countries, and the majority of learners were in non-western countries. In these cases, interaction among learners was limited, partly due to time and technical constraints. Despite these caveats, reflecting on these courses led to questions about how learner support is regarded and valued, especially in 'marketised' open and distance learning.

In all three cases cited here, learner support was a very significant component of the distance learning experience, in terms of time investment and impact on learners. Although distance education experience has generally confirmed the importance of learner support, there has been a trend among academic providers to scale it back (Paul, 1988; Lentell, 1995). Recently, as Lentell notes in this volume, there has been an increased focus on tutorial support, especially in online courses. However, this in turn raises the question: if there was the same investment in tutorial support in conventional distance courses as in on-line courses, would learner outcomes in conventional distance courses be comparable with the improved outcomes of on-line courses? In other words, is it the technology that is helping learners, or the tutorial support?

Although larger institutions are moving towards more customised courses with greater learner support, there are signs that these enriched approaches may not survive beyond the inaugural phases. Davis (2001) notes that new technologies, especially on-line delivery, enable institutions to shift away from large-scale course development to designing more flexible resources that can be customised for specific sub-groups of learners. Calder (2000) also observes that institutions have started to move away from teacher-centred curricula towards more client-centred curricula. However, Davis points out that it is not clear whether the more flexible delivery model will be sustainable in large institutions that count on economies of scale, and he questions whether there will be sufficient savings in course development to cover the additional cost of more intensive, focused tutoring.

There are many differences between marketised ODL and the three situations discussed in this article: we can only speculate whether any of these differences affected the attitude towards, and investment in, learner support. You are invited to consider whether any or all of these factors has an impact on the nature and extent of learner support in ODL:

1   The courses were not offered to 'paying customers' seeking an academic credential.
  •   How well does the academic structure and drive for accreditation, match the needs of situated learning? Does a situation without market orientation and without formal accreditation make it easier to provide flexible learning that learners could apply to their context?
  •   How well does the human interaction of caring learner support flourish in an environment of measurement and cost recovery? How well do the needs of open learning fit with the drive for standardisation and profitability?
2   The courses served relatively small numbers: the largest had 200 participants at any one time, but each tutor worked with no more than twenty-five learners, making it possible to respond individually to each person.
  •   Although many forms of ODL claim economies of scale, how well does mass education serve individual learning goals?
  •   Do distance learners have a right to individualised support?
3   Relatively simple communication technologies were used for individual learner support. In two of the three courses, email was the only means of tutor–learner contact, because it was the only medium that was feasible for learners dispersed worldwide. In the third situation, phone and email were used for communication between learners and mentors.
  •   Are communication technologies more effective if they are used for individualised support rather than as a generalised 'all points bulletin'?
  •   To what extent are advanced communication technologies used to substitute high intensity activity for meaningful interaction?

4   Situated learning introduced an element of reciprocity in the tutor–learner relationship. Tutors or mentors had to learn about their participants' context in order to respond appropriately to their assignments: this exchange of knowledge between tutors and learners encouraged mutual respect for each others' areas of expertise.

- What strategies are best suited to ensuring that adult learners are treated appropriately and respectfully?
- How well does the view of 'learner as customer' address the potential power imbalance between learners and an accrediting institution?

Conclusion

In North American parlance, the 'lost and found' is the place in a public building, usually a dark corner room, where forgotten personal items are kept until the owner claims them. After some time, unclaimed articles are discarded or sold, and a new owner benefits. Proponents of learner support have often claimed that it is the least visible and most easily ignored aspect of open and distance learning. In marketised open learning, learner support has been sidelined by the tenet that technology is the most important instrument for achieving cost effective mass education and profitable niche programmes.

What may be lost, for market-oriented providers of open and distance learning, is the value of addressing social inequalities by providing equitable access and appropriate learner support. What may have been found is a non-competitive model of providing open and distance learning through organisations whose social goals are more compatible with providing genuine learning experiences. Newer providers, following the basic principles of learner-centredness articulated throughout distance education literature, are finding more creative and flexible ways of responding to learners. Unhampered by a belief that the course materials do all the teaching, or that the demands of credentialism must define the power balance between learner and provider, organisations newly engaged in distance learning are demonstrating that it is possible to offer a learner-responsive and cost effective educational experience.

Acknowledgements

Thanks to Donna Chiarelli and Gillian Martin-Mehers at LEAD International; to those associated with the UNHCR course; Maree Bentley, course author, and Claire Carigi and Angela Kwan of the Commonwealth of Learning; and to Daniel Larocque, project leader for AlphaRoute Phase 2.

References

Calder, J. (2000) Beauty lies in the eye of the beholder, *International Review of Research in Open and Distance Learning*, 1 (1) (June), www.irrodl.org.
Chiarelli, D. (2001) *Evaluation of Pilot Test, Writing Project Proposals: A LEAD Distance Learning Module* (London: LEAD).

Commonwealth of Learning (2001) Interim Reports on Effective Writing for UNHCR, internal documents, mimeo.

Davis, A. (2001) University: conversion from traditional distance education to on-line courses, programs and services, *International Review of Research in Open and Distance Learning*, 1 (2) (June).

Franklin, U. (1990) *The Real World of Technology* (Toronto: Anansi Press).

Larocque, D. (1999) *AlphaRoute Phase 2: A Research Report* (Toronto: Centre AlphaPlus).

Leach, J. (1999) Learning in practice: support for professional development, in Tait, A. and Mills, R. (eds), *Supporting the Learner in Open and Distance Learning* (New York: Routledge).

Lebel, C. (1989) Le support à l'étudiant en enseignement à distance, *Journal of Distance Education*, 4 (2).

Lentell, H. (1995) Giving a voice to the tutors, in *One World, Many Voices: Quality in Open and Distance Learning*, selected papers from the ICDE conference, Birmingham, England.

Mills, R. (1999) Diversity, convergence and student support, in Tait, A. and Mills, R. (eds), *The Convergence of Distance and Conventional Education* (New York: Routledge).

Paul, R. (1988) If student support is so important, why are we cutting it back?, in Sewart, D. and Daniel, J. D. (eds), *Developing Distance Education* (Oslo: ICDE).

Schön, D. (1987) *Educating the Reflective Practitioner* (San Francisco: Jossey-Bass).

Tait, A. (1999) The convergence of distance and conventional education: some implications for policy, in Tait, A. and Mills, R. (eds), *The Convergence of Distance and Conventional Education* (New York: Routledge).

Tait, A. (2000) Planning student support for open and distance learning, *Open Learning*, 15 (3).

Tait, A. (2000) Students and attachment: the nature of electronic relationships, *Adults Learning*, 11 (10) (June).

Yates, C. and Bradley, J. (eds) (2000) *Basic Education at a Distance* (London: Routledge).

Web sites

Commonwealth of Learning: www.col.org
LEAD International: www.lead.org

13 Challenges in adjusting to new technology in supporting learners in developing countries

Jason Pennells

This discussion is prefaced with two fictionalised case studies of distance learners in developing countries on an international distance education course. These case studies are included to make more tangible some of the generalities which follow.

Case study 1: Zeinab Ali

Zeinab Ali has recently moved to a new job at the Ministry of Education as student services manager on a national distance education teacher training project.

Zeinab has a wide circle of friends, colleagues and contacts with whom she enjoys keeping in touch by email. She checks her work email and personal Hotmail daily, at the office and at home. Zeinab enjoys gaining more experience in using the web, and is excited at the on-line course she has enrolled on through the project.

Zeinab has found the introductory activity compulsive and stimulating, as she reads the documents she has downloaded, thinks about the questions raised and discusses them with other course participants in the conference. She has agreed to be rapporteur for her group in this introductory task and will be spending the weekend compiling the group's responses to post to the plenary in time for the Monday morning deadline which she has negotiated with the course moderator.

Zeinab cannot imagine going back to the days before she had the Internet. She sighs when she thinks how letters would take forever to arrive (if they did) or had to be sent by expensive courier, and all the problems of fighting the fax machine. She felt so cut off in those days, and now she feels the whole world is open to her.

Case study 2: Magumbe Johnson

Magumbe Johnson is a tutor in a teachers' college and is a zonal student support officer in a national distance education teacher training project. Magumbe is responsible for supporting sixty local tutors and three hundred students. The electricity supply in the town where Magumbe works is erratic, and at the college it is even less reliable. For the past week, there has been a general problem and no power.

With financial support from the project, Magumbe has enrolled on an on-line course to develop his knowledge of distance education. So far, Magumbe has not been able to make much progress. In the week before the present power cut, he did spend as much time as he could spare outside his teaching and other commitments and before his journey home in the evening, at the Internet café in town, trying to log on in order to download the first reading and carry out the introductory activity. However, he couldn't get far. The Internet connection was down for much of the time; when he did manage to connect he found it very slow; and often the computer would seem to freeze up completely, and the café owner would have to reboot it.

When Magumbe did manage to maintain a connection and access the course web site, he found he could not download and open the documents he was supposed to. Several days ago, he sent an email to the course moderator, but has not yet received a reply. Magumbe feels he is slipping behind as the introductory task is due to be finished by the end of the week and he has not yet been in contact with any other participants. He is losing confidence and becoming depressed. He is beginning to think the course he took last year was much easier for him to fit in with his life, with its printed materials and audio-tapes and assignments he faxed to his tutor for marking and feedback. He still uses the folders of course material he was sent for that course, especially when he is preparing tutor training workshops.

Introduction

The International Extension College (IEC) is an educational non-governmental organisation (NGO) based in Cambridge, UK. IEC is concerned with helping governments, institutions and projects in developing countries to improve equitable access to good quality, relevant education to support development, using open and distance education approaches.

Our focus remains as it has been since our foundation by Michael Young in 1971. Essentially, we are not essentially concerned to be at the cutting edge of what technological education approaches might feasibly offer to privileged minorities, but to help developing countries to address their educational challenges by judiciously applying innovative methods. Broadly, the challenge has typically been to provide effective access to key areas of education to the most needy sectors of the population, on a large scale, at the lowest cost. As in any enterprise, balancing these priorities in any specific case involves compromises and creative thinking.

As well as working in-country on consultancy and training for specific projects, IEC also conducts general access training and education in open and distance education for international audiences. Such open courses attract participants from around the world, predominantly Africa, followed by Asia, South America and the Caribbean, with some representation also from the South Pacific, Europe and North America. We have also had a reciprocal course exchange arrangement with the *MA in DistanceEducation* of an Australian university.

This chapter gives a general overview of an area of current concern in IEC: the challenges our students and we as an organisation face in planning to adopt 'new' (computer-mediated communications) technologies for supporting learners in developing countries.

IEC's established course offerings

IEC's established course offerings include both distance and face-to-face training and study. A regular face-to-face course which IEC conducts is an annual four-week course with the Institute of Education at the University of London, *Distance Education for Development*. IEC also runs tailored face-to-face workshops ranging from one day to several weeks, for individual clients, both in the UK (generally in Cambridge) and, more often, overseas on the site of the client project or institution.

Through distance education, IEC offers an *MA and Diploma in Distance Education*, again with the Institute of Education as our partner, through the University of London External Programme. The participants for this programme (which comprises a range of courses) are located around the world. This distance-taught MA is based on a set of specially prepared print materials, supported by audio and video tapes. Tutorial support is provided by correspondence, one-to-one, between the student and course tutor. Administrative and counselling support use the same means. There is no group activity among students.

Since the MA programme was designed and launched, use of the Internet has developed rapidly. Over 70 per cent of our current postgraduate distance students now have access to email. This has enabled IEC and our students to engage in much more frequent interaction than was the case earlier. However, there remain many students who do not have access to email. These continue to rely on courier, post and fax communications for their interactions with IEC and their tutors.

IEC's newly emerging course offerings

IEC has offered versions of the above courses and workshops over a number of years, essentially using face-to-face or traditional distance education media. As mentioned above, in recent years email has become an optional facility for tutorial, counselling and administrative communication, if a student has access to the technology. We are now developing courses incorporating Internet-based communications in a more integral way. Various virtual learning environments (VLEs) are involved.

We have developed and run a web-based course concerning *Globalisation*, using asynchronous text conferencing, structured modular group activities and web-based resources, together with course books supplied for the core readings around which initial discussion of issues is based. For this course, we have used the University of Hull's Merlin VLE. We are also currently developing a distance version of the *Distance Education for Development* course, initially for use with a specific overseas partner. This places little reliance on electronic communications, as it is designed to be accessible to college staff who do not have computer or Internet facilities. As with the existing MA, it will use email as an alternative to post, courier or fax for supporting students, where email is available and preferred.

IEC's most substantial current course development activity, however, places Internet-mediated communication and study at its core. The *MA in Distance Education* is being revised into a model using computer conferencing and web-based resources along with some print material as resource. As an intermediate step in this process, IEC has developed and run with the University of London Institute of Education an MA module *Education and International Development: Concepts and Issues*, using FirstClass computer conferencing software. As with its predecessor, the new MA which we are developing is part of the University of London External Programme, which is undergoing extensive modernisation, through a 'Virtual Campus Project', to offer many of its component programmes on-line. For the *MA in Distance Education*, this involves updating and rewriting or replacing courses. The new versions are being completely redeveloped both in content and in design and concept, to suit the computer-based medium involved in course delivery and student support. The result will be a new *MA in Open, Distance and Flexible Learning*.

To study a module of the new MA, students will use a printed module reader, set books and a study guide, along with on-line conferencing and web-based resources. Participation in the on-line collaborative and cooperative group activities will be monitored and is likely to form part of the student's assessment portfolio, through submission of a study journal and other means of evidence. There will be no face-to-face meetings among students or between students and tutors as part of the course plan. The necessary computer conferencing client software, and possibly a collection of library resources, will be distributed to students on CD. Additional support will be provided outside the conferencing system by email where this would be more effective or appropriate. Students may have access to a complimentary virtual library service which is concurrently under development on a project basis at the University of London.

As a prerequisite for participation, students will need to have access to the Internet and regularly spend time on-line in the electronic conference undertaking web search and evaluation activities. Unlike on the previous programme, where assignments and feedback were one-to-one between student and tutor, in the new MA, students will be expected to undertake much of their study activity jointly with fellow students, either working collaboratively on a single task or cooperatively, sharing and discussing one another's parallel, individual tasks. Similarly, a substantial proportion of the feedback and support provided by tutors, moderators and technical support personnel will be to the course group rather than to individuals.

Issues and challenges

Adopting on-line course approaches entails various issues and challenges, impacting both on the students and on IEC as an organisation. Some implications of a move to on-line courses are as follows.

Equity

Students who are more remote from facilities and less well resourced will be excluded from an on-line course in a way in which they would not be, and have not been, from the print and correspondence-based courses. Dependence on technology for course mediation is likely to fail some students, for technical rather than academic reasons.

Costs to the student

The cost of course materials is pushed from the providing institution (IEC and the University of London) onto the student. This includes the costs of printing and binding material if desired, having a suitable computer and maintaining or paying to access Internet and computer facilities and services. In selecting the VLE to use, great importance has been placed by the External Programme on one which enables students to disconnect and study off-line, rather than needing to remain on-line while in the VLE. Also, a VLE which provides a full range of facilities for carrying curriculum content was desired, rather than a predominantly conferencing package. In view of these criteria, the university has chosen to use Lotus Domino/ Notes.

The burden on support staff

Skills in on-line course design, management and learner support need to be developed in the academic, technical, counselling and administrative staff involved, and students need to acquire on-line study skills. Students will expect turnaround of communications and assignments to be far quicker than by traditional methods. Students and the institution (including contracted tutors not on IEC staff) need to establish mutually acceptable, viable and realistic expectations of support levels and turnaround speed. We are also aware of the potential burden and cost of extensive tutor time on-line and the need for tutors to have access to the on-line medium. The same applies to any complementary electronic conference moderators and facilitators and to staff providing administrative, technical and counselling support.

Educational quality

Computer conferencing provides an opportunity for linking students from different professional and personal backgrounds, countries, languages and abilities. It also enables constructivist approaches to course design and support to be adopted effectively. However, connecting students with one another is not in itself sufficient to ensure they will work together, and some students may have entrenched learning expectations of receiving course content ('knowledge') rather than of developing it with colleagues in a constructivist way.

In revising and designing course specifications, we have been concerned – on grounds of educational quality and of cost to the student – to avoid simply loading up course materials onto the web and 'shovelling' them at students. Similarly, we need to consider the tasks we set and the web links we provide in the on-line course. We need to ensure these are viable and will not require the student to pay additional software or site registration fees.

Institutional learning and change

The External Programme of the University of London has a long and noted history in earlier modes of distance education. Within the much shorter time frame of the existing *MA in Distance Education*, academic and administrative staff also have established patterns and structures for supporting students. Changing from such a *status quo* brings into play considerations that are different from those which would apply to an organisation and staff setting out to create a new on-line programme from a point without any former distance education background. Challenges of institutional learning and adjustment involve rethinking across the board. Examples of this include tutors agreeing hours and the limits of student access to their support; course writers designing modules and tasks which are workable and not too intensive or ambitious; overcoming inbuilt institutional conservatism to achieve assessment methods appropriate to the medium; and providing access to the support services, resources and library services students will need on-line. However, in many respects, these are simply familiar stories in new guises for experienced distance educators.

Reasons for a cautious approach to adopting new technology for our courses

Further to these issues and challenges and in view of our expected student profile, we are acutely aware of reservations about pursuing an on-line strategy. Some key areas of concern and questions which we have to address satisfactorily follow.

Will our students have access?

Access to the necessary technology is likely to be a major determining factor in participation. Access is *qualitative* and can mean a range of things: it is not simply a question of having or not having a computer with an Internet connection. Having the use of a computer connected to the Internet will itself be limited to relatively few people. Fewer will have a good connection or their own machine. The technology which on-line courses depend on is particularly vulnerable for our students. Connections may be slow and intermittent. Power supplies may be very unreliable. Access to the web may be filtered through national proxy servers, seriously limiting and slowing the on-line experience. Technical support may be unavailable or expensive. The computers our students use, and the software which runs on them, may well be several generations out of date compared to the requirements of the VLE and the assumptions of course designers.

Some students may rely on using computers in Internet cafés or other places where they cannot download or install software. This would limit their access to the course, as the off-line capability of the client Lotus software would not be available to them. If able to participate at all, they would have to use a web-based version of the programme and remain connected throughout each conferencing session, which would be expensive and slow. The course design assumes students have the ability to access the VLE, download the current update of the conference then disconnect and read and write while disconnected but still within the VLE, finally to reconnect to send their contributions and download any further updates. For many, if not most, computer access will be limited to opportunities in the workplace or a public computer, whereas paper-based course materials could be studied at home or in any other convenient place.

Will our students be able to afford it?

Cost will also be a factor in designing courses, and the course fees will be at least as high as for the traditional courses. Yet students will probably have to spend more, on top of the course fees, to access the courses, through computer access and printing documents, than they would for a paper-based course where the package of materials was supplied. For some prospective students, the cost of Internet connection will be prohibitive, with expensively metered charges. Against this higher real cost to the student, the globalised access to an increasing range of courses which the advent and growth of Internet offerings is bringing means there is greater choice for our potential students and greater competition facing IEC and the University of London. Those who fund students (mostly, in our experience, this has been sponsoring agencies or projects, but the same applies as acutely for self-financing students) can be expected to use marketplace price competition as a determinant of selecting programmes. We have to ensure the value we offer, in terms of quality as well as cost, is attractive in this context.

Will our students and staff have the necessary skills?

Among those students who can overcome the hurdles of cost and access, only some will be in possession of high level computing and Internet navigation skills. A sizeable majority of those who are able to use email will be near novices in other Internet use, and likely in many cases to lack suitable technical support and training opportunities. Where participation in the programme is entirely dependent on engaging through the electronic medium, this risks excluding some students and places a heavy burden of responsibility on the technical support services we provide and on the course designers to produce glitch-free packages. Similarly, as already noted, both course developers and student support staff will need technical and andragogical skills to operate effectively in their roles in the on-line programme.

Can we guarantee the quality of the study experience?

The quality of the educational experience available to students, assuming they can access the course on-line, is a prime concern. Course design needs to encourage the best use of the on-line environment, so that it delivers a richer, rather than an impoverished, learning experience. This is an issue of continuing student support, not one limited to initial course package design. For example, the experience of working on-line may be highly fragmented, with any purposeful study being punctuated by hours of unstructured web browsing, email exchanges, casual social chat and technical 'administration'. Rather than this, we would wish to facilitate the focused pursuit and discussion of knowledge contributing to the achievement of the student's clearly identified learning outcomes. Tutors and activities need to facilitate such satisfactory and purposeful learning. Support services need to provide students with the skills, help and information resources they need to pursue their learning.

The individualisation and group interaction possibilities of on-line learning invite the benefits of constructivist course design. However, these characteristics also have a downside: in contrast to traditional distance education based on standard packages of materials and centrally quality-assured tuition, the course 'received' and participated in by each student may be far more variable and dependent on local conditions. With our student body from around the world, the variations are likely to be dramatic. There is far greater dependence on the vagaries of peer participation and an effective dynamic within a moderated on-line study group than in the 'bilateral' student–tutor relationship of the older model of distance education. There is also new and unfamiliar pressure on the group moderator or tutor to manage the learning process and to ensure it works. If the process fails to get off the ground or falls flat midway, the moderator or tutor may resort to intensive on-line interaction with individuals or groups in an attempt to stimulate and generate activity or even to lead students through the activity they were expected to proceed through autonomously. This in some ways is analogous with cases of traditional print-based distance education where face-to-face tuition has expanded and become in effect direct teaching to compensate for print materials which have failed to persuade, activate or teach the students.

Will our students suffer loss of independence?

For some students, a study process based on group interaction and collaborative or cooperative work may be a deterrent rather than an attraction. The independence and privacy of traditional means of distance study might be preferred, regardless of the technological possibilities and posited benefits of studying on-line. With a student body widely diverse in aspects such as location, varieties and mastery of English language, educational experience, computer skills, facilities, culture and motivation, some students may not flourish with this means of studying. Compared to traditional, print-based distance education, the collaborative or cooperative on-line group model may impose a greater degree of synchronicity (lockstep) among students. This may be beneficial, as a pacing mechanism helping to nudge students through their study successfully; or (as in the second case study which started this chapter) detrimental, as students who do not keep to the schedule of the group may soon feel excluded, academically and socially.

Is the on-line model relevant to our students?

Using an on-line model may be perceived as implying that less technologically sophisticated means of distance education are invalid. Allied to this, the student will not experience, as they would through studying through a well designed and implemented print-based course with audio cassette and correspondence support, how effective such earlier generation media can be. The combination of these two effects may discourage the student in a developing country from implementing appropriate and affordable distance education in their own environment. On-line education is unlikely to be a realistic choice for most of them for the foreseeable future.

A combination of these factors and others is likely to exclude some people who would have been able to participate beneficially in our existing distance education MA. Further, students' performance on on-line courses may become more dependent on their web skills and levels of access than on their educational strengths.

Potential benefits of adopting new technology for our courses

Despite all these reservations and more, there are persuasive reasons for IEC's pursuit of VLE-based courses.

Efficient communication

Information sharing possibilities are much better on-line – faster, cheaper and multi-directional – than by means of post.

Constructivist learning

Constructivist approaches to education can be brought to course design, so that courses can be anything but simply 'pumping out information'. Though we believe our established courses have avoided the latter, both in their materials and assignment design and in the tutorial support provided, nevertheless the possibilities offered by effectively using VLEs are especially rich (as Diana Laurillard originally pointed out some years ago in *Rethinking University Teaching*).

Flexibility

On-line learning allows for variation to suit individual learners and groups, and for updating progressively, including supplementation of the core materials, references and activities by tutors and by course members as a course progresses. It is especially suitable in this regard for encouraging learners to contribute and use their own experiences as a resource in the course. This is extremely valuable for students who have widely differing characteristics and needs and who are working in very diverse situations.

Reducing isolation

For remote and scattered students such as ours, possibilities for peer support and for a feeling of belonging to a learning community are far greater in a successful on-line course compared with the traditional print and correspondence model.

Students experience, rather than only read about, on-line learning

Through studying on-line, students have the opportunity to experience and evaluate on-line learning 'from the inside', which itself constitutes part of their learning and better equips them to consider the use of VLEs for their own institutions' purposes.

Environmental pressures to adopt new technology

Aside from the internal strengths and weaknesses associated with VLEs for IEC's courses and student body, there are conditions in the wider environment which exert a pressure to move in the direction of on-line courses.

Funding

Over the past years, anecdotal evidence suggests the funding available for students to attend face-to-face courses in the UK has been greatly reduced, as a result of changed policies, economic circumstances and increased UK fees. This has appeared to have had a very marked impact on enrolment on our UK-based courses, as it has with other institutions and courses. Although course fees for the on-line *MA in Open, Distance and Flexible Learning* will not be less than for a face-to-face MA in London, studying at a distance offers a way of avoiding the associated cash and opportunity costs and other inhibiting factors associated with studying in the UK.

Public perceptions and profile

Expectations – among funders, competitors, educators, learners, policy makers and the general public – are that on-line courses offer the most up-to-date, economical and convenient form of distance education. The perception, valid or not, that a distance course offered without the use of VLEs is out of date is increasingly prevalent. Thus, if only for face validity, it is increasingly important that we offer on-line options.

Offering students up-to-date learning

With the growth and incorporation of on-line learning into the mainstream, we have to include our students in this world or run the risk of under-serving or indeed ghettoising them by remaining in the realm of the more traditional media.

The web as a mainstream medium

Some resources are most easily, cheaply and readily available through the web (increasingly, for example, this is true of publications, references, databases and current information services). When this factor is allied to the rapid interactive possibilities among course members and facilitators which the Internet offers, on-line learning becomes the baseline norm.

Competition in a global market

If we are not reaching our students on-line, those with Internet access are increasingly likely to pass over IEC in favour of alternatives available from around the world on-line, regardless of the respective merits of the quality or relevance of the curricula on offer.

Conclusion

The innovative and appropriate application of available technologies to solve educational challenges for disadvantaged groups remains central to IEC's purpose. We therefore have an interest in examining and applying on-line models for our purposes, albeit critically and with reservation where such media are less suitable.

However, IEC must remain committed above all to the primacy of fitness for purpose. This applies to the application of VLEs for our courses as much as it does to any other media, material, service or resource we use. We do not wish to adopt a technology simply on the grounds of it being possible or fashionable to do so; we wish to adopt it if it will be beneficial in terms of educational effectiveness, access and economy.

Thus as we develop and use on-line courses, we must remain continually reflective, asking whether this medium or collection of media can be used for our purposes; if so, how it can best be used, and whether this is the best way to serve our students. We must therefore remain focused on our end goals. To reach those goals, we need to consider issues of equity – access, cost, and how what we offer will ultimately serve the interests of people at the margins in developing countries. We also need to keep thinking about being innovative in the application of open, distance and flexible learning for development ends, choosing the most appropriate, effective and efficient means for the job.

The prospects for the future

The adoption of on-line learning touches the core of IEC's purpose and raises vital issues for us.

- Certainly, technology is able to help us achieve our purposes and the Internet has become eagerly adopted by those of our students who have access to it.
- Using on-line approaches can both provide for our students greater richness of learning experience and also equip them to be in the forefront of developing the education system in their institution or country.
- However, relying on the Internet and VLEs also excludes from participation, wholly or partially, many who would be able to access our established format

of print-based courses with individual one-to-one tuition rather than conference discussion with fellow students.

• Though access to and reliance on the Internet is growing and seems set to continue to do so, in Africa as elsewhere, nevertheless our move to an on-line model is likely to push the demographic profile of our student enrolment towards better resourced markets, such as people interested in distance education and development work who live in Europe or North America, or who are resident in a developing country on an expatriate basis, and the more cosmopolitan higher level officials of institutions or ministries in developing countries.

• To IEC and the External Programme of University of London as organisations, and to our course developers, administrators and tutors as individuals, adopting on-line methods of offering courses brings challenges and benefits of grappling with new ideas, new ways of working and new skills.

• To all of us, developing our capacity to embrace and exploit the possibilities of on-line learning is vital to our continuing professional relevance and survival.

• We must not, however, allow this new technology to distract us from supporting where appropriate the high quality and cost-effective exploitation of combinations of older media such as face-to-face, print, radio, audio and video, or the essentials of well planned and implemented student support services.

• Overall, IEC foresees that we will offer an increasing proportion of our courses using the Internet for student support, whether by simple email tuition, web-based resources or more comprehensive on-line courses using VLEs. We also see the need to balance our response to the forces which draw and push us towards reliance on 'new technology' on the one hand, against, on the other hand, our commitment to the principle of making our courses accessible as cost-effectively as we can to those who will best convert the fruits of their study to the ends of furthering international development.

Acknowledgements

In preparing this chapter, I have benefited from ideas of colleagues within IEC and elsewhere, drawing on recent discussions, workshop sessions, bibliographies and 'grey literature'.

References

Bates, T. (2001) The continuing evolution of ICT capacity: the implications for education, in Farrell, G. M. (ed.), *The Changing Faces of Virtual Education* (Vancouver: The Commonwealth of Learning). Available at http://www.col.org/virtualed/virtualpdfs/V2_chapter3.pdf (last accessed 25 May 2002).

Burge, E. J. and Haughey, M. (eds) (2001) *Using Learning Technologies: International Perspectives on Practice* (London: Routledge).

Butcher, N. (2000) KnowledgeBank paper 3 – distance education in developing countries. Available at http://www.imfundo.org/knowledge/articles.htm (last accessed 25 May 2002).

Cyranek, G. (2000) Virtual learning in the African context, paper prepared for PALOP workshop, 14–15 November 2000, Maputo, Mozambique (Addis Ababa: UNESCO).

Farrell, G. M. (ed.) (2001a) *The Changing Faces of Virtual Education* (Vancouver: The Commonwealth of Learning). Available at http://www.col.org/virtualed/index2.htm (last accessed 25 May 2002).

Farrell, G. M. (2001b) Issues and choices, in Farrell, G. M. (ed.), *The Changing Faces of Virtual Education* (Vancouver: The Commonwealth of Learning). Available at http://www.col.org/virtualed/virtualpdfs/V2_chapter8.pdf (last accessed 25 May 2002).

Fillip, B. (2000) *Distance Education in Africa: New Technologies and New Opportunities* (Washington, DC: Japan International Cooperation Agency).

IEC (2001) *Imfundo: A Review of Experience with Information and Communications Technologies in Education Projects* (Cambridge: IEC). Available at http://www.imfundo.org/knowledge/articles.htm (last accessed 25 May 2002).

Jensen, M. (1998) African Internet connectivity: summary of international ICT development projects in Africa, http://demiurge.wn.apc.org/africa/projects.htm (last accessed 25 May 2002).

Kirkwood, A. (2000) Shanty towns around the global village? Reducing distance, but widening gaps with ICT, paper presented to the Conference 'Distance Education: An Open Question?', Adelaide, South Australia, September 2000.

Laurillard, D. (2001) *Rethinking University Teaching*, 2nd edition (London: Routledge).

Perraton, H. (2000a) Information and communication technologies for education in the south, report on a study for the Department for International Development (Cambridge: IRFOL).

Perraton, H. (2000b) *Open and Distance Learning in the Developing World* (London: Routledge).

Rumble, G. (2001) E-education – whose benefits, whose costs? Inaugural lecture, The Open University, 28 February 2001. Available at http://www.iec.ac.uk/resources_online.html (last accessed 25 May 2002).

Ryan, Y. (2001) The provision of learner support services on-line, in Farrell, G. M. (ed.), *The Changing Faces of Virtual Education* (Vancouver: The Commonwealth of Learning). Available at http://www.col.org/virtualed/virtualpdfs/V2_chapter5.pdf (last accessed 25 May 2002).

Simpson, O. P. (2002) *Supporting Students in On-line, Open and Distance Learning*, 2nd edition (London: Kogan Page).

14 Delivering learner support on-line

Does the medium affect the message?

Marion Phillips

This chapter considers the development of an on-line service for learner support at the UK Open University (OU UK). The basic principles that underpin the provision of a service to support open and distance learners remain the same whatever learning technology is employed, but the way that technology is engaged can change the nature of the service. How can the web be harnessed to provide effective student support services and what are the advantages and disadvantages of using web technologies?

Introduction

Many providers of open and distance learning for adults are turning to the widescale use of the new technologies as their chosen media for course delivery. The World Wide Web not only offers the opportunity to deliver course materials but also to facilitate communication and interactions between students, their tutors and host institutions. It is inevitable that students, many of whom already use 'on-line' facilities to study their course, will wish to use electronic media to access information and learner support services from the University.

At the OU UK the brief of the New Technology for Supporting Students (NTSS) Team has been to develop the use of new technology for the provision of advice, guidance and learning support for students and potential students. In reflecting on our experiences of developing on-line learner support materials, it has become clear that the *way* we employ the technology for these developments can have a profound effect on the nature of the experience for users. To illustrate these effects I will refer to the materials we have developed: some of these materials are currently live on the Internet in an area known as *The Learner's Guide to the Open University* (www.open.ac.uk/learners-guide) (Figure 14.1), some are available only for our registered students on a password-protected web site and some are purely experimental and not yet part of the learner service that we offer.

The basic principles that underpin the provision of a service to support open and distance learners remain the same whatever learning technology is employed, because these principles are driven by the needs of the students who use the service. A learner service must focus on learners and learning; they, rather than the technology, represent the key issues (Burge, 2000).

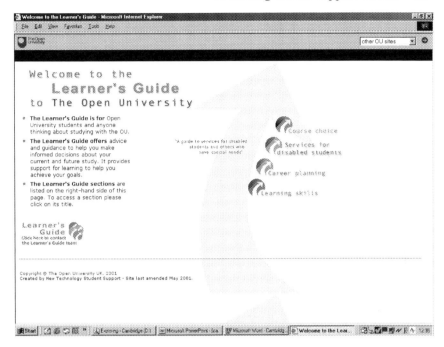

Figure 14.1 The Learner's Guide to the Open University

However, the use of the new technologies for the delivery of student support services provides us with an opportunity to consider *how* we provide learner support for our open and distance students. Are there new and better ways of doing things, rather than simply using new technologies to provide the same old services? How does the use of new technology impact on learning at a distance? Does the use of the new technologies affect the service that we offer to our learners? To answer these questions it is necessary first to return to basic principles and consider what are the needs of our students and how we can best support these needs at a distance.

Who are our learners?

At the OU UK all of our students are adults who study 'at a distance' that is at home, in the workplace or elsewhere. The University offers open access (at undergraduate level), open and distance higher education. There are no entry requirements and no selection processes for any of the 250 or so modules offered in the undergraduate programme. Students can choose to study single modules or can group their course credits together for specific qualifications such as undergraduate or postgraduate certificates, diplomas and degrees. There are also a wide variety of other courses available at pre-degree and post-graduate levels including opportunities for professional development and updating. The 'open' policy enables students to select modules for study in any order they wish and thus create their own individual curriculum.

Since the study pathway of any individual is not set by the institution, it is not possible to meet their needs, such as their developmental learning skills requirements, directly through the modules/course being studied (Macdonald *et al.*, 2002). Instead we meet these needs through a non-course based 'learner service' which aims to assist very large numbers of enquirers and students from diverse backgrounds, on a wide range of courses and programmes of study (Tait, 1998).

What is learner support?

The term 'learner support' describes a holistic approach to the provision of non subject-based support for the individual learner in the context of a study career which operates from the first enquiry to the completion of studies. A learner support service offers advice, guidance and study support as developmental factors in the whole learning process and aims to identify and remove barriers to learning. It should be responsive to the actual needs of learners, which vary from individual to individual, course to course and year to year (Brindley, 1995).

For example, students may need:

- information and admission guidance prior to enrolment
- guidance about module/course choices and qualification planning
- careers guidance to enable them to link study plans to their career interests
- guidance about study requirements and available facilities for those with disabilities
- induction advice both as new students of the institution and because for many this may be their first exposure to 'study at a distance'
- support for study at a distance
- guidance about the University's administration
- advice about, and opportunities for, study preparation and the development of learning and study skills
- opportunities to monitor and review their progress
- support for academic progress

To be at its most effective, the guidance and learner support should be tailored to meet the needs of each learner. The learner support service needs to be available at every stage of a student's career: at entry, during study, between courses and at the end of the study programme. It should be driven by the development of a relationship with the student and should provide a framework to guide students through their studies. Students expect to make decisions for themselves and to be 'in charge' and it is essential that the support framework is learner-centred (Kelly and Fage, 2002).

On-line: why, how, what, and what not!

The UK Open University (OU UK), was founded on a multi-media teaching, learning and support system which has developed as new technologies have become available. A variety of media including print, television and video, radio and audio cassettes and face-to-face, telephone and correspondence tuition and guidance are exploited to teach and support student learning (Tait, 1999). Now that the new technologies have developed as mass media, computer-mediated communication and the Internet are also becoming widely used. The OU UK has decided to assume access by students to on-line facilities within the next few years (Open University, 2001). As a result more of our students are expecting on-line facilities for all features of their academic life including the provision of a learner support service (Phillips and Kelly, 2000).

When developing on-line learner support, it is essential to consider issues of accessibility. This is of particular importance to us at the UK OU where our strategic aim is to provide a university education, for *anyone* who wishes to experience it (Open University, 2001). For those unable or unwilling to purchase computer equipment for use at home, or for those whose Personal Computer (PC) is not working, computer-based services need to be made available through public-access centres. Through its *Opening up IT* initiative the OU UK has developed a network of local partnerships to enable students to take advantage of local IT provision for their study. Details of these local centres are held on an on-line database, accessible for anyone to search and view. For those who do not have Internet access, details of the centres can be obtained from our Regional Centres where advisory staff can assist students in finding the most appropriate learning centre to meet their needs. We anticipate that in the UK public access to computer study equipment is likely to remain an important issue for some time. For those parts of the world where the numbers of potential learners who have access to computers for study is considerably less, public access to PCs may be crucial.

It is also important to think about the type of equipment and Internet connections available to our students. Although in 2002 approximately 80 per cent of OU UK students are 'on-line' and using the University's on-line services and applications, there is evidence that the majority of these learners rely on limited modem access rates and only very few currently have broadband connections. This restricts the kind of learning and teaching material which can be offered on-line to text, audio and low to medium resolution images (Greenburg, 2002).

Consideration also needs to be given to the ongoing costs of using on-line resources. How long a student is required to stay on-line in order to study is an issue for many learners since telephone bills can be costly for those without an all-inclusive tariff for Internet access. There may also be costs for students associated with printing on-line resources. If a document or a resource is better suited to the printed medium, it should be made available in this form by the institution. It is not enough merely to provide printed documents in electronic format.

Resources provided on-line should be either adapted for this environment or preferably constructed specifically for the electronic medium. The consensus is that screen-based information takes up to 20 per cent longer to read than print-based. Materials designed to be studied on-line need to be presented in 'small chunks' which can be accessed individually so that the user gets precisely the information or activity required at that time without having to wade through numerous 'pages'.

When developing student support provision in the context of new technology, it remains essential to use the medium most appropriate for the task in hand. It is important to consider not only how best to use the new media to deliver the service but also whether on occasions the 'old media' will remain the best option. The new technologies offer new opportunities, but they are unlikely to be the answer to every issue for every student at all times. There is likely to remain a need for printed materials for certain tasks and activities. Likewise, group sessions or one-to-one discussions with academic or advisory staff might remain the best method for the provision of part of the learner service. A new service needs to integrate the old with the new to provide a total service for all using the appropriate medium for the task in hand.

Developing learner support on-line

In developing a support service that can be accessed from the Internet for the OU UK, our intention has been to provide a service which exploits the new media and offers on-line advice, guidance and learner support opportunities for the growing number of students and enquirers who use the Internet.

The *Learner's Guide to the Open University* (www.open.ac.uk/learners-guide) offers a learner service through a new medium, but the underpinning philosophy and approach remains the same as that for the existing support service for OU UK students. The on-line service adopts a student-focused approach, which puts the needs of the students at the heart of the guidance service; it provides a base for informed decision making through pathways that enable users to ask and answer questions of themselves and to access appropriate resources and information. However, there are a variety of ways in which the new technologies can be deployed and the use of these different applications can affect the type of service offered and the quality of the students' experience when using the on-line support service.

Integrated text-based advice systems

The use of text as the basis of a web site ensures both easy access (anyone who has access to the Internet will be able to view these pages) and quick download times. These are important considerations for any on-line learner service developed for 'distance students', many of whom will work from home without access to the latest computer specifications. Unless the on-line learner service is easy and quick to access, students are unlikely to use it however good it may be.

We have used hypertext-based advice systems to provide web sites that support students in choosing appropriate courses, and for planning their study. A full range of information can be offered that in paper form can (and often does) overwhelm the student by making their own hyperlinks, students are able to follow only those pathways that meet their needs.

The use of hypertext environments for learning are now well documented, having been used to help learners acquire and construct both a broad appreciation of a topic and more specific knowledge (Carver *et al.*, 1992). Some developers however, have cautioned against the use of hypertext because it can undermine comprehension (Plowman, 1996) and users can 'get lost' (Marchionini, 1988).

For us, the key has been to provide an integrated system: easy access web-based advice and guidance *embedded within* information about the institution's courses. This approach enables potential students to mentally 'tick-off' some of the worries or uncertainties they may have about selecting a course. It can also help ensure that students choose courses suited to their own needs by encouraging them to ask the right questions, such as:

- do I want to improve or change my job prospects?
- do I want to work towards a qualification?

The OU UK web site, *Learner's Guide Course Choice* (www.open.ac.uk/learners-guide/course-choice) (see Figure 14.2) aims to provide such an integrated system. The web site offers students and enquirers advice and guidance on a variety of course choice issues alongside information about the courses and qualifications available and the opportunity to register on-line. The course choice sites have been live on the OU web site since the year 2000 and by 2001 over one third of all course registrations were administered on-line. Students are accessing the on-line facilities in large numbers and the trend in the use of on-line resources continues to grow.

The guidance elements of the on-line course choice and registration sites are essential in ensuring that students register on courses that meet their needs and aspirations; without such guidance, there is a risk of high student dropout when students commence their studies. By making a student aware of aspects such as the level of study involved or what study skills are required, there is a better chance of that student staying the course, and thus of improving overall retention rates.

The initial course choice area of the web site was expanded at an early stage to include access to advice and guidance about *services for students with a disability* (www.open.ac.uk/learners-guide/disability) (Figure 14.3). This site contains details to enable students to consider their study needs and to find out what specific services are available from the OU to help them study effectively.

A third web site, *Career Planning* (www.open.ac.uk/learners-guide/careers) (Figure 14.4), completes the trilogy of sites primarily concerned with course choice. The *Career Planning* site provides information for career development with sections on 'thinking about yourself', 'looking for job ideas' and 'relating study to career options'.

Reading large quantities of text on-line can be tedious and so we have provided several options with which students can interact. For example, the Careers site includes a Toolkit which combines activities with more detailed advice on such topics as 'age and employment' and 'how to seek employment' and 'prepare for

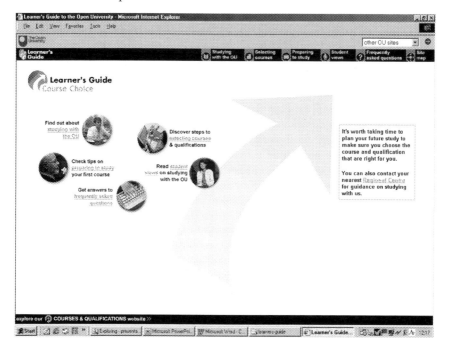

Figure 14.2 The Learner's Guide: course choice

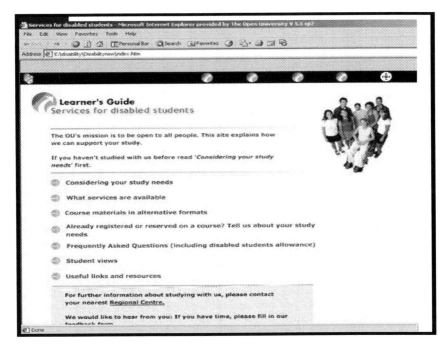

Figure 14.3 The Learner's Guide: services for students with a disabilitiy

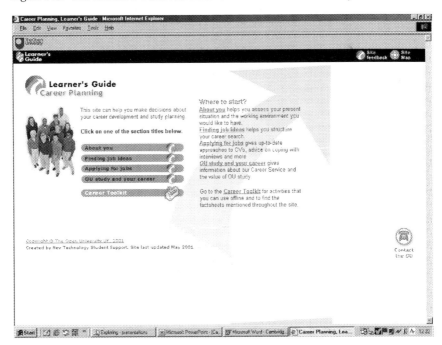

Figure 14.4 The Learner's Guide: career planning

interviews'. In addition, all of the guidance sites give access to a real person; local support is provided from Regional Centres in the UK and some parts of Continental Western Europe and the on-line service is used to give easy access to telephone numbers and email facilities.

The use of computers in the provision of learner advice and support services does not make personal support with real people redundant. Students tell us that they do not want to be asked to choose between traditional methods and the new electronic media. They want whatever works best for them. However, offering on-line Learner Services can often increase student understanding of the issues confronting them and thus save time and money; for example, it can mean the student is better informed before entering into discussion with learning support staff thereby making that discussion more effective.

Real time interactions

Providing telephone numbers through our web sites as a means of accessing real people in real time can provide an essential link for conversations with advisory staff who can answer queries relating directly to the individual circumstances of the student. However, the new technologies can also be harnessed to offer real time interactions. Such a service can provide seamless support for the learner who can access text-based information and guidance and then move to a conversation with advisory staff in the same medium, without the need to disconnect from the Internet. Thus the on-line service is able to be responsive in meeting the needs of the individual as well as providing easy-to-access information and guidance for the student body as a whole.

At the OU UK we have experimented with this concept to provide a *virtual course choice session* in real time (http://kmi.open.ac.uk/projects/rtag/resources.html).

This service offers students access to resources, and opportunities to ask questions and receive answers from OU advisors in real time. Through the use of streaming technology, we can also provide audio and video capabilities thus enabling the students to see the people who they are talking to. The individual has a sense of talking with a real person rather than a machine and the 'human face' of the distance learning organisation is immediately evident. Also students can easily and quickly gain reassurance by checking 'is this right for me?'

The 'web-cast' is available to anyone who logs in and so, although only a small percentage of people may actually ask a question, many can be aware of it and receive the 'answer' (in many ways it acts like a radio phone-in programme). This is therefore a cost effective way of providing a responsive and personalised service to our students.

Although our virtual course choice session experiment was popular with those students who were able to access the site, there were a number of students who told us that they would have liked to 'visit' this session, but were unable to do so because they had slow Internet connections that made the use of streaming media out of the question. While the use of multimedia is attractive because it is so engaging, the use of streaming media remains problematic for most users and especially those with slower Internet connections. It seems likely that we will need to wait for mass broadband connection before we can mainstream the use of streaming media. Nevertheless, the idea of individuals receiving guidance in real time on the Internet remains compelling and we hope to carry out further experiments using readily accessible, text-based communications in real time.

Interactivity

A major aim of our learner service is to help students become autonomous, and as a result students may need help to learn how to learn, to learn study skills and to learn how to plan for their development. Brown (1978), and Flavell (1987) coined the term 'metacognition' to describe this approach to learning. Effective learners are those who are aware of their strengths and limitations and find ways to remedy the latter (Bransford *et al.*, 1999). When learners are engaged in metacognitive activities such as self-assessment, monitoring their own progress or revising, their learning is enhanced (White and Frederiksen, 1998). However, many researchers (for example, Chi *et al.*, 1989; Lin and Lehman, 1999) have shown that students do not engage in metacognitive thinking unless they are explicitly encouraged to do so through carefully designed instructional activities. In considering how metacognitive activities can be designed, Lin (2001) emphasises the importance of prompting and helping students to develop knowledge about self-as-learners. A key point for Lin is that self-knowledge needs to be nurtured alongside that of the subject domain being studied. Support for 'metacognition' and the development of knowledge of self-as-learner is therefore an important aspect of any learner support service.

Our conviction is that to support metacognition we need to engage the student in *active* learning. Learning by experience is as important 'on-line' as elsewhere (Alexander and Boud, 2001). Interactive activities not only help users engage with the learning resources provided but also help to make them more meaningful for each individual user. Interactivity plays a powerful part in providing a true web-based learner service. The best systems will also provide feedback to the learner.

The *Learning Skills* area of the Learner's Guide (www.open.ac.uk/learners-guide/learning-skills) (Figure 14.5) contains a variety of resources that include on-line interactive activities to support the development of study skills.

The 'Improving your English Language Skills' area for example, includes activities and advice on 'assessing your own writing' along with activities for practising essay writing and dealing with grammar. The 'Exams and Revision' site offers reassurance for those who experience anxiety and stress at exam time as well as practical advice about how to use revision and examination time effectively. Both the areas contain activities for the user to complete. Some limited feedback, in the form of completed activity 'exemplars', is also provided.

Feedback is most effective if it can be provided for the student as a response to work completed. This is difficult to do without providing feedback from an

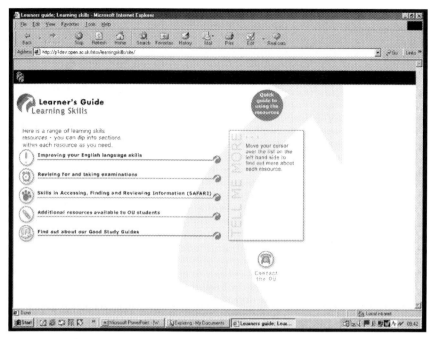

Figure 14.5 The Learner's Guide: learning skills

individual such as an advisory member of staff or a tutor. However, new technology can be harnessed to provide some feedback to responses completed by individuals.

An example of such an interactive activity is the time management exercise developed for the *Learner's Guide Course Choice* site (http://www.open.ac.uk/learners-guide/choose/02.htm) (Figure 14.6).

This activity asks users to plot how many hours they think they have available per week against the suggested hours of study for the course. Depending on their answer, appropriate advice is given and links to further advice about how to find a suitable study pattern is provided. Such an activity can make a real difference in helping prospective learners to engage with the need to set aside sufficient time to study. We know from the feedback of students who 'drop out' that awareness of time pressures can be crucial to their success. However, this issue is difficult to deal with at a distance. We have had limited success through passive paper resources in persuading students of the need to actively consider the time required for study. The use of new technology allows this issue to be tackled in an interactive manner and can really help the student to identify clearly how they can set aside the time they will need to be a successful 'distance' student.

The interactive activities within the Learner's Guide enable users to become active learners and to 'make it their own'. In addition, such activities are more engaging than merely reading text. On-line interactivity also enables students to make mistakes 'in private' and thus helps to boost confidence. The downside of introducing interactivity again relates to the issues of accessing the technology.

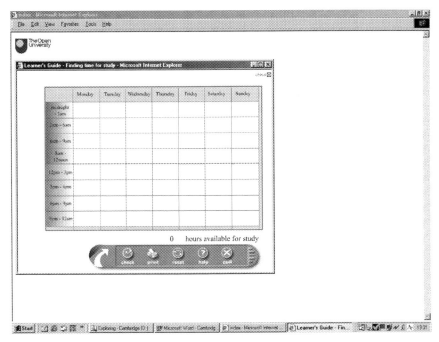

Figure 14.6 The Learner's Guide: time management

As soon as a site becomes more than text, it can cause difficulties for users of low-specification computers. Using interactive activities can also increase the length of time that users need to remain on-line. For those who use the Internet via a modem and phone line, this increased time on-line can be expensive. It is for this reason that we ensure that all interactive activities are also available in printable form so that they can be completed offline. However, providing direct feedback in these instances remains a problem.

Putting learning support in context

The resources discussed thus far rely on the student or prospective student identifying an appropriate route through the various resources available on-line through the use of hyperlinks. Since the resources are available to all via the Internet, we have had to ensure that these materials are 'generic' in nature. As such, they may be consistent with the needs of learners at any one time, but there is the danger that learners may not recognise that they are relevant to them since they are not set within the context of the subject domain being studied. Context plays an important role in the implementation of any learning event (Shambaugh and Magliaro, 1997) and tight linking of learning skills development with the curriculum being followed by a student has also been shown to be more effective than a generic approach to skills development (Martin and Ramsden, 1987). However, such considerations can provide particular problems for us as we attempt to design a non-course based learner service which is available and appropriate for all our students.

One approach which might help to overcome these difficulties is to ask learners to 'sign in' to the on-line service so that we can 'recognise' who they are; this affords the opportunity to tailor the content of the web site to the course or qualification that the student is studying. If this can be done 'automatically' by technology, then so much the better.

We have made a first step in this direction with our *on-line induction* pilot study. The main challenge has been to 'marry' generic and course-specific induction materials so that the user is provided with a single set of information which is set in the context of the course that they have chosen to study.

To achieve this objective, we are using XML-backed technologies (extensible markup language) and a content management system. The content has been written using 'learning objects' (small pieces of 'learning material' which might be information or guidance, or an activity). Each learning object is labelled through the use of 'metatags'. Finally, the system is backed by a database which is used to link the relevant information (generic and course-specific) together.

In this example, the specific use of XML technology allows us to store, organise and maintain information as well as to ensure that the course information is delivered with the relevant generic elements. It will also eventually allow individual faculties and course teams to update their induction materials independently and automatically. This is an important refinement for an institution as large as the OU UK. The use of the technology allows us to provide induction opportunities, set within the context of the course that any one student is studying, without having to write a specific induction site for each of our 500 or so modules. It also provides a better experience for students, since although we use hyperlinks to enable the student to select appropriate pathways for whichever pathway they choose, all the information is both relevant and set in the context of *their* course.

The future: individualised personal learner support on-line?

To develop an effective service for the future, we need to select the appropriate types of resource that will provide 'added value'. We will need to keep in touch with our learners and to ensure that the on-line service is subject to ongoing evaluation and usability testing. Users will continue to seek resources through a variety of media and will value a service that knows them and treats them as an individual. To be fully effective our service needs to be both proactive and reactive to the needs of our students.

Student Support Services must be designed to accommodate the needs of individuals. Our students expect timely delivery of materials, feedback and replies to queries or concerns. New technologies can help us to deliver such a service if we employ them appropriately. Our work to date indicates that the particular advantages that can be gained include the effective use of hyperlinks, interactivity combined with feedback, real time interactions, use of multimedia, and the provision of a service set in the context of the subject being studied.

The ultimate aim of any learner service is to provide a service that is not only set in the context of the course or qualification that the student is studying, but is

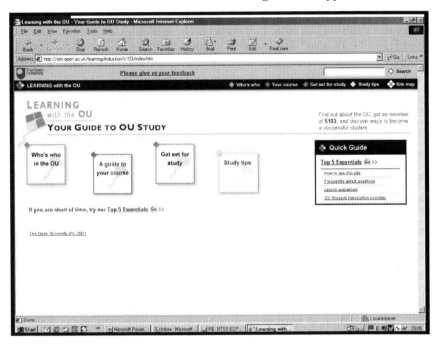

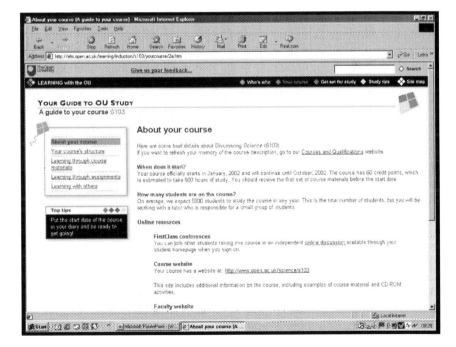

Figure 14.7 The Learner's Guide: your guide to OU study

also customised for the individual. In this way we will be able to provide a Learner Service which both fulfils all the generic functions and is tailored towards the personal needs of each student. Such a service would take into account the student's past experiences, present circumstances and future aspirations, and be proactive as well as reactive. A truly personalised service will also take into account the individual's learning styles, learning strategies and study intentions in order to build interactive learning solutions that recognise, match and support critical factors that influence how individuals learn (Martinez, 2001). Can the new technologies be employed to develop such a system available to all students 'at a distance'? Researchers are now making rapid progress realising the personalised learning dream using object architecture and adaptive learning technology. Is this the future of on-line student support in open and distance education? We think it likely that it is.

Our induction project is a first stage in what we plan to extend to a student Personal Development Planning initiative. We have high hopes for this to act as a framework through which we can support student learning and development throughout the student's learning 'life', which in the context of life-long learning, could well span a very large numbers of years.

For example, in the induction area, one of the exercises prompts the students to reflect on their needs as a student and to self-assess their study skills (see Figure 14.7). We could collect further material about a student's study intentions and their learning styles. Why not use the technology to collect this and other information that the student is willing to share out, which will then enable us to tailor a service for the student that is capable of taking into account their individual needs and progress. Such a service could provide targeted support for an individual (see Figure 14.8).

As a first step at the OU UK, we have been working with other colleagues at the university to develop a student bulletin board. Using the OU systems databases, we can identify students who fit certain criteria and send a message to them. At the moment, our databases contain mostly administrative information so our current 'messages' tend to be administrative in nature but the implications for learning support are clear. Such a system offers the potential to provide a tailor-made service for each of our students which will enable them to receive personalised support which is both appropriate to *their* needs and set within the context of *their* studies.

References

Alexander, S. and Boud, D. (2001) Learners still learn from experience when on-line, in Stephenson, J. (ed.), *Teaching and Learning On-line: Pedagogies for New Technologies* (London: Kogan Page).

Bransford, J. D., Brown, A. L. and Cocking, R. R. (1999) *How People Learn: Brain, Mind, Experience and School* (Washington, DC: National Academy Press).

Brindley, J. (1995) Learners and learner services: the key to the future in open distance learning, in Roberts, J. M. and Keough, E. M. (eds), *Why the Information Highway? Lessons from Open and Distance Learning* (Toronto: Trifolium Books).

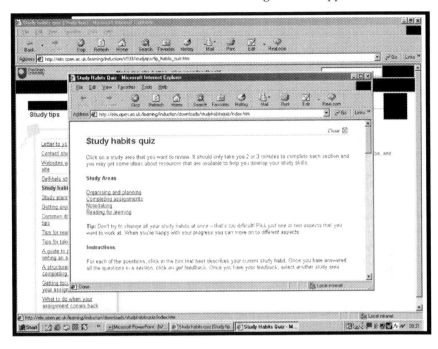

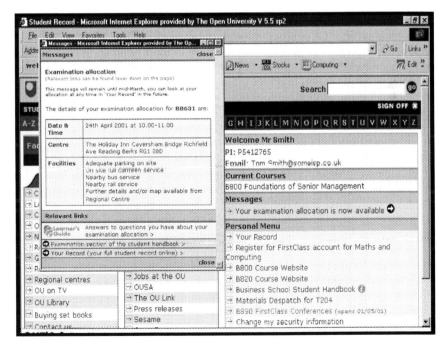

Figure 14.8 The Learner's Guide: example of individualised resources and information

Brown, A. L. (1978) Knowing when, where and how to remember: a problem of meta-cognition, in Glaser, R. (ed.), *Advances in Instructional Psychology*, 7, pp. 55–111 (New York: Academic Press).

Burge, E. J. (ed.) (2000) *New Directions for Adult and Continuing Education: The Strategic Use of Learning Technologies*, Number 88 (San Francisco: Jossey-Bass).

Carver, S. M., Lehrer, R., Connell, R. and Erickson, J. (1992) Learning by hypermedia design: issues of assessment and implementation, *Educational Psychologist*, 27 (3), pp. 385–404.

Chi, M. T. H., Bassock, M., Lewis, M. W., Reinmann, P. and Glaser, R. (1989) Self-explanations: how students study and use examples in learning to solve problems, *Cognitive Science*, 13, pp. 145–82.

Flavell, J. H. (1987) Speculations about the nature and development of metacognition, in Weinhert, F. E. and Kluwe, R. H. (eds), *Metacognition, Motivation and Understanding* (Hillsdale, NJ: Lawrence Erlbaum Associates).

Greenburg, J. (2002) *Broadband: Current Position and Future Projections*, internal publication: Open University Learning and Teaching Innovation Committee papers, February 2002, Milton Keynes, Open University.

Kelly, P. and Fage, J. (2002) *A Framework for Student Support and Guidance*, internal publication: Student Services Planning Office (Milton Keynes, Open University).

Lin, X. D. (2001) Designing metacognitive activities, *Educational Technology Research and Development*, 49 (2), pp. 23–40.

Lin, X. D. and Lehman, J. (1999) Supporting learning of variable control in a computer-based biology environment: effects of prompting college students to reflect on their own thinking, *Journal of Research in Science Teaching*, 36 (7), pp. 1–22.

Macdonald, J., Barrett, C., Goodwin, V. and Phillips, M. (2002) What makes a good skills web site? Optimising the impact of study skills advice using web based delivery, *Proceedings 9th Improving Student Learning Symposium, 2001*.

Marchionini, G. (1988) Hypermedia and learning: freedom and chaos, *Educational Technology*, (Nov), pp. 8–12.

Martin, E. and Ramsden, P. (1987) Learning skills or skill in learning?, in Richardson, J., Eynsenck, M. and Warren Piper, D. (eds), *Student Learning: Research into Education and Cognitive Psychology* (Milton Keynes: Open University Press).

Martinez, M. (2001) Key design considerations for personalised learning on the Web, *Educational Technology and Society*, 4 (1).

Open University (2001) *Learning and Teaching Strategy*, www.open.ac.uk/ltto/LTstrategy (Milton Keynes: The Open University).

Phillips, M. and Kelly, P. (2000) Learning technologies for learner services, in Burge, E.J. (ed.), *New Directions for Adult and Continuing Education: The Strategic Use of Learning Technologies*, Number 88 (San Francisco: Jossey-Bass).

Plowman, L. (1996) Narrative, linearity and interactivity: making sense of interactive multimedia, *British Journal of Educational Technology*, 27 (2), pp. 92–105.

Shambaugh, R. N. and Magliaro, S. G. (1997), *Mastering the Possibilities: A Process Approach to Instructional Design* (Boston, MA: Allyn and Bacon).

Tait, A. (1998) Guidance and counselling in the Open University, in Crawford, M., Edwards, R. and Kydd, L. (eds), *Taking Issue: Debates in Guidance and Counselling in Learning* (London: The Open University and Routledge).

Tait, A. (1999) Face to face and at a distance: the mediation of guidance and counselling through the new technologies, *British Journal of Guidance and Counselling*, 27 (1), pp. 113–22.

White, B. Y. and Frederikson, J. R. (1998) Inquiry, modelling and metacognition: making science accessible to all students. *Cognition and Instruction*, 16 (1), pp. 3–118.

15 Rethinking learner support in the Open University UK

A case study

Alan Tait

Introduction

This chapter reviews the range of factors both internal and external that makes imperative a review of the ways in which learners are supported in the OU UK, and by extension more widely in open and distance learning. The factors include, from within the institution: declining retention figures; the nature of learner expectations in the change of status from 'student' to 'customer'; changes in the division and distribution of labour brought about by ICT; pressures on costs and the effect of competition; and from the external perspective the nature of consumer behaviour; the deterioration of time available for study with the increase of long working hours; difficulties with space for study in the context of increasing domestic overcrowding; and changes in the characteristics of learner populations with the impact of lifelong learning as governmental policy arena. The discussion concludes with what supports student 'engagement'. All of these lead to the observation that a fundamental review of learner support in the OU UK is necessary after some thirty years of teaching and learning. As the OU UK has been so significant in the modernisation of open and distance learning from the perspective of learner support as much as in multi-media course design, it is felt that an analysis of change in this field is of broad interest and significance.

Discussion of change is structured in this debate within categories of those driven from inside and outside the institution: such a structure has its limitations as the institution is itself, of course, part of its environment, and the reader will find common threads in both parts.

Internally driven change

Student retention

The immediate context for a review of learner support in the OU UK proposed here, undertaken, it should immediately be said, on a personal basis, is the decline in student retention over the last five years of some 5 per cent, or to put it another way, that in the teaching year 1997/8 of 166,000 registered students, 95,000 completed and passed their courses (Open University Retention Project Report,

2001, p. 1). That is a non-completion and failure rate of some 43 per cent. Declining student retention figures, with their implications for the access mission of the OU UK, led to the establishment by the university of the Retention Programme, a significant action research project at strategic level tasked with the identification of a range of retention-supportive activities. This report makes its recommendations under four broad headings, namely:

1 Managing open entry: increasing student progression by rewarding achievement.
2 Reducing student workload.
3 Building stronger relationships with students: paying attention to the key role of the Associate Lecturer (tutor).
4 Changing the focus of funding of central academic units.

The most significant areas of attention it addresses include, first, the need to provide more obvious markers of success for students, e.g. a student who successfully completes part but not all of the continuous assessment in a year should be able to carry forward that part to a succeeding year, rather than suffer the de-motivating experience of effectively losing all that work. Second the need for course teams to manage the workload they create for students more effectively; it seems that little has been learned over the last thirty years about how student workload is created. This has been complicated by the introduction of new technologies for learning and teaching, including electronic conferencing and CD-ROM resources, where timing of workload has in some courses been badly misleading, although at the same time recognised as providing effective and motivating learning resources. Third, the need to embed more firmly the support that students gain from their tutor, that is in the OU UK system the part-time teacher who assesses and teaches each individual student through his or her assignments during the course. The tutor role in being able to support students through the difficulties of study is recognised as absolutely central, although at the same time the learning environments have become so complex that the tutor is less able than ever to offer comprehensive information and guidance to the learner, and needs to be supported by teams of staff involved in what is termed 'student services', both in the thirteen Regional Centres as well as at headquarters in Milton Keynes. Lastly, faculties and schools in the university should, as the university as a whole does, receive an element of funding on student success and not just on student recruitment.

A little history

It would be helpful initially to have a little history as to how the OU UK has got to where it has in the development of discussion. The university was remarkable in establishing itself for teaching in 1971 in recognising that one of the core ways in which it would take forward and revolutionise the tradition of correspondence education would be to offer student support alongside professionally designed multi-media teaching materials, in particular through individualised tutoring and counselling and a range of local study centres. Student support was conceived for a single programme, with which the OU UK was originally established, namely the undergraduate programme. The most significant change in that overarching design has been the removal of the counselling system, that is in OU UK terms, support of an educational but non-course-specific kind. In the undergraduate programme where it was developed this led to the core concept of 'continuity of counselling', that is that the tutor supporting a student in his or her first year remained as the counsellor for an entire five or six years' degree, thus giving an individual student a continuity of acquaintance over and above the range of tutors who would be specific to a course each year (see Tait, 1996, pp. 60–1 for an account of the original design of learner support in the OU UK). As the first Vice-chancellor Walter, now Lord, Perry wrote in his personal account of the OU UK:

> I am sure that Robert Beevers (the first Director of Regional Tutorial Services, AWT) was fundamentally correct in deciding that students would need con-tinuous counselling, but it was not a view that was shared widely by academics. They tended to believe that most of the advice that students would want would come best from the academic staff who were teaching them (the tutors) and that counselling would become a relatively peripheral and minor activity. This runs counter to the experience of most people who have worked in the field of adult education, where the belief is fairly general that adults need a great deal more supportive help, in areas divorced from their purely academic studies, than do students in conventional residential institutions.
>
> (Perry, 1976, p. 113)

This counselling system has been removed, and the reasoning behind this derived from a complex of internal and external pressures including the need to control costs at a time of expansion (Tait, 1998, p. 124). We have in fact arrived at the situation where support is most significantly given by the tutor, who may or may not feel that he or she wants the range of questions raised by a student whom the tutor barely has time in many instances to get to know at all during a nine-month or less course of study at a distance. Second, the student may seek support from a team of student advisors based in Regional Centres (typically say for the OU in the East of England, a team in the region of 3.5 Advisors supported by 25 Student Support Assistants for some 17,000 students). It is clear in the latter case that students have almost no opportunity to get to know anyone apart from their tutor, as the student advisor and Student Support Assistant is offering support on the 'Call Centre' model, which has an efficiency which does much to please the institution, but for all of us who use such services in other contexts offers frustration as much as it offers rewarding communication. This chapter challenges whether such 'light touch' relationships are adequate in the context of adult higher education, in particular in supporting student 'engagement'.

However, while the non-completion of students as already noted has increased over recent years there are newer developments already bringing change although without any evidence yet of their impact on completion. These derive principally from the new opportunities for communication through electronic conferencing between students and tutors, and students and each other, and second, from the opportunities through web-based information and guidance systems to make available to students on a 'self-help' basis more and more of what they need in more manageable, attractive and dynamic ways than can be done with the production of student handbooks and support materials. These offer not only opportunities to supplement what has been available, but also to change the overarching pedagogic assumptions to those that have constructivist ideas at their core, namely that students can rely less on prepared materials and more on exploration of information and resources, creating their own learning and support to a greater extent than ever before.

Does place still matter?

Some 30 years ago when the OU was established there was a need to be 'near' the students, that is to say the fundamental shape of the organisation was defined in the form of a headquarters-periphery model. It was at the headquarters that the writing of courses took place, together with central organisational direction and core administrative and operational services. However, a network of thirteen Regional Centres was established more or less at the same time to support the even greater network of some 260 study centres, where in turn students met tutors. The primary locus of contact for students was the tutor in her or his region, and the services provided by the Regional Centre. There was no other way to conceive proximity at that time within the context both of technology and the social culture of learning and teaching. The impact of ICT on this core design characteristic is only just being understood, and has yet to be acted on in any consistent and agreed way. For example, now that course teams located at the headquarters can and do relate to their tutors through electronically supported conferences, this radically changes the division of labour which hitherto has meant that almost all support given to tutors has been delivered from faculty staff based in Regional Centres.

The greater complexity of programmes of study leads now to more than eighty awards being available, as against the one award of the BA with or without Honours back in the early 1970s. The greater plurality of programmes, including the emerging importance of work-related programmes such as social work and initial teacher training with their relationships to employers and workplaces, brings a plurality of students with distinct, in addition to common needs. On the volume side, registered student numbers have grown to some 200,000. The combination of the dimension of scale and complexity also throws up significant challenges to the imperatives of accuracy and timeliness of information and support to students: who knows the answers to the questions that the students now ask, and how quickly can that expertise be found in order to be able to respond in an acceptable way? Thus the former ways of working with generalists available everywhere are having to give way to expertise available from perhaps only one location. Where a programme is supported for the whole of the UK and

Continental Western Europe from one location, rather than the 'traditional' distribution of labour across all thirteen regions, the question quickly comes into focus as to why the concept of a Regional Centre is needed, at least for the smaller and more specialist programmes of study. In what sense do these students relate to any regional sense of identity, or do they rather relate to a 'Programme identity' which is geographically independent and electronically free of location. In other words, does place still matter? Further, in the context of the regionalisation of HE and the increased importance of the workplace as a setting for learning with associated partnerships with employers and trades unions, it is necessary to ask whether the traditional headquarters-periphery model represents a dated structure. It may be possible to conceive a networked institution, with faculty distributed across the UK rather than based in the centre of England. This may be particularly the case for the curriculum areas with strong links to the professions such as education, health and social welfare, and management. Place and proximity can be expected to remain important in the organisation of services for learners, albeit at least in part for different reasons. Re-thinking the purposes of the Regional Centres in many distance teaching institutions founded in the 1970s and 1980s thus represents a core task for the next five to ten years.

In all of this it can be seen how the advent of ICT demands a fundamental examination of the ways in which the core tasks of supporting enquiry, application, teaching and assessment can be carried out, and that these affect in deep, not surface, ways the organisational structures in education, as in other service industries such as insurance or banking.

External factors

Consumer behaviour

The identification of the learner as a consumer has been most consistently attended to by Field (1994; 2000). The main thesis is that when institutions are in competition, working practices have to foreground the student interest as a consumer, and therefore the student should be constructed as the customer. It is certainly true in the UK that the OU had in the beginning a near monopoly in most parts of the country in serving adult students with part-time degrees, challenged only and to a limited degree by the University of London External Studies Programme and the tutorial colleges that supported it, and by Birkbeck College in London for those who could attend it. The situation thirty years later would have seemed incredible then: that of the 130 or so HE institutions now in existence the majority offer some part-time study, and many also offer some opportunity for distance study. Some universities have as many as 50 per cent of their student body as 'mature' students. The multi-mode university is on the horizon, where students can move between full and part-time, and campus and distance based modes, in a relatively seamless way according to their life situation over a number of years. This offers a very serious challenge to the single mode distance teaching university. The OU UK has to work harder and harder and to spend more and more money on advertising and promotional activities in order to meet government directed recruitment targets in such a competitive situation, as the following suggests:

> The cost of attracting a new undergraduate student and converting them to registration in response to advertising or direct marketing was £395 in the year 2000.
>
> (Open University Retention Project report, 2001, p. 1)

While one could question the wisdom in the UK context as a whole of using public finance to pay for publicity for so many universities to compete against each other, there is considerable truth in that students can first choose in many instances between institutions in ways that were never before possible, and second, that they bring expectations from other contexts like shopping or travel and expect to find a level of service that regards their interest as primary rather than secondary to university academics and systems. This is reflected in the time now expected for queries to be answered, and what is termed the 'complaint culture', that more and more complaints are received about the quality of service. This last change has been influential in changing the ways in which services to students have been organised, with a move towards the Call Centre supported by web-provided information and guidance, and a centrally-based student complaints office.

It is worth noting that the rise of both consumerism and the notion of the student as customer derives from a number of streams in social development. Core to these is the construction of education as a commodity, with its providers as competitors in a market. Thus while on the one hand the elevation of the student to the status of customer may enhance her or his self-esteem, and no doubt removes the legitimacy of using academic status as an excuse for ignoring the needs of learners, it can only be done at the same time as market-related fees and institutional competition are introduced for education, in an overarching context of neo-liberal approaches to social policy. In such a scenario the individual who cannot afford the fees cannot become a customer (or student). The notion of the student as customer is therefore not 'ideology free', but belongs to a larger agenda of the endorsement of neo-liberal approaches to policy very dominant at present in industrialised countries.

The extent to which the customer notion can work effectively in the educational context (as well as other similar areas of practice such as medicine) is problematic. The issue can be highlighted by the term the 'naïve customer', i.e. in the educational context can she or he really know what is on sale when the ability to judge derives to a significant extent from what is gained from study itself. In other words, the act of purchase often takes place with inadequate customer understanding, and must be supported by professional advice. Further, for as long as educational institutions such as universities carry the authority for credential award, i.e. the right to award or not to award qualifications, the customer cannot always be right, or at least cannot always have what she or he wants. However, because educational institutions cannot control the environments in which they work, they must respond to the trend that sees students behaving as consumers and customers. Sewart has argued that this means educational institutions must behave in many ways as a service industry, with systems and quality standards to match (Sewart, 2001a).

Working hours

Working hours in the UK are the highest in the EU (Business in the Community, 2001). The Paid Educational Leave Campaign has also stated that:

> Research demonstrates that lack of time is one of the biggest barriers to people taking up learning. Research has also highlighted the high social costs associated with training outside of work. For example, a recent study into the effects on the home and family life of nurses, midwives and other NHS staff found that 49% of interviewees undertaking continuing education courses in their own time found it a strain, 10% thought it was causing serious detrimental effects.
>
> (Paid Educational Leave Campaign, n.d.)

Thus, while at one and the same time we have governmental policy which places lifelong learning more and more as an imperative both for the economic success of the UK and for individuals in order to stay employable, it can be surmised that pressures from the workplace have made success more and more difficult. Certainly, increased pressure from work is jointly cited as the largest single difficulty contributing to withdrawal by OU students, along with pace and workload of the course, both being cited as the principal reason by 36 per cent of students who withdraw (and these could of course represent some common causal explanation) (Open University Retention Project Report, 2001, p. 20). The issue is such that the Paid Educational Leave Campaign has been established within the UK, supported by the OU. The campaign was initiated within the Trades Union movement and aims to promote legislation that would permit time off as a statutory right for study in organisations above a certain size (Paid Educational Leave Campaign, 2002). Such legislation, already in place in the majority of EU member states, typically gives five or six days paid leave for study of an approved type (this was implemented in Sweden as long ago as 1974). This development is of particular importance for those concerned with open and distance learning, which has unfortunately assisted in masking the real implications of time for study in its rhetoric about flexibility. (This has implicitly and even explicitly at times promoted the idea that study by adults, especially in vocational contexts, can be shifted into the individual's private time and out of paid time ('You don't need to send your employees to college', is not an unfamiliar promotional statement to employers from providers of open and distance learning). The increasing acceptance by employers of open and distance learning methods is thus a double-edged sword in terms of the lives of employees.

In conclusion, the intensification of working hours in many industrialised countries, reinforced by the greater distances that many people now have to travel to work and the decreasing quality of road and rail infrastructure, makes the pressure on learners more and more intense when they engage in part-time study of any sort, but especially so when that study does not involve time which can be clearly marked out to employers as involving attendance at an institution. Lifelong learning policy masks a pincer movement of driving the population more and more towards compulsory or semi-compulsory learning throughout one's life in a credential-led society, and at the same time making it increasingly difficult. Thus new categories of elites and the marginalised are unwittingly created, and social divisions reinforced by the very institutions and ideologies that were established to challenge them. In rethinking what the institution can do about managing hours of study for learners, the external dimension of societal change cannot realistically be ignored, either in the institution's interest, or in the interest of the student. Large universities do, however, have the capacity to influence policy both individually and through national organisations such as the Vice Chancellors' Committee (now entitled Universities UK), and have responsibility to act on the external dimension in support of their sphere of activity, as indeed do most large commercial organisations.

Living conditions

A further dimension of external social change relevant to the OU is the nature of living conditions, and their suitability for home-based study. The adoption of distance and flexible learning methods has seen the positing of the home as a campus over the last thirty years, and the advent of the World Wide Web has redoubled that trend, seeing the arrival of a range of resources including world class libraries in potentially every house on the street, along with the PC as a workstation. However, while the digital divide is well written about, the relationship of homelessness, temporary accommodation and overcrowding to education is relatively little studied. Shelter, a UK housing NGO, produced a research report in 1995 which examined this issue from the perspective of children whose education suffers because of temporary accommodation following homelessness, and noted that there had been a four-fold increase in homelessness between 1980 and 1994. In that latter year, there were in the UK some 54,000 homeless families living in temporary accommodation including 60,000 children (Power, Whitty and Youdell, 1995, p. 8). This figure excludes street sleepers. By 2002 the number of children living in homeless households had risen to 102,000, while the number of households living in temporary accommodation had risen to 78,000, representing an 8.5 per cent rise from the previous year (figures relate to England only). Once again Shelter explicitly comments on the negative effects on children's education, as well as on health and happiness (Shelter, 2002). In the same period it was also reported that 'The number of households in England has overtaken the number of homes for the first time since records began', identifying overcrowding as an increasing problem (*Observer* newspaper, 2002). The point to be drawn out in this context is that discussion of learner support for adults as well as for children should take into account the needs of those in overcrowded conditions or temporary accommodation, and should not assume that potential learners have space and quiet in which to pursue their studies (this issue has been addressed in the South African context: see SAIDE, 1999). While it might be argued that in terms of a hierarchy of need, education is not going to be high on the list of street sleepers (although I have had one homeless student with the OU UK who used the post office as a mailing address), this is surely not the case with those who have accommodation even if of an inadequate kind, and for whom education may provide an essential route for personal and vocational development to better circumstances. The need therefore remains in the UK context for a minority of students and unknown proportion of potential students for study space in study centres, libraries, Community Centres, or the newer development of 'Telecentres' where ICT facilities represent an additional and increasingly important service for the marginalised (Latchem and Walker, 2001). While this sort of need might be thought to be restricted to developing country contexts, increased divisions in the industrialised world create first and third world conditions in the same society. Services to learners cannot therefore simply ignore the mapping of study facilities for students, especially the substantial minority of the population of the UK who live outside the magic circle of financial adequacy and stability. Any attempt to widen partici-pation further in higher education will surely need to address learner support from this perspective.

The impact of government policy

Governmental policy in the UK impacts in this context with two further main pressure points. First, the expansion of participation in higher education to 40 per cent of the population at school leaving age, with the intention to drive this upwards to 50 per cent, and the supplementary reward through funding of recruitment of traditionally non-participative populations, means that competition from other higher education institutions for part-time adult students has, as already noted, become intense. It also means that the pool of 'second chance' students is changing in nature to one where support, it could legitimately be argued, is more not less important. Second, the government's commitment to reshaping the ways in which we understand the UK as a looser collection of regional groupings is seen most dramatically in the granting of a significant degree of devolution to Scotland with its own Parliament driving educational policy amongst other areas. Within England the Regional Development Authorities are also increasingly demonstrating their interest in regional dimensions of HE provision, with funding made available for a range of research and development as well as course provision activities (Higher Education Funding Council for England, 2001). Thus a university founded on a political settlement from the 1970s, and a division of labour that suggests essentially that programmes and courses are uniformly delivered across all four nations of the UK, has significant challenges to its core concept, its division of labour, and its cost effectiveness, which all impact on the ways in which structures to support learners are organised. While the uniformity of the ways in which services have been organised across thirteen Regional Centres may diminish with the advent of electronically delivered communication for significant elements within the range of learner support services, there may at the same time be the need to grow the OU presence in regions and the nation states that make up the UK in order to be able to play an adequate role in the ways in which HE is going to be organised in the future. This may represent an essential element in any strategy for re-thinking learner support organisational structures in the OU, and indeed more widely in a 'Europe of the Regions', as has already been the case with EuroStudyCentres (see European Association of Distance Teaching Universities, 2002).

Engagement

Finally, this chapter examines contemporary developments, in particular as they relate to ICT and Call Centres, that support and/or threaten student 'engagement'. The term 'engagement' helps us to reflect on the elements that support the persistence of students, i.e. their desire and capacity to relate strongly to the institution and persist with a programme of study. For many students in more conventional situations this is likely to come from their families and peers, and from one or more members of staff who attract significant interest and admiration, and/or offer significant support of one kind or another. This is no less true for mature adult students than it is for young adults going to college at the age of 18 or so (Earwaker, 1992; Asbee and Simpson, 1998). Marton and Säljö's well-known distinction between surface and deep learning, much used at a certain period in discussion of learning in distance education (see Morgan, 1993), allows us to posit that students may also engage emotionally and learn in deep and surface ways (and indeed these are likely to be closely related). While the pressures of time and the formally or informally compulsory nature of lifelong learning may push some students towards a more and more instrumental approach to learning opportunities, thus reinforcing both shallow engagement and learning, there is no evidence that for most adults the activity will be affectively 'lite'. Rather we can expect it to continue to offer significant opportunity and/or threat to self-esteem and personal development. A core challenge for learner support for the OU as well as for other distance learning providers will therefore be to find ways to support that engagement in the face of the pressures of time, etc. sketched out in this chapter, within the light-touch environments of the World Wide Web and Call Centres that are increasingly influential. Distance teaching institutions have to recreate the traditional ways in which attachment can be created, whose intensity is generated through place and individuals across time.

It is precisely this mix which the OU UK is at the first stages of adumbrating for the future. While for a small minority of programmes there will be the replacement of all other media by web-supported environments, policy for teaching and learning as well as for student support proposes a mix for the majority, the so-called blended learning environment (see Stenning and Hemsworth, 2001 for a recent account of the importance of 'putting a name to a face' in the OU UK context). While more than 70,000 students relate to the OU through electronic means at least in part, the variability of practice with regard to computer con-

ferencing, legitimately seen as offering opportunity for peer–peer support, ranges
in fact across the extremely successful to the wholly unsuccessful. The blended
learning environment might draw from mainstream organisational experience, to
wit that there is an informal hierarchy for communication which moves from email
to telephone in the advent of a certain level of complexity or delicacy, and again
from telephone to face-to-face when that is further felt to be necessary. There is
no evidence in academic continuing professional development that face-to-face
meeting is on the decline – viz. the increased number of conferences advertised
and attended – and thus no reason to think that anything other than a blended
environment would be attractive and adequate for the majority of learners and
programmes of study, at least for the foreseeable future. In this context Sewart
insists on the continued importance of personal intervention as a strategy of 'attack'
for the OU UK, seeking out students who find themselves in need of support, for
example when the information system picks up that they have not sent in an
assignment, or at the time of year when choices about future study should be
made (Sewart, 2001b). In this way a 'real' human being intervenes by telephone
as a result of prompts from a sophisticated management information system. It is
planned that continuity of interest (the generation of engagement across time)
will be supported by the student's own WebPage, which offers a record of progress
and reflection on study which can be shared with tutors and student advisors (the
OU response to the HE Funding Council demands that all HE institutions support
the building by each student of a 'Personal Development Portfolio').

Evidence of what works

There remain crucial and as yet relatively unresearched aspects of learner support,
despite thirty years of modern distance education. Primary amongst these are
answers to the question as to what evidence there is as to the actual effects of
learner support systems and services in all their variety. For example, if student
success is taken as the primary output of an ODL system, at what point does the
law of diminishing return begin to reduce the worthwhileness of further investment
in learner support? We have evidence that students find learner support useful,
that they like it and indeed want more of it. But the difficulty from the ethical
point of view of setting up control groups of registered and paying students who
do not have access to services available to others has made it impossible to give
answers to such questions. Where we have had systems with little learner support
at all, such as unsupported students in the University of London external system
or that of UNISA in South Africa until the recent past, the evidence is so complicated by variables, in the latter case of the effects of apartheid, that it is very difficult
to say with surety that we know what the results of not having learner support in
distance education are, over and above the general observation that systems with
little or no learner support seem to have high levels of drop-out and non-completion
(Tait, 1994). While it may currently be the case that commitment to learner support
services are substantially driven by values, culture and expectations in a particular
social and educational context, the increased role of business management methods

in education as a whole means that more evidence-based practice is rightly necessary. Evaluation of changes make an invaluable contribution, although too often in the press of events that drive institutional change, evaluation seems to be overlooked, even in relatively wealthy and sophisticated institutions.

Conclusion

In sum, the range of issues discussed in this chapter lead to the conclusion that a fundamental review is needed of learner support in the OU UK and in distance education more widely. Signs of such a review taking place in the OU UK are indeed in evidence at the time of writing, although the recognition of the issues of time and place for study are not in this writer's view adequately foregrounded. A learner-centred rather than an institution-centred review would need to begin with an assessment of the learner's world, beginning with the challenging question of 'Who is the learner?' (see Tait, 2000 for discussion of a planning mechanism for learner support in distance education). The review would need to address how learner support impacts on the core issues of study/life conflict management and student workload, academic support, space and facilities for study, and lastly student 'engagement'. It would need to take into account the external influences on learners' lives as well as the internal levers available to the institution. The role of the workplace as a site of learning and the impact of devolution and regionalisation within the UK will demand recognition, perhaps even bringing about the possibility of a networked rather than a centre-periphery model. Such a review would need to be prepared to reshape organisational structures while identifying and incorporating lasting values. Further, it would need to acknowledge change in learner behaviour brought by the migration from student to consumer/customer status as well as the role of ICT, in particular as it relates to place. Above all, there must be a recognition that the plurality of learners found in the variety of programmes of study that exist in any large institution will demand a plurality, not uniformity of approaches. While this challenges the cost-effectiveness of the 'one size fits all' systems that have characterised large scale distance teaching over the last thirty years, there is no way back to a simpler world from the point of view of either curriculum or learner support.

References

Asbee, S. and Simpson, O. (1998) Partners, families, and friends: student support of the closest kind, *Open Learning*, 13 (3), pp. 56–64.

Business in the Community (2001) British workforce allegedly fed up with working so hard, *Business in the Community web site 07/01*, http://www.business-impact.org/bi2/news/see_news_item.cfm?newsid=282&specific=Jul01 (site visited July 2001).

Earwaker, J. (1992) *Helping and Supporting Students* (Buckingham: Society for Research into Higher Education/Open University Press).

European Association of Distance Teaching Universities, EuroStudyCentres Info, www.eadtu.nl/eurostudycentres/escinfo/content.htm (site visited May 2002).

Field, J. (1994) Open learning and consumer culture, *Open Learning*, 9 (2), pp. 3–11.

Field, J. (2000) *Lifelong Learning and the New Educational Order* (Stoke on Trent: Trentham Books).

Higher Education Funding Council for England (2001) *Higher Education and the Regions,* HEFCE Policy Statement, www.hefce.ac.uk/pubs/2001/01_18.htm (site visited April 2002).

Latchem, C. and Walker, D. (2001) *Telecentres: Case Studies and Key Issues*, Perspectives on Distance Education Series (Vancouver: Commonwealth of Learning).

Morgan, A. (1993*) Improving Your Students' Learning: Reflections on the Experience of Study* (London: Kogan Page).

Observer newspaper (2002) New homes crisis hits UK families, 28 April, www.observer. co.uk_news/story/0,6903,706559,00.html (site visited 1 May 2002).

Open University, Retention Project Team (2001) *Report of the Student Retention Project 'A Strategy for Improved Student Retention'*, Internal Document OU/01/1 (Milton Keynes: Open University).

Paid Educational Leave Campaign (n.d.) Special briefing for members of Learning Skills Councils (London: UNIFI).

Paid Educational Leave Campaign, www.paid-educational-leave.org.uk (site visited April 2002).

Perry, W. (1976) *Open University* (Milton Keynes: Open University Press).

Power, A., Whitty, G. and Youdell, D. (1995) *No Place to Learn: Homelessness and Education* (London: Shelter).

SAIDE (South African Institute for Distance Education) (1999) *Learner Support in Distance Learning: a South African Perspective* (Johannesburg: SAIDE).

Sewart, D. (2001a) The future for services to students, in papers presented to the 20th World Conference of the International Council for Open and Distance Education, Düsseldorf, 7–12, Student Services, Open University, Milton Keynes.

Sewart, D. (2001b) Pro-active Student Support in a Developing Electronic World, Student Policy Board SPB/8/22, mimeograph, Open University, Milton Keynes.

Shelter (2002) Press Release 11 April 2002, www.shelter.org.uk/about/press/viewpress release.asp?PressReleaseID+87 (site visited 30 April 2002).

Stenning, M. and Hemsworth, M. (2001) Wanting to put a name to the face, *Adults Learning*, 13 (4), pp. 21–23.

Tait, A. (1994) The end of innocence: critical approaches to open and distance learning, in *Open Learning*, 9 (3), 27–36.

Tait, A. (1996) Conversation and community: student support in open and distance learning', in Mills, R. and Tait, A. (eds), *Supporting the Learner in Open and Distance Learning* (London: Pitman), pp. 59–72.

Tait, A. (1998) Guidance and counselling in the Open University, in Crawford, M., Edwards, E. and Kydd, L. (eds), *Taking Issue: Debates in Guidance and Counselling in Learning* (London: Routledge), pp. 115–27.

Tait, A. (2000) Planning student support for open and distance learning, *Open Learning*, 15 (3), pp. 287–99.

16 Collaborative on-line learning

Transforming learner support and course design

Mary Thorpe

Posing the question

Open and distance learning (ODL) is characterised by a more diverse range of practices than ever before. Some of the traditional print and correspondence models are still viable and in use, while we have also developed the most advanced on-line environments to complement the more interactive technologies of CD-ROM and the web. ODL feels like a radically different experience for those practitioners who can look back from the most advanced technologies of today, to review what we were doing twenty or so years ago (Cochrane, 2000).

The purpose of this chapter, however, is to review the implications for how we conceptualise learner support of on-line-intensive and interactive forms of learning and teaching. The focus therefore is on courses where students have electronic access to resources and where they are expected to be in regular contact on-line with their peers and tutor(s). The key feature will be that they work in a virtual learning environment, which begins and ends with on-line interaction. Collaborative forms of learning where these are achieved provide a particularly demanding context for both tutors and learners and one which challenges our conventional models of learner support.

In a context such as this, the substance and meaning of on-line activities is determined by the particular students who work together on-line. Their tutor may play a very direct role also, helping shape these interactions, sometimes designing the activities themselves in order to suit particular needs of the current group. There may be little if any fixed body of content common to all learners. The OU's Masters in Open and Distance Education is one such programme, and includes courses with a much smaller proportion than usual of course material prepared by the course team. Since students may also surf the Net to find articles that fit their interests, it is not even clear that there *is* a defined body of material which creates a shared framework for all students.

This raises the question of where the boundaries now lie between learner support and course design and development. As an author of postgraduate course material for students of open and distance learning (Thorpe, 1999), I find this an interesting dilemma. Traditionally, learner support is seen as that which happens *after* the course materials have been made. Its function is usually defined as enabling learners to study successfully and to develop their own understandings of the material. As Tait (2000) defines it, the common assumption is that student support is 'the range of services both for individuals and for students in groups *which complement the course materials* or learning resources that are uniform for all learners and which are often perceived as the major offering of institutions using ODL'.

Such boundaries, however, no longer hold in on-line courses where collaborative learning plays a major role. If much of the content of such a course is generated through on-line interaction and collaborative activities, how can we consider course design without also dealing with learner support at the same time? And where does one locate on-line interaction – within course design or learner support? Where so much of the content of the course cannot be specified in advance because it is the process and substance that takes place in the on-line interactions, course design and learner support start to merge. Furthermore, since learner support is no longer an add-on to a predefined course, but itself defines what the course becomes, the old model of course design first, learner support second, should be questioned and possibly reversed. Only when we have decided what can be delivered through on-line interaction, will we be in a position to design 'content' and create course materials.

Learner support as a technical term in open and distance learning (ODL)

Learner support is a technical term for a particular set of practices, which have been developed within ODL, and it is with this technical meaning that I am concerned here. The everyday meaning of 'support', particularly the idea that all aspects of ODL should facilitate learning and the learner's well-being, is still relevant but not my primary concern here. We can assert that *all* aspects of an institution's provision, from the enquiry desk through to the quality of the interface on the CD-ROM, should be supportive in the sense of fostering high quality learning. However, distance education practitioners have developed the term 'learner support' to identify a distinctive and important set of practices carried out at a different time and often (though not necessarily) by a different group of people from those producing the course materials – up until, that is, the use of on-line and collaborative learning.

'Learner support' is not a term that has much currency within campus-based higher education. In that context, it often refers to provision that must be made for handling personal difficulties which grow too great for the student to handle alone. Such provision is oriented to *exceptional* needs arising for a minority of students, although there has also been a growth in services such as careers guidance and study skills, that are relevant to the student body as a whole. Learner support in ODL refers to the meeting of needs that *all* learners have because they are central to high quality learning – guidance about course choice, preparatory diagnosis, study skills, access to group learning in seminars and tutorials, and so on. These are the elements in systems of learner support that many practitioners see as essential for effective provision of ODL (Keegan, 1996; Moore and Kearsley, 1996).

However, important though many of those writing in this field believe it to be, Sewart (1993) notes that a review of key areas of the literature back to 1978 did not reveal any comprehensive analysis of learner support services (see also Robinson, 1995). It is therefore particularly challenging to address the issue of learner support in on-line learning. Can we just 'add on' the web and CMC as a new medium through which support is provided, or do we need to reconceptualise learner support?

In what follows I shall occasionally use Nipper's terminology of 'second generation' and 'third generation' to indicate large-scale shifts in the way we teach at a distance brought about by the use of the web and CMC (Nipper, 1989). However, this should not be used to over-simplify such technology applications and their effects. Third generation ODL will not necessarily be collaborative and constructivist (Jonassen *et al.*, 1995; Garrison, 1997) just by virtue of the use of these technologies. The social interaction and virtual presence that can be delivered, require the integration of both pedagogy and technology and practical commitment to collaboration in learning. Whether or not third generation ODL *is* collaborative and constructivist, will depend on how the technology is used.

Meanings of learner support

ODL sub-systems with distinctive roles – learner support individualising, humanising

Keegan (1996) identifies two distinct sub-systems within distance education: course development and student or learner support services, which he characterises as 'the essential feedback mechanisms that are characteristic of education', distinguishing it from the publishing house or materials producer (Keegan, 1996, p. 156).

Tait has expanded this emphasis on learner support as the key means through which uniform course materials are articulated with the interests of diverse groups of students, as individuals and as learning groups (Tait, 1995). He sees this role as complementary to that of the materials, and he has also drawn attention to the humanistic tradition embodied in systems which provide for interpersonal interaction, identifying conversation and community as values which should not be lost in technicist approaches to system or learning management (Tait, 1996). Research into the experiences of individual learners has stressed how important this dimension of enjoyment and relationship can be in fostering personal transformation (Evans, 1994; Lunneborg, 1994, 1997).

Institutional intermediaries

Sewart defines learner support as the means through which individuals are enabled to make use of institutionalised provision. Learner supporters are 'intermediaries', able to talk the language of the student/learner and to interpret the materials and procedures of complex bureaucratic organisations (Sewart, 1993). While course production might work within a management model appropriate to manufacturing industry, he likens learner support to a service industry, in which the needs of customers are paramount. Learner support activities are produced and consumed simultaneously, a process in which the learner/consumer must participate actively, as well as the tutor/supporter (Sewart, 1993, p. 7).

Interpersonal response

Thorpe has focused less on system implications and more on how to construct a definition which will locate the *functional essence* of what distinguishes learner support from other elements in the system (Thorpe, 1994, 1999). Learner support is defined as *all those elements capable of responding to a known learner or group of learners, before, during and after the learning process.* Course materials prepared in advance of study, however learner-centred and interactive they may be, cannot respond to a known learner. Even interactive programmes which react to input from the learner cannot make a response to the particular learner Jane Brown or Adam Smith, in the light of knowing Jane or Adam or their study group, as particular people studying here and now.

This is an important distinction, at a time when computer-based programmes are being developed with 'tutor' and similar terms in the title, although they cannot respond to a known learner or group of learners (Albert and Thomas, 2000). They offer automated supports or frameworks that structure on-line learning and reduce the load on human tutor or other support staff. They may therefore play an important role within a course or the support system loosely termed, but they are not as yet fully responsive to particular people and their actions as they learn.

The key function and elements in learner support

If we can no longer assume that there will be two distinct sub-systems with contrasting roles, does this imply that we no longer need a concept of learner support? In practical terms we have certainly found that on-line learners continue to need support. The difficulty comes where we try to conceptualise this in terms of two sub-systems or of a complementary addition to course materials, neither of which really fits where courses are taught through a collaborative on-line process.

However, this is where a functional rather than a systems-related definition is particularly helpful. If learner support is defined as 'all those elements capable of responding to a known learner or group of learners, before during and after the learning process' (as outlined above), no assumptions are made about the nature of the course or the sub-systems and structure of the provision in question. This definition also brings together elements that are a common feature of other definitions and uses of the term, and provides an effective starting point. Instead of relating learner support to types of system, it relates it to its key function of response and responsiveness, in relation to three essential and inter-related elements – *identity, time/duration and interaction.*

Identity

Identity is crucial because it indicates that a learner support system must include the possibility of responding to and interacting with a person or group known to the learner supporter. Note that relating to the individual may or may not be central here. Individualisation is not essential on those programmes where the key learning 'unit' is the group. Learner support therefore should not be tied only to efforts which support individual learners, albeit that for many systems response to individual learners is a key capacity in learner support and one of its most exploited features.

However the important point is that the learner supporter knows that the enquirer or learner is a person with an identity that influences their response. Such information about identity as it exists may be slight – perhaps not much more than gender and date of registration, but even that can make a material and significant difference to the content and style of interactions for the purpose of learner support. It does also signify that learner support is essentially to do with interpersonal interaction – until such time as we have machines in use that can be conscious of human identity in the way described here.

This reveals of course how culturally specific learner support is and therefore how important it is to be alert to cultural differences between learners and their supporters, as well as across the learner population itself. On-line learning that crosses cultural and national boundaries will need to be especially sensitive to these issues. All learner support needs to be sensitive to the way in which identities change in parallel often with progress through a course or programme of study. Support needs to be modulated not only in relation to the person but to the stage they are at and the changes they have experienced.

Time and duration

Time and duration are therefore already foregrounded in focusing on identity. But they are also essential in the sense that learner support is about a 'live' process which has duration – it is the process experienced by individuals and groups, from the point of considering study, choosing whether or not to study, through studying and then ending study or progressing further. By contrast, course design is about planning for something to happen – the designer may be very active in creating the course but 'the course' or more properly the course material, is an object without duration until the moment it is taught or studied. Learner support is a process defined by the duration of actions performed by actual and potential learners, which in turn are affected by the actions of their supporters, whether planned and intended or not. Learner support is in that sense therefore a dynamic process, in which the impact of interventions is never wholly predictable. Not only must the supporter respond or act within a particular time frame, but their response will also influence what happens in future and the speed of the response. This will be the case even where learner support occurs asynchronously, because it will still be by definition within the real time of that learner or learner group's study activity.

Interaction

Interaction, specifically interpersonal interaction, is key to all main theories of learner support because it is the only way of addressing the needs of learners *in the terms in which those learners wish to express themselves.* The distinctive capacity of persons is that they can respond whatever the input, providing they understand the language used. An 'interactive' CD-ROM for example allows inputs from the learner but within a tight prespecified framework and with a response based on a limited set of predicted inputs. By contrast, a tutor can respond appropriately virtually whatever input a student makes, and can develop a dialogue from that input, addressing specifically whatever it is that concerns that particular person or group of people. Interpersonal interaction thus is part of the functional essence in that it represents the most flexible and open-ended form of interaction we can deliver.

Contexts for learner support

There are two contexts within which the interactive process of learner support happens: the institutional context and the course or teaching context. The availability at times of need arising within both contexts is crucial to provision of effective support. Learners need support with regard to their operation within both:

1   institutional systems (such as knowing what is on offer, how to apply, how to claim a refund, make a payment, choose a course, etc.) before, during and after course study; and
2   the course they are studying, such as how best to complete a particular assignment, how to contact and work with other students on the course, how to make sense of something in the course materials, whether their contributions to the course conference are relevant, well conceived or otherwise, and so on. It is in this area particularly that CMC and the web are challenging our concept of learner support.

Learner support is essentially about roles, structures and environments, therefore: support roles and supportive people, together with support structures and supportive environments. On-line teaching and learning is generating new forms of support and challenging our existing view of ODL systems. Where learner support is available on demand at any time, from the learner's perspective, such services are probably a more continuous and available feature of ODL than any other.

The impact of collaborative on-line teaching and learning

On-line teaching impacts on both the institutional context and the course study context for learner support. There is currently a mixed economy for many institutions, in terms not only of whether CMC and the web are used but how essential they are for the achievement of learned outcomes (Moran and Myringer, 1999).

However, my purpose here is to identify the categorical changes being brought about by the collaborative on-line model, and this is the focus for what follows.

Interaction built-in to course design

Collaborative on-line courses are designed from the beginning in order to take advantage of the interactive potential of on-line learning. In this context, the on-line tutor represents a new kind of animal in ODL. Let us suppose here a model where the tutors of the course carry authority to create the detailed course teaching as it progresses over the duration of the course, rather in the way a conventional university lecturer might decide how they were to teach introductory history, working within the broad parameters of what their department had decided that 'introductory history' should be. Such tutors must of course be content experts, but they will also need even more skills of learning facilitation than the conventional tutor of a second generation distance education course.

In the case of this and other similar courses, the traditional model of learner support does not hold. Learner support will not be about complementing a pre-existing and self-contained set of materials designed for individual study. There may be some course materials prepared in advance, but probably fewer than the conventional course, and if existing resources on the web are used, these will come with virtually none of the structure that we would expect to be built-in to a second generation distance education course. It is the purpose of the on-line inter-action *to use the learners themselves as a resource*, and to build on their experience, reading and perspectives.

This is the design of teaching being used in on-line masters courses such as those taught at the OU UK. In the case of two courses in the OU Masters in Open and Distance Education for example, a relatively small volume of text-based resources has been designed in advance to launch each section of the course and to provide 'bearings' to guide a programme of on-line interaction and much less structured reading. The major focus for student learning is the programme of activities, which their group tackles on-line, in conferences facilitated by their tutor and increasingly by the group itself. Stimulation of a critical grasp of knowledge, and deep processing of the meanings of both resources and practice in ODL, are fostered by continuous assessment and by the on-line discussions in tutor groups. These number about a dozen students to each tutor/facilitator, who is contracted to spend several hours every week in on-line interaction and support of various kinds. Staff/student ratios at the OU UK are more usually one tutor to twenty to twenty-five students on average, with much lower hours for interaction with students expected of the role.

A constructivist approach to teaching and learning

The pedagogical design of these courses builds on a constructivist approach to teaching and learning. Learners and tutor work together intensively on personal meaning construction in which learners seek to integrate their own experience with resources provided by the course team or teaching institution. In the case of the OU MA in Open and Distance Education a strongly collaborative approach has been built onto this approach, emphasising the values of peer facilitation and mutual support through construction of an on-line learning community. In this context not only do students get to know each other on-line very quickly and in some depth, but groups can take on a different character and quite different experiences can be had depending on which group a student happens to be in. A student also has the choice of how they present themselves, and can to some extent manipulate the kind of personality they present through their words and actions. Studying together will certainly bring their identities into play, possibly more intensively than even face-to-face study opportunities typically allow.

Such a model is now a familiar idea and rallying ground in the literature of ODL. It is in fact easier to conjure up the ideal model of collaborative and conversational learning as a construct than as lived reality. It takes considerable ingenuity, design and appropriate educational goals in order to achieve a course where interaction on-line is *absolutely essential in order to pass*, rather than a highly desirable enrichment. Nonetheless, it is often celebrated in terms which draw attention to its ideal features, by contrast with those of large scale 'industrialised' forms of distance education. Garrison and Anderson, for example, contrast the two in terms of 'big and little distance education', in an article which extols the values of LDE (little distance education) for the elitist research universities (Garrison and Anderson, 1999).

While the contrast may be over-drawn, on-line teaching which does not include the highly designed course materials of second generation courses, but which *does* aim for the intensive on-line constructivist model of learning, is a radical change. There is a challenge to the basic assumption of two sub-systems, the one coming after the other and being primarily concerned with learning facilitation not with course production. A fixed body of knowledge has not been created 'out there' for both tutor and learner to relate to. Who and what is 'in authority' may be less clear, and the relationship between learners and supporters similarly more fluid and open.

Second generation DE and on-line, collaborative learning compared

To draw the contrast more clearly we might envision the second generation model of learner support (Figure 16.1) as a three-way traffic around the 'triangle' of course materials, tutor and learner, with the learning group an occasional 'event' on the side, for those students who choose to take up the option for a tutorial, face-to-face or otherwise. The lines of communication between both tutor and student are quite heavily used, showing the overt interaction that is possible in a second generation ODL system with developed learner support enabling the individualisation of learning, counter-balancing the course materials. The model can also include intensive 'interaction' between the learner and the course materials,

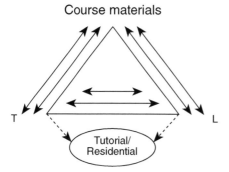

Course materials

T   L

Tutorial/
Residential

Key: T = Tutor L = Learner

Figure 16.1 Second generation ODL – learner support model

if they are designed for learner engagement and include many activities and approaches designed to encourage an active learning process.

On-line teaching by contrast (Figure 16.2) must include a fourth point of orientation, since the learning group itself creates such a focus of attention and study time (Burge, 1995). This constitutes a largely new source of ongoing interaction. Indeed the group process *is* the course to a great extent, and although resources are provided, their authority is deliberately lower than that of the conventional course, and the requirement on students to construct their own knowledge structures takes priority.

The availability of learners to each other and to the tutor asynchronously as well as synchronously, has the potential to overturn the emphasis on distance education as an individualised form of learning. The potential to create extensive dialogues and interchange electronically means that on-line teaching is often prioritising the learning group as the chief resource for learners and the focus for the tutor, rather than the needs of each individual learner, though these too can be accommodated if the pedagogical design supports that.

Implications for learner support and ODL systems

Drawing together the impact of the changes discussed above reveals a number of themes.

Creation of on-line or 'virtual' learning environments

The software interface and the design of web sites and conferencing architecture are new and powerful tools that institutions can use to shape the learning 'space' and influence learner use. Some of the earliest critics recognised the need to create an on-line culture which replaces the face-to-face and other cultures in which we feel confident about speaking and contributing. Feenberg's account of the loss of

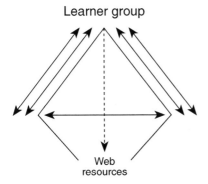

Figure 16.2 On-line and collaborative ODL – learner support model

all the usual cues of gesture, tone and indexicality of face-to-face communication is telling (Feenberg, 1989). Lacking these cues and scripts for interaction in familiar settings, misunderstandings and communication breakdown are an ever-present threat. Communication anxieties and identity management become issues for most contributors. Feenberg aptly comments: '*playing at computer conferencing consists in making moves that keep others playing. The goal is to prolong the game and avoid making the last move*' (Feenberg, 1989, p. 27). Mason (1994) has observed the persistence of reluctant minorities, who seem unwilling or unable to overcome the barriers and contribute effectively. Jones and Cawood (1998) document how students can and do subvert the purposes of on-line courses, and use existing methods of communication to make short cuts in achieving the ostensible goals of the on-line context.

Feenberg also refers to Goffman's term 'absorption' to account for the pleasure to be found when a group works well, each member sharing the purpose of the interaction and committing themselves to a community, albeit one established on a temporary basis. He and others have emphasised the need for participants to experience intrinsic rewards from participation, without which interaction may be spasmodic and ineffectual. Stratfold has summarised the essential features of conferencing systems designed to foster rewarding interaction (Stratfold, 1998).

Increased importance of learner support as a delivery mechanism

In the on-line teaching context, the quality of the learning experience is heavily dependent on the resources the group brings to bear and on the skill and commitment of their on-line tutor (Musselbrook *et al.*, 2000; Salmon, 2000). Where these both work well, the technology and social interaction truly enable the 'defeat of distance'. The content experts or course team can 'speak' directly to learners and if necessary become tutors themselves, thus teaching at a distance without the need for intermediaries in the form of tutors or other learner supporters.

However, teaching on-line, particularly fostering collaboration and a constructivist approach, requires novel skills and attitudes for many educators. Skills
required for the on-line teaching role are being defined by several authors (see
particularly Salmon, 2000). Indeed particular systems may benefit from setting
up several specialist roles, to manage different aspects (Tolley, 2000). A definitive
account of learner support at this stage is not feasible, given the new possibilities
opening up for video and audio communication. If global teaching and web sites
designed for cross-cultural participation increase as anticipated (Mason, 1998),
awareness of a wide range of cultural norms and expectations in the educational
context will also be needed. These will certainly require sensitivity to and accommodation of a variety of communication styles and preferences for formality (Collis
and Remmers, 1997).

A wider range of learning outcomes

The use of interactive technologies is also increasing the range of learning outcomes
achievable through learner support. Collaborative learning and IT skills development are new dimensions in ODL, made feasible by CMC in ways which neither
tutorials nor residential options could deliver. In courses which use the full potential
of the web and CMC, interactivity between learners is set up as the medium through
which many key course learning goals are to be achieved (Macdonald and Mason,
1998; Weller, 2000). A large element of the course is in effect what would be
called 'learner support' under second generation terminology. While the term now
sits rather awkwardly with the activity of on-line teaching, many practitioners
emphasise the enlarged importance of the quality of interactions set up and sustained
during course presentation.

The new group and community potential of distance education

The concerns of particular communities can now be addressed through bringing
local groups together and negotiating learning programmes. This is an enrichment
of the traditional 'independent learning' orientation of ODL, and an enlargement
of its value, in so far as individuals can work now within effective groups on a
continuing basis, as well as realise their own individual learning needs and
preferences (Garrison, 1997).

New skills and capabilities for learner supporters/learning facilitators

We can be assured that there will be no single model of on-line learner support.
We can anticipate that a variety of roles and titles will continue to develop, incorporating the range of local needs for support to the communication and discursive
requirements of particular courses and learning groups. Currently we are learning
new ways of creating social presence through textual and audio-visual communication, and how to design for supportive synchronous and asynchronous interaction

and collaboration on-line. Global teaching, and increased use of virtual presence through video and voice communication will bring new challenges and new combinations of content expertise and process expertise, to suit local needs.

Systemic changes within the institution as a whole

As Moore and Kearsley (1996) emphasise, such far reaching change in one area of a system brings change elsewhere. Learners can now interact on-line for all registration and administration functions, with on-line advice and support available in parallel with course-based support. There are also changes within the large scale capital-intensive institutions where the front-end loading of course production is changing. Lower initial production costs are feasible but costs during presentation are likely to increase, to sustain the IT infrastructure and realise the benefits of continual updating and learner support on-line.

Conclusion

In sum, 'learner support' is the arena within which transformations in the nature and the scale of activities made feasible by on-line teaching, are generating widespread change in pedagogies and learning communities, and across institutions as a whole in ODL. These are clearly manifest in both large and small-scale variants of ODL, and we are seeing the evolution of existing second generation approaches as well as the introduction of completely new on-line forms. The connotations of 'support' can foster misleading and unfortunate imagery – the crutch, leaning post or parental guide for example. Whereas our best on-line tutors are developing what Romiszowski (1997) has described as 'the technology of conversation' and our researchers are identifying the skills we require to develop as expert 'knowledge workers' (Eisenstadt and Vincent, 1998).

Technologies themselves do not guarantee progressive education, but they do provide certain affordances (Laurillard, 1993). The communicative dynamics that can be created through intensive design and build of on-line learning groups afford the possibility of greater communication – and greater challenge – for both learners and tutors/course creators. Learners can and do challenge the pedagogical assumptions as well as the knowledge claims of those in authority within such learning contexts. Naturally the challenge can extend to the values that as educators we are currently assigning to collaborative learning. Distance learners in some contexts have identified reduced freedom to study at their own pace and place, as a result of on-line collaborative approaches being used in their courses (Thorpe, 1998). Their right to surface both dissatisfaction as well as satisfaction, around this and other issues, and to engage their course tutors and the teaching institution in discussion of the choices available to them, is one of the more desirable potential outcomes of on-line communication. What matters is less how we line up with regard to our priorities and preferences, and more that we are open and willing ourselves to engage in the process-intensive and time-consuming on-line debate with both learners and colleagues. In the light of that assertion, collaborative teaching and learning support on-line offers distance educators an additional and a powerful means of achieving desirable educational goals.

References

Albert, S. and Thomas, C. (2000) A new approach to computer-aided distance learning: the 'automated tutor', *Open Learning*, 15 (2), pp. 141–50.

Burge, L. (1995) Electronic highway or weaving loom? Thinking about conferencing technologies for learning, in Lockwood, F. (ed.), *Open and Distance Learning Today* (London: Routledge).

Cochrane, C. (2000) The reflections of a distance learner 1977–1997, *Open Learning*, 15 (1), pp. 17–34.

Collis, B. and Remmers, E. (1997) The World Wide Web in education: issues related to cross-cultural communication and interaction, in Khan, B. H. (ed.), *Web-Based Instruction* (Englewood Cliffs, NJ: Educational Technology Publications Inc).

Eisenstadt, M. and Vincent, T. (2000) *The Knowledge Web: Learning and Collaborating on the Net* (London: Kogan Page).

Feenberg, A. (1989) The written world, in Mason, R. and Kaye, A. (eds), *Mindweave* (Oxford: Pergamon).

Garrison, D. R. (1997) Computer conferencing: the post industrial age of distance education, *Open Learning*, 12 (2), pp. 3–11.

Garrison, D. R. and Anderson, T. D. (1999) Avoiding the industrialization of research universities: big and little distance education, *American Journal of Distance Education*, 13 (2), pp. 48–63.

Harry, K. (ed.) (1999) *Higher Education Through Open and Distance Learning* (London: Routledge with the Commonwealth of Learning).

Jonassen, D., Davidson, M., Collins, M., Campbell, J. and Haag, B. B. (1995) Constructivism and computer-mediated communication in distance education, *American Journal of Distance Education*, 9 (2), pp. 7–25.

Jones, C. and Cawood, J. (1998) The unreliable transcript, contingent technology and informal practice in asynchronous learning networks, in Banks, S., Graebner, C. and McConnell, D. (eds), *Networked Lifelong Learning: Innovative Approaches to Education and Training Through the Internet* (The University of Sheffield: Centre for the Study of Networked Learning).

Keegan, D. (1996) *Foundations of Distance Education*, 3rd edition (London: Routledge).

Laurillard, D. (1993) *Rethinking University Teaching* (London: Routledge).

Lunneborg, P. (1994) *OU Women:Undoing Educational Obstacles* (London: Cassell).

Lunneborg, P. (1997) *OU Men: Work Through Lifelong Learning* (Cambridge: Lutterworth Press).

Macdonald, J. and Mason, R. (1998) Information handling skills and resource-based learning in an Open University course, *Open Learning*, 13 (1), pp. 38–42.

Mason, R. (1994) *Using Communications Media in Open and Flexible Learning* (London: Kogan Page).

Mason, R. (1998) *Globalising Education: Trends and Applications* (London: Routledge).

Moore, M. G. and Kearsley, G. (1996) *Distance Education: A systems view* (Belmont, CA: Wadsworth Publishing Company).

Moran, L. and Myringer, B. (1999) Flexible learning and university change, in Harry, K. (ed.), *Higher Education Through Open and Distance Learning* (London: Routledge with the Commonwealth of Learning).

Musselbrook, K., McAteer, E., Crook, C., Macleod, H. and Tolmie, A. (2000) Learning networks and communication skills, *ALT-J*, 8 (1), pp. 71–9.

Nipper, S. (1989) Third generation distance learning and computer conferencing, in Mason, R. and Kaye, A. (eds), *Mindweave* (Oxford: Pergamon Press).

Phillips, M., Scott, P. and Fage, J. (1998) Towards a strategy for the use of new technology in student guidance and support, *Open Learning*, 13 (2), pp. 52–8.

Robinson, B. (1995) Research and pragmatism in learner support, in Lockwood, F. (ed.), *Open and Distance Learning Today* (London: Routledge).

Romiszowski, A. J. (1997) Web based distance learning and teaching: revolution or reaction to necessity?, in B. H. Khan, (ed.), *Web-Based Instruction* (Englewood Cliffs, NJ: Educational Technology Publications Inc).

Salmon, G. (2000) *E-moderating: The Key to Teaching and Learning Online* (London: Kogan Page).

Sewart, D. (1993) Student support systems in distance education, *Open Learning*, 8 (3), pp. 3–12.

Stratfold, M. (1998) Promoting learner dialogues on the Web, in Eisenstadt, M. and Vincent, T. (eds), *The Knowledge Web: Learning and Collaborating on the Net* (London: Kogan Page).

Tait, A. (1995) Student support in open and distance learning, in Lockwood, F. (ed.), *Open and Distance Learning Today* (London: Routledge).

Tait, A. (1996) Conversation and community: student support in open and distance learning, in Mills, R. and Tait, A. (eds), *Supporting the Learner in Open and Distance Learning* (London: Pitman).

Tait, A. (2000) Planning student support for open and distance learning, *Open Learning*, 15 (3), pp. 287–99.

Thorpe, M. (1994) Planning for learner support and the facilitator role, in Lockwood, F. (ed.), *Materials Production in Open and Distance Learning* (London: Paul Chapman Publishing Ltd).

Thorpe, M. (1998) Assessment and 'third generation' distance education, *Distance Education*, 19 (2), pp. 265–86.

Thorpe, M. (1999) Learner support – planning for people and systems, H804 The implementation of open and distance learning, Block 3 Overview Essay (Milton Keynes:The Open University).

Tolley, S. (2000) How electronic conferencing affects the way we teach, *Open Learning*, 15 (3), pp. 253–65.

Weller, M. (2000) Creating a large-scale, third generation distance education course, *Open Learning*, 15 (3), pp. 241–52.

Index

Printed in the USA/Agawam, MA
February 6, 2012

563924.150